10 SECRETS *of* THE LAIDBACK KNITTERS

A GUIDE TO

Holistic Knitting, Yarn, and Life

VICKI STIEFEL AND LISA SOUZA

PHOTOGRAPHS BY VICKI STIEFEL

ST. MARTIN'S GRIFFIN
NEW YORK

Book Design by Deborah Kerner

ISBN 978-0-312-61200-9

First Edition: May 2011

10 9 8 7 6 5 4 3 2 1

Vicki ~

To Cindy's Knitters~
  Heather Dalrymple
  Jody Simpson
  Kim Brady
  Marcia Schwartz
  Nancy Musarra
  Pat Fairchild
  Peggy Howard
  Sara LeFebvre
  Chris Huntington
  Gail Hoffmann
  Margit Porter
  Dorine Ryner
  Cindy Johnson~
I couldn't have done it without you,
    and
To my beloved Billy,
who always believed in me.

Lisa ~

To my high school sweetheart
and life mate, Rod,
who has always helped me
to bring my dreams to life,
    and
To my mother,
who always made me work for it.

10 SECRETS *of* THE LAIDBACK KNITTERS

ACKNOWLEDGMENTS

*t*his book was a huge group effort. We struggled, we got feedback, we queried, we questioned, and we got lots of help. So we bow to those whose time and effort and thoughtfulness and care helped make the *10 Secrets* a reality. We ♥ you all.

To models Wayan Suarni; Chris Huntington; Heather Dalrymple; Robin Young; Cameron, Cole, and Emily Dexter; Grace and Gabrielle Ramsden; for your beauty and grace under fire.

To our marvelous knitters, Elizabeth Risch and Tami Sutter, who knitted several of our patterns into reality.

To the yarn companies and individuals who graciously gave us their yarns for our projects.

To our hardworking, inventive, and spirited designers. What talent!

To Therese Chynoweth, for her amazing tech editing, patience, and sense of humor.

To Amy Finlay at KnittingHelp.com, for her conversation and help.

To all the LaidBack Knitters (& Crocheters) in our Ravelry Group, for being who you are.

To Gabrielle Clarke, Audrey's daughter, for allowing us to share her mom's pattern.

To the Blodgett-Johnson Girls: Ruth, Deb, Becca, and Lexie, for their constant support and inspiration.

To Linda Roghaar, for her brilliant agenting and friendship.

To Peter Rubie, for his understanding and faith.

To BJ Berti, our amazing editor, for her enthusiasm and encouragement, and for giving us freedom, yet showing us the way.

To Jasmine Faustino, for her able assistance.

To Deborah Kerner, for her gorgeous book design.

To Cheryl Krementz, for her superb copy editing.

To Lorrie Hunter, for helping Lisa through a very challenging year.

To Andrea Urban, for her constant encouragement and caring.

To Brenda Patipa, for her creativity and buzzing in Lisa's ear.

To Kim Brady, whose deep friendship kept Vicki on the road.

To Peter, Kathleen, and Summer, who helped turn chaos to sanity.

To the Animals—Gracie, Muffin, Cranberry, Zoey, and Sally—as well as all the sheep and goats and llamas and alpacas who added warmth and spirit to our project.

To Blake and Ben and Mike and Melissa and Sarah and Kate and Corey, for their patience, their caring, and their love.

CONTENTS

VICKI'S FIRST MODELING GIG—1950S PATTERN BOOK,
FASHIONS IN WOOL FOR LITTLE TOTS.

INTRODUCTION

*t*his book evolved from two knitters—one knowledgeable expert and one passionate amateur—bouncing around ideas about the world of fiber and knitting and, well, more. Lots more.

We're both pretty laidback knitters. Nowadays, we knit for the joy of it. We have fun. We don't compete. We're relaxed, even giggly, about knitting and our love of it.

We weren't always like that. Tense, uptight, competitive, obsessive—those adjectives used to fit us much more. But we changed. And we started thinking about the bouillabaisse of people and yarn and patterns and worlds that contributed to that change.

We really wanted to do a book that was more . . .

. . . more than patterns . . . more than yarn . . . more than style.

A book that spoke to all levels and types of knitters; a book that enhanced and expanded any knitter's experience in both joyful and substantive ways.

Some of the paths we take in the book are well trod, but with novel perspectives. Other journeys are new ones, where knitters will tread fresh ground. And a few of our travels will be echoes of things knitters may have once known but are now long forgotten.

Our book is a holistic one.

Holistic Knitting: The knitting world can't be explained by its component parts alone. Rather, the whole of the knitting world—more than simply the sum of its parts—has an existence all its own.

Knitting is Abundant, Inclusive, Organic.

10 Secrets of the LaidBack Knitters gives knitters permission to relax and have fun with their knitting; to see that knitting is as much about process as product; and to know that the stitches they knit can express the inner joy they feel.

~Vicki Stiefel and Lisa Souza

REALITY CHECK

Our book isn't a be-all, end-all kind of knitting book. We expect some of you will have to look up a few terms and methods, such as "short rows" or "provisional cast-on" and such. Rather than re-create every diagram and instruction for various knitting terms and techniques, our goal is to give you a spectrum of tools and sources for methods, definitions, sizes, colors, and more that will enable you to always find just what you need.

In the spirit of the book, and just for fun, we've adapted some of the skill-level definitions of the Craft Yarn Council of America.* Here they are:

SKILL LEVELS FOR THE LAIDBACK KNITTER

Recliner ~ Talk about relaxing! For first-time and beginner knitters. Uses basic knit and purl stitches; minimal shaping. (**Beginner knitter**)

Rocking Chair ~ Still pretty relaxing, but you might have to perk up for a bit. Uses basic stitches, repetitive stitch patterns, simple color changes, and simple shaping and finishing; some knitting in the round. (**Advanced Beginner knitter**)

Wing Chair ~ Sit up, pay attention, but it's still darned comfy; check the pattern once in a while, when you get to the "next part." Uses a variety of stitches, such as basic cables and lace and simple intarsia; double-pointed needles and knitting-in-the-round techniques; and mid-level shaping and finishing. (**Intermediate knitter**)

Dining Chair ~ Laid-back only in your approach to the project; it'll be fun, but challenging, too. Uses advanced techniques and stitches, such as short rows, Fair Isle, intricate intarsia, cables, lace patterns, and/or numerous color changes. You'll need tools nearby, a ruler on your chart, the whole nine yards. So spread 'em out on that dining room table. (**Advanced knitter**)

~Vicki and Lisa

*The names of the levels are ours (of course!), but the definitions are based on the Craft Yarn Council of America's Yarn Standards (www.YarnStandards.com).

x

I like making a piece of string into something I can wear. ~AUTHOR UNKNOWN

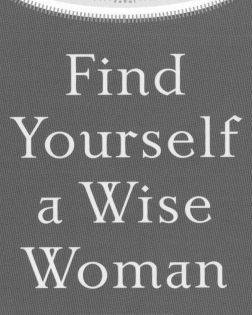

OUR 1ST SECRET

Find Yourself a Wise Woman

She's the One Who Sets You on the Path

A Wise Woman is many things to many people. But most of all, a Wise Woman is a mentor. Funny how so many knitters have "Wise Women" in their lives—women they've learned from, admired, watched, tried to emulate. Women who've helped them, guided them, steered them to the right path. These Wise Women often set the bar high—not for perfection but, rather, for commitment. Wise Women tend to be admirable in many ways. Find one, and you've found treasure.

Vicki: I've been thinking about our secrets, our knowledge, our people that we see as . . . cool. I've been thinking about Anne Hennessy. She's been a guru in New England for more than 30 years. So I'm thinking she could be our Number One Secret: Find Yourself a Wise Woman. Whaddaya think?

Lisa: I think that is right on. I always think of EZ (Elizabeth Zimmermann) when I channel a Wise Woman. I only had one in book form. You had the real thing.

Vicki: EZ was definitely a Wise Woman. I wish I'd met her.

Lisa: Me, too. I would love to meet Anne.

Vicki: I bet you will.

On a New England May day budding with life, a friend and I pulled up to an 1800s house with a sky-blue door on a seldom-traveled road. Neither of us had knit in years, but we thought it might be worth another try.

Beside the old farmhouse, sheep grazed in a field, chickens pecked in the dooryard, and the tabby on the windowsill licked a paw. The sign said THE WOOL ROOM.

The dark of aged pine greeted us inside a hall lined with shelves stuffed with brightly colored skeins of yarn. To the right, in a beamed, low-ceilinged room, a woman with a halo of snowy hair sat pressing pedals on a small spinning wheel. She was transforming a cloud of wool into yarn.

"I'm Anne," the spinner said. "Please, look around."

Wood, steel, and bamboo needles. Alpaca, merino, and linen yarn. Lime and turquoise and smoke colors. Crochet hooks, ball winders, stitch counters. So much. And the books! They spilled from the shelves, with patterns on Nordic knitting and socks and felting and stash.

Stash?

My fingers twitched to knit. I bought two skeins of soft merino the color of chili peppers and a pair of bamboo needles, and I began casting on.

Nothing happened. Nothing. My hands froze. "It's been a long time."

Anne's blue eyes smiled. "Your hands will remember. Try again."

I did. Twice more. Frozen. And then, my hands remembered. And I cast on.

I fumbled as I knit. It felt odd, awkward. I snagged stitches, knit too tight, too loose. I had no rhythm.

"Relax," she said. "You'll feel the flow..." It took a while, but Anne was right. I did.

My first project complete in more than two decades, I wrapped the colorful scarf around my neck. But as my ever-exuberant pup, Burt, bid me farewell, he snagged a loop. A monster "string" dangled from my new scarf.

I cursed. I growled. The scarf was ruined. And then I heard Anne's voice: *What a glorious opportunity for a design element!*

I used the strand to stitch a charm to the scarf. Perfectly adorable. An epiphany—my knitting didn't have to be perfect, but it did have to bring me joy. Knitting was as much about the process as the product.

Anne Hennessy had guided me down a path I hadn't even known I was on.

ANNE HENNESSY

Born into a world slower and more bucolic than ours, *Anne Hennessy* contracted whooping cough when she was 5. Shipped off to her grandmother's, she learned to knit. And to knit well.

She grew and she kept knitting, and after college, after teaching the deaf in Santa Fe and New Hampshire, Anne married Brian and they bought a farm in rural New Hampshire. Led there by the wool gods, Anne says.

To keep her three babies warm, Anne knit. And knit. Soon, she began selling her socks and sweaters and hats. She learned to spin, raised her own sheep. "Nothing like spinning wool from my very own sheep." But she missed teaching.

In the early '80s, Anne opened THE WOOL ROOM. Women found her out-of-the-way farm, and Anne taught them to knit and to spin. They found commonality and community, and as Anne's fame as a spinner and teacher grew, students came from all over New England.

Today, her kids are grown. Sock No. 600 just went out the door. She's taught hundreds to knit and spin. And the famed New Hampshire Wool Arts Tour, which she co-founded, just celebrated its twenty-eighth year. So is Anne satisfied with all she's accomplished?

"No," she says. "I think you should have something you want to do better. I'd like to be a marvelous great-wheel spinner—it's a dance when properly done."

Perhaps that's part of her Wise Womanhood—along with teaching, Anne has never stopped learning.

When asked what matters to her today, Anne pauses. "Can I survive well?" she finally answers. "And with grace?"

Anne Hennessy has graced this Earth for more than seventy years.

She is my Wise Woman. ~ VICKI STIEFEL

"A knitter must have a headlamp."

— NORAH GAUGHAN DURING THE ICE STORM BLACKOUT OF 2008

LISA'S WISE WOMAN

As a knitter, the turning point in freeing myself to create knitted pieces without following Rules and Regulations was in the early 1970s, when I bought *Knitting Without Tears* by *Elizabeth Zimmermann*. In her easy and conversational style of writing, EZ gave me permission to follow my artistic muse and blend my painter's art with the three-dimensional craft of knitting. As a kid, I made lots of weird things, and it was always a solitary pursuit. EZ led me to my only *Aha!* moment. Elizabeth Zimmermann gave me permission to be weird.

I laugh to think of her calling a mistake a Design Element, and I've quoted her many times when talking to hand-spun yarn customers embarking on their own fiber journey.

The most freeing day of my knitting career was when I raised scissors to the body of my first steeked colorwork cardigan. I heard the voice of Elizabeth telling me that I would survive the sewing and cutting of that piece of work and could then go lie down in a dark room, without shame, to recover. I crossed that big challenge off of my fear list, thanks to her.

~ LISA SOUZA

WHAT'S IN A WISE WOMAN'S NOTIONS BAG?

NEEDLE PROTECTORS • PEN • CROCHET HOOK • SCISSORS • DARNING NEEDLES • TAPE MEASURE • NEEDLE SIZER • OPENABLE STITCH MARKERS OR SAFETY PINS • CABLE NEEDLES • ROW COUNTER

6 GREAT KNITTING WEB SITES:

WWW.KNITTINGHELP.COM
WWW.RAVELRY.COM
WWW.KNITTY.COM
WWW.TWISTCOLLECTIVE.COM
WWW.KNITTERSREVIEW.COM
WWW.TECHKNITTING.
   BLOGSPOT.COM

GOING HER OWN WAY

We suspect Althea Crome's a Wise Woman, too. Talk about going your own way when it comes to knitting. *Althea Crome* has done just that. Her miniature knit pieces inspire awe. The Rembrandt of miniature knitters, Crome produces work that is breathtaking in both detail and style, not to mention size. Her sweaters and gloves were worn by the tiny Claymation star of the film *Coraline*. (www.BugKnits.com)

We love her tips to knitters:
• If you're tired, put the needles down. You are bound to make mistakes, and it isn't worth it. Finish the row and go to bed.
• Try to design something from your imagination—if I can do it, you can do it! Start by altering someone else's patterns until you feel confident enough and then move on to making something that is truly your own.
• Make things that are beautiful to you—push yourself just a little bit further each time. Do what feels exciting to you.
• Bring your knitting everywhere—kids' games, meets, meetings, airplanes.
• Go through some of your pattern books that you haven't looked at in a while and get inspired.
• Share your knowledge generously and help new knitters tap into their knitting mojo.

ANNE'S WINGS ...
Designed by Anne Hennessy

This design is adapted and refined from classic Faeroese shawl patterns. The neat thing about this shawl is that it literally curves. Why so cool? It'll cling to your shoulders with ease. The edging comes from *Barbara Abbey's Knitting Lace* (Schoolhouse Press). My Wise Woman, Anne Hennessy, has been knitting and teaching this design for decades. It's a multipurpose, fit-for-anything shawl. It works as a scarf, too. ~ VICKI

Skill Level: ROCKING CHAIR

Things You'll Need to Know
• Short row shaping
• Increasing stitches by knitting into the front and back of the loop
• Simple lace knitting
• Attaching a lace border as you knit

Finished Measurements
Width: 59" [150cm] from edge to edge, including edging
Length: 23½" [59.5cm] from neck to bottom edge, including edging

Yarn
Hand-spun *Corriedale* (100% Corriedale wool); approximately 250 yards; worsted/medium weight [4]; 6¾ oz. [191g], shown in color Violet; also Mulberry, Lavender, Evergreen

Needles
Size US 8 (5mm) needles, 16" (40cm) and 32" (80cm) circular needles, or size needed to obtain gauge
Size US 8 (5mm) needles, set of 4 or 5 double-pointed needles; 2 needles will be used to knit the edging

Notions
Stitch markers
Blunt tapestry/yarn needle

Gauge
15½ sts and 34 rows = 4" (10cm) in garter stitch
Gauge for this project is not critical. So relax. Have a ball.

together through the back of the loop so the wrap falls to the wrong side. On wrong-side rows, purl to the wrapped stitch, lift the wrap up from the right side and over the stitch, then purl both wrap and stitch together.

Abbreviations

beg begin(ning)
dpn(s) double-pointed needle(s) • **k** knit
k2tog knit 2 stitches together (1 stitch decreased)
kfb knit into the front loop, then through the back loop of the same stitch (1 stitch increased)
ndl(s) needle(s) • **p** purl
pm place marker • **rem** remaining
rep repeat • **sl** slip
st(s) stitch(es) • **tog** together
w&t wrap and turn • **wyb** with yarn in back
wyf with yarn in front • **yo** yarn over

Tips

• If you think you've lost your place, keep track of where you're at in the short row portion of the shawl by checking for wrapped stitches just below the needle. Removable stitch markers in different color, placed along the side edges can help you keep track of which short row you're working.

• Embellish your shawl to customize it. Try a lace edging, a ruffle, buttons, fringe, or whatever you can dream up.

• The size can be varied by using lighter or heavier yarn and can be worked to any desired length or width, and made with or without a border.

• This shawl can become wide, so make sure you have space to spread out as the fabric grows, such as a circular table with a circumference of 24"–32".

SHAWL

Using shorter circular ndl, cast on 1 st.
ROW 1: Kfb—2 sts.
ROW 2: Sl 1 wyf, kfb—3 sts.
ROW 3: Sl 1 wyf, k to last st, kfb—4 sts.
Rep row 3 until shawl measures about 17" (43cm) from bottom point; end with an odd number of sts.

Techniques

WORKING SHORT ROWS: As this shawl is worked in garter stitch, all short rows are worked the same way. Knit to where you need to turn, bring the yarn to the right side, slip the next stitch purlwise, bring the yarn back to the wrong side, slip the stitch back to the left needle, then turn (wrap & turn; w&t). Check out www.KnittingHelp.com's great videos on short rows.

PICKING UP AND WORKING WRAPS: On right-side rows, knit to the wrapped stitch, lift the wrap up and over the stitch, knit both wrap and stitch

SHORT ROW SHAPING

Pm at center st of row, then place another marker 12 sts before and after the center st.

ROW 1 (SHORT ROWS): Sl 1 wyf, k to first marker, w&t. K back to last st, kfb—1 st increased.

ROW 2: Sl 1 wyf, k to last st, picking up wrap and knitting it together with the st it wrapped, kfb—1 st increased.

ROW 3 (SHORT ROWS): Sl 1 wyf, k to first marker, w&t. K back to last st, kfb—1 st increased.

ROW 4: Sl 1 wyf, k to last st, picking up wrap and knitting it together with the st it wrapped, kfb—1 st increased.

Rep these 4 rows until shawl measures about 20" (51cm)–21" (53.5cm) from bottom point. Bind off loosely.

LACE EDGING

Using longer circular ndl, beg at one side edge and pick up 1 loop of each slipped st along side, 1 loop at cast-on edge, then 1 loop of each slipped st along rem side of shawl (total number of loops on ndl should be a multiple of 4 + 3).

Using a dpn, cast on 5 sts. K4, then k tog last st with first loop on edge of shawl, turn.

ROW 1: Sl 1 wyb, k1, k2tog, yo, k1.

ROW 2: K1, (k1, p1, k1, p1, k1) in yo, yo, k2tog, k last st tog with next loop on edge of shawl, turn—9 sts.

ROW 3: Sl 1 wyb, k1, yo, k2tog, k5.

ROW 4: K6, yo, k2tog, k last st tog with next loop on edge of shawl, turn.

ROWS 5 & 7: Rep row 3.

ROW 6: Rep row 4.

ROW 8: Bind off 4 sts, k1, yo, k2tog, k last st tog with next loop on edge of shawl, turn.

Rep rows 1–8 along edge, around bottom, then up along rem side edge. At bottom edge, work rows 4 and 6 in the same st at cast-on edge. On last row, bind off all sts, knitting together last st of edging with last loop on edge of shawl. Fasten off.

Thanks to Beth Pulsipher for this great knit trick:
Once you've joined stitches in the round, exchange 1st & last
stitch to avoid both gap and an 'unbuttoned' looking 1st row

SWEATER FOR CHILLIN'...
Designed by Lisa Souza

Light as a feather and just warm enough, this pull-over was a staple that I could knit up for clients in a couple of days. A laidback knitter's project that is simple and luxurious and, with a strand of supersoft kid mohair and a strand of wool, can be knitted with big needles in a weekend. It's a perfect gift for any Wise Woman you know. ~ LISA

  Skill Level: **RECLINER**

Things You'll Need to Know
• Decreasing stitches
• Working in the round
• Picking up stitches

Sizes
S (M, L)
Instructions are given for size S, with larger sizes in parentheses. When only one number is given and no size is mentioned, that number applies to all sizes.

Finished Measurements
Bust: 40 (42, 44)" [101.5 (106.5, 112)cm]
Length: 22 (23½, 24½)" [56 (59.5, 62)cm]

Yarn
COLOR A: Lisa Souza *Hand Dyed Blue Faced Leicester Worsted* (100% Blue Faced Leicester wool); 250 yds [229m]/4 oz [113g]; worsted/medium weight [4]; 2 (2, 3) skeins, shown in color Mars Quake
COLOR B: Lisa Souza *Hand Dyed Kid Mohair* (90% kid mohair, 10% nylon); 500 yds [457m]/4 oz [113g]; worsted/medium weight [4]; 1 (1, 1) skein, shown in color Ruby

Needles
Size US 13 (9mm) needles, straight and double-pointed needles (set of 4 or 5), or size needed to obtain gauge

Notions
Stitch holder
Stitch marker
Blunt tapestry/yarn needle

Gauge
12 sts and 14 rows = 4" (10cm) in stockinette with 1 strand of each color held together
You know you want to take the time to check your gauge, right? Please.

Abbreviations
beg begin(ning) • **cont** continu(e)(ing)
dec decrease • **dpn(s)** double-pointed needle(s)
k knit • **k2tog** knit 2 stitches together (1 stitch decreased) • **ndl(s)** needle(s) • **p** purl
pm place marker • **rem** remain • **rep** repeat
rnd(s) round(s) • **RS** right side(s) • **sl** slip
ssk slip, slip, knit: Slip one stitch from left needle to right needle, knitwise (as if to knit), slip second stitch same way, insert left needle through front of loops on right needle, then wrap yarn around right needle. With left needle, bring loops over the yarn wrapped around the right, which will knit them together through the back of the loops (1 stitch decreased).
st(s) stitch(es) • **St st** stockinette stitch
WS wrong side(s)

Tips
• This pullover is worked with 1 strand of each color held together throughout.

BACK
With straight ndls, cast on 60 (63, 66) sts.
K 6 rows.
Beg St st and work until piece measures 12 (13, 14)" [30.5 (33, 35.5)cm] from beg; end with a WS row.

ARMHOLES
Bind off 8 sts at beg of next 2 rows—44 (47, 50) sts.

Cont even in St st until armhole measures 10 (10½, 10½)" [25.5 (26.5, 26.5)cm]. Bind off all sts loosely.

FRONT

Work front same as back until armhole measures 7 (7½, 7)" [18 (19, 18)cm] for a portrait neck, or 8 (8½, 8)" [20.5 (21.5, 20.5)cm] for a turtleneck; end with a WS row.

SHAPE NECK

K14 (15, 16) and sl to st holder for left shoulder, bind off next 16 (17, 18) sts for neck opening, then k rem 14 (15, 16) sts for right shoulder.

RIGHT SHOULDER: Next row (WS), p.

NEXT ROW (RS): K1, ssk, k to end—13 (14, 15) sts.

Rep last 2 rows once more—12 (13, 14) sts. Work even until armhole measures 10 (10½, 10½)" [25.5 (26.5, 26.5)cm]. Bind off all sts loosely.

LEFT SHOULDER: Return sts from holder to straight ndl. Reattach yarn at neck edge and work 1 row on WS.

NEXT ROW (RS): K to last 3 sts, k2tog, k1—13 (14, 15) sts.

Rep last 2 rows once more—12 (13, 14) sts. Work even until armhole measures 10 (10½, 10½)" [25.5 (26.5, 26.5)cm]. Bind off all sts loosely.

Sew front and back tog at shoulders.

NECKBAND

PORTRAIT NECK: With RS facing, beg at left shoulder and, with dpns, pick up and k64 (66, 70) sts evenly along neck edge. Pm for beg of rnd. Join to work in the rnd.

Work 4" (10cm) of St st. Bind off loosely knitwise. Fold neck band to WS and loosely sew edge to neck edge where sts were picked up.

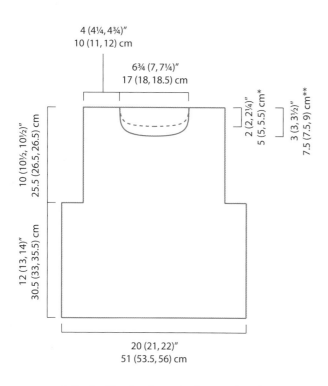

4 (4¼, 4¾)"
10 (11, 12) cm

6¾ (7, 7¼)"
17 (18, 18.5) cm

2 (2, 2¼)" cm*
5 (5, 5.5) cm*

3 (3, 3½)" cm**
7.5 (7.5, 9) cm**

10 (10½, 10½)"
25.5 (26.5, 26.5) cm

12 (13, 14)"
30.5 (33, 35.5) cm

20 (21, 22)"
51 (53.5, 56) cm

* Depth of front neck opening for portrait neck
** Depth of front neck opening for turtleneck

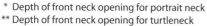

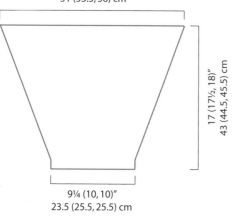

20 (21, 22) cm
51 (53.5, 56) cm

17 (17½, 18)"
43 (44.5, 45.5) cm

9¼ (10, 10)"
23.5 (25.5, 25.5) cm

TURTLENECK: With RS facing, beg at left shoulder and, with dpns, pick up and k56 (58, 62) sts evenly along neck edge. Pm for beg of rnd. Join to work in the rnd.

Work 6" (15cm) of k1, p1 rib. Bind off loosely in rib.

SLEEVE (make 2)

METHOD 1: With RS facing, use straight ndls and pick up and k60 (62, 62) along straight edge of armhole; do not pick up sts along bound-off edges at bottom of armhole.

Beg St st and, AT SAME TIME, dec 1 st each end

every RS row 8 (7, 6) times, then every other RS row 8 (9, 10) times—28 (30, 30) sts.

Work even until sleeve measures 15 (15½, 16)" [38 (39.5, 40.5)cm]; end with a RS row.

K 5 rows. Bind off loosely knitwise.

METHOD 2: With straight ndls, cast on 60 (62, 62) sts.

Beg St st and, AT SAME TIME, dec 1 st each end every RS row 8 (7, 6) times, then every other RS row 8 (9, 10) times—28 (30, 30) sts.

Work even until sleeve measures 15 (15½, 16)" [38 (39.5, 40.5)cm]; end with a RS row.

K 5 rows. Bind off loosely knitwise.

Finishing

If you made the sleeves using Method 2, sew sleeves into armholes along long and short straight edges. Sew side seams and underarm seams. Weave in ends.

SOLVANG WEEKEND VEST...
Designed by Kathleen Day

Straight lines become curves in this great vest created by a woman we consider deep and wise. Perfect for a casual lifestyle, the design is a quick knit, stylish, and cozy. We bet you'll want several in your wardrobe!

 Skill Level: ROCKING CHAIR

Things You'll Need to Know
- Provisional cast-on
- Picking up stitches
- Twisting stitches without a cable needle

Sizes
S (M, L)
Shown in size Large

Finished Measurements
Bust: 31¼ (33¼, 35)" [79.5 (84.5, 89)cm] with rib relaxed
Length along center back: 24 (25½, 26½)" [61 (65, 67.5)cm] to bottom edge

Yarn
Cascade Yarns *Eco+* (100% natural Peruvian wool); 478 yds [437m]/8¾ oz [250g skein]; chunky weight/bulky [5]; 1 (1, 1) skein, shown in color Spruce #8426

Needles
Size US 8 (5mm) needles, 24" (60cm) circular needle, or size needed to obtain gauge
Size US 7 (4.5mm) needles, 24" (60cm) circular needle

Notions
Stitch holder
Removable markers or safety pins
Blunt tapestry/yarn needle
Waste yarn for provisional cast-on
Buttons, snaps, or frogs (optional)

Gauge

28 sts and 23 rows using larger needles = 4" (10cm) in rib with Eco+

Please, please, please check your gauge, gauge, gauge.

Techniques

PROVISIONAL CAST-ON: Choose a smooth yarn of similar weight to the vest (chunky/bulky). Cast on the number of stitches as normal, knit one row in the waste yarn, then start knitting your vest with the actual yarn. When you remove the waste yarn, unravel it one stitch at a time and pop that stitch onto the needle.

Abbreviations

beg begin(ning) • **k** knit

m1 make 1: With tip of left needle, lift strand of yarn between the last stitch worked and the next stitch by inserting the needle from front to back, then knit through the back of the loop to twist it (1 stitch increased).

ndl(s) needle(s) • **p** purl • **rep** repeat

RS right side(s) • **RT** Knit 2 stitches together but do not remove from left needle, knit the first stitch again, then slip both stitches from left needle.

sl slip • **st(s)** stitch(es)

tog together • **WS** wrong side(s)

Tips

• Please read through entire pattern before beginning.

• The vest starts out as a long ribbed scarf that forms the back yoke and both fronts. The back stitches are picked up along one long edge and worked from the top down. The remaining long edge folds back to form a shawl collar.

• The rib for the lower edge of the body is formed by removing the provisional cast-on from the beginning end of the long section and picking up those stitches, then picking up stitches along the lower edge of the back and the remaining short end of the long section.

• The ribbing at the lower edge can be worked with either the same size needle or a smaller needle, if you prefer a more body-hugging fit. The same fit can sometimes be achieved by twisting the stitches as you work them instead of changing needle sizes.

• When you remove the provisional cast-on from the bottom edge, there will be one less stitch than was cast on. To maintain continuity of rib, one stitch is increased on the first row.

FRONT AND BACK YOKE

Using larger ndl and provisional method, cast on 60 (64, 68) sts. Work back and forth.

ROW 1 (RS): K1, *p2, k2; rep from * to end, ending last rep k1.

ROW 2 (WS): K the k sts and p the p sts.

Rep these 2 rows until piece measures 54 (58, 60)" [137 (147.5, 152.5)cm. Place sts on st holder or scrap yarn.

With RS facing, divide one long edge into thirds and place removable markers 18 (19¼, 20)" [45:5 (49, 51)cm] from each end; you should have about 85 (91, 92) rows between markers.

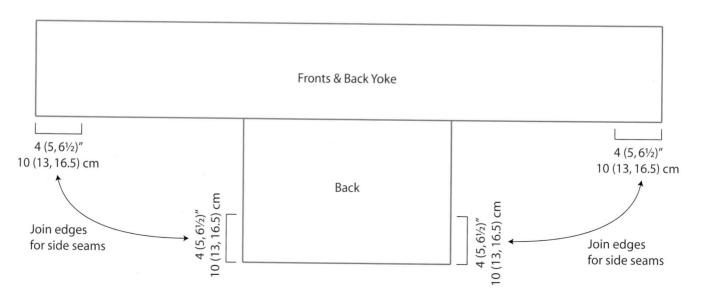

Fronts & Back Yoke

4 (5, 6½)"
10 (13, 16.5) cm

4 (5, 6½)"
10 (13, 16.5) cm

Join edges
for side seams

4 (5, 6½)"
10 (13, 16.5) cm

Back

4 (5, 6½)"
10 (13, 16.5) cm

Join edges
for side seams

BACK

Using larger ndl, beg at one marker and pick up and k1 st in each row to next marker—85 (91, 92) sts. Turn.

ROW 1 (WS): K8 (4, 1), m1, *k5 (7, 6), m1; rep from * 13 (11, 14) more times, then knit to end—100 (104, 108) sts.

ROW 2 (RS): K1, *p2, k2; rep from * to end, ending last rep k1.

ROW 3: K the k sts and p the p sts.

Rep the last 2 rows until piece measures about 11½ (12, 12¾)" [29 (30.5, 32.5)cm] for a deeper bottom edging, or about 13¼ (13¾, 14½)" [33.5 (35, 37) cm] for a narrower bottom edging.

Cut yarn, leaving a tail about 6" (15cm) long to weave in.

BOTTOM EDGING

Remove waste yarn from provisional cast-on and sl sts from both ends of front to same ndl with back sts, making sure not to twist pieces—219 (231, 243) sts. Change to smaller ndl.

With RS facing, reattach yarn to left front.

ROW 1 (RS): K1, *p2, RT; rep from *, increasing 1 st where cast-on edge of front joins back, end last rep k1—220 (232, 244) sts.

ROWS 2–4: K the k sts and p the p sts.

Rep these 4 rows 3 more times, or to desired length, ending with row 1; a deep 3¾" (9.5cm) edging was worked for the Eco+ vest, and a narrow 1½" (4.5cm) edging was worked for the Big Wool vest.

Bind off in rib pattern.

Finishing

Weave in ends. Sew fronts and back tog for about 4 (5, 6½)" [10 (13, 16.5)cm] above bottom edging for side seams, leaving rem of edge open for armholes.

If desired, sew buttons, frogs, or snaps to front edges; if using buttons, sew button loops to other side of front opposite buttons.

Lightly spray with water and lay flat to dry; do not steam or press, as this may flatten the rib.

Discover Slow Knitting

It's Not What You Think

Vicki: I want to talk about slow knitting.

Lisa: Slo-o-o-o-w knitting, like something that takes a year to make?

Vicki: No, no, slow with a capital *S*, like the Slow Food Movement.

Lisa: Mmmm, Slow Food like osso buco?

Vicki: Exactly! Slow knitting as a metaphor for knitting with yarn that comes directly from shepherds or artisan spinners and dyers. You know, the Good Stuff that's straight from the source.

Lisa: I know what you mean—like people who raise Heritage breeds of sheep, small spinning mills, or artists who spin amazing yarns. Things to savor, just like osso buco. Are you getting hungry?

Vicki: Starved!

Working with artisanal yarns is good for your soul, whether you have a big collection or a small bowl of pettable skeins. The yarns don't have to be of a costly fiber; it's the care taken in their production that makes them so special. The Slow Food movement has brought people back to the land, to the process of growing what we eat. Slow Food nourishes our souls as well as our bodies. Slow Knitting can be just as fulfilling.

17

Why not visit a nearby sheep or alpaca farm? Maybe go on a wool tour. Or make your way to one of the dozens of sheep-and-wool festivals scattered across the country. There, you can meet the cashmere goat and her proud goatherd, the artisanal dyer and the hand-spinner, as well as familiarize yourself with a variety of sheep breeds. You can touch the lanolin-rich fleeces that will eventually become wonderful knitting yarns and talk to the artisans who can show you the evolution of raw fleece to roving to hand- or small-mill-spun yarns.

Slow Knitting is about savoring the pleasure of working with yarn that has taken the same low-tech journey for hundreds of years. If you know only commercially produced yarn, we urge you to dabble in the Slow Knitting movement and sample some yarn from the soul.

Join the Fiber Festival Festivities

Sheep and llama and goats. Fried dough, lamb kebabs, and burgers. Silk skeins and merino fleeces and cashmere roving. Hand-dyes, spinning wheels, drum carders. Contests, sheepherding trials, the blare of the PA, blue ribbons, 4H. And acres and acres of yarn. All that and more can be found at fiber festivals, not to mention hugs and babies and laughter and community. A visual, auditory, and tactile feast, fiber fests are not-to-be-missed events for anyone with a love of knitting, crocheting, spinning, and/or weaving.

Arguably the largest and most famous, the Maryland Sheep & Wool Festival will be 38 years old in 2011. Hot on its heels in size and fame, the New York State Sheep and Wool Festival will mark its 39th birthday that same year. Yet in this instance, size doesn't really count. Numerous midsized and small fiber fests abound.

How and where do you find fiber fests? The best resource we've found is Knitter's Review (www.KnittersReview.com), which lists just about every fiber fest in the U.S., along with some international entries. You can also Google "sheep and wool festival," with satisfying results.

WHAT THE HECK IS A FIBER CSA (COMMUNITY SUPPORTED AGRICULTURE)?

Many of us know of or even subscribe to an agricultural CSA, where, for X number of dollars, you purchase a one-season share of a local farmer's crops. Thus, the farmer sells local, you buy local, and you eat local. That's what the Slow Food movement is all about.

In 2007, *Susan Gibbs*, a burgeoning sheep and goat farmer, thought the CSA model might work for animal farms and yarn. Folks would buy shares of her flock, and when it came time to shear, clean, and spin the wool, those same folks would be the recipients of some incredibly lovely skeins of locally grown yarn. In other words, "slow" fibers.

Gibbs posted her Martha's Vineyard Fiber Farm (now Juniper Moon Farm) on Etsy in 2008. For each share, an investor would receive 1 percent of the farm's shearings, either as yarn or as roving. Gibbs also included a shareholder certificate, updates on the farm and its critters, and an invitation to the farm's Shearing Day Celebration. The shares sold out, and the fiber CSA movement was launched. What Gibbs imagined in 2007 has snowballed. (See Resources on page 159 for a variety of fiber CSAs.)

Why Do We Throw?

The English (or throw) method of knitting (as opposed to the continental method) came about because ...

Folks believed it to be more refined and ladylike. The throw method was also known during the Victorian era as the "drawing room position." As hand-knitting segued from a way to earn a livelihood to more of a pastime, throwing was deemed more attractive for upper-class ladies.

Is the Continental method of knitting better than the English method? Or vice versa? We're not getting into that. The whole point of being LaidBack is enjoying what you do. So do whatever floats your boat.

WASH AND WEAR? YUP!

We love to relax as we knit, but one thing we do not find relaxing is wearing scratchy, rough yarn. Amazing how some of the most magical yarns in the world—Icelandic, llama, and artisanal yarns—can feel rough to the touch initially, but soften after washing in a gentle, biodegradable soap.

HERE ARE SOME SUGGESTIONS:

EUCALAN is a fully biodegradable, phosphate-free, no-rinse soap. It's enriched with lanolin and eucalyptus oil. (www.Eucalan.com)

SOAK is also a fully biodegradable, phosphate-free, no-rinse soap. (www.SoakWash.com)

KOOKABURRA WOOL WASH, yet another no-rinse soap, is made with lanolin and tea tree oil; is water-based and completely biodegradable; and contains no enzymes, phosphates, peroxide, or alkali. (www.KookaburraCo.com)

SO HOW DO I WASH IT?

Clean your sink, stopper it, fill with cool water. Then pour about one teaspoon of soap into the water. Place the item in the water and let soak for 15 minutes. Gently squeeze out the water. No need to rinse. Lay knit items flat to dry.

*If the color bleeds ... soak with warm water and a couple of tablespoons of white vinegar, which will allow any errant dye molecules to settle back on and bond with the yarn.

Not only will these products clean your soiled hand-knits; they will soften and relax rough fibers, including linen.

One more note: Clara Parkes of Knitter's Review tests all her knit pieces for review using Ivory liquid soap. Lisa uses Dawn liquid soap for her knit pieces.

PEASANT-BREAD TUNIC ...
Designed by Kimberly K. McAlindin

As an old hippie, I reacted in a visceral way to my first sight of Kimberly's pattern. The tunic seemed so contemporary, yet it also hearkened back to that Age of Aquarius I remember so well. Using an artisanal yarn, spun at a small mill and hand-dyed, made the tunic feel even more "of the earth."

The sweater itself has an ebb and flow as you knit—equal parts easy and thinking knitting. The lace embellishment totally works for me, yet the piece would still be beautiful with only garter-stitch edges and a simple stockinette. ~ VICKI

 Skill Level: DINING CHAIR

Things You'll Need to Know
- Lace knitting
- How to knit an I-cord
- Working short rows
- Kitchener stitch
- Three-needle bind-off

Sizes
S (M, L, XL, XXL)
Instructions are given for size Small, with larger sizes in parentheses. When only one number is given and no size is mentioned, that number applies to all sizes.

Finished Measurements
Bust: 33¾ (37½, 41¼, 45, 48¾)" [85.5 (95, 105, 114.5, 124)cm]
Length: 26½ (27½, 28, 28½, 28½)" [67.5 (70, 71, 72.5, 72.5)cm]

Yarn
Decadent Fibers *Marshmallow* (80% alpaca, 20% merino wool); 315 yds [288m]/4 oz [113g]; 3 (4, 4, 4, 5) skeins, shown in color Honey Butter

Needles

Size US 7 (4.5mm) needles, 16" (40cm) and 32" (80cm) circular needles, and 1 set of double-pointed needles, or size needed to obtain gauge
Size US 6 (4mm) needles, circular or straight needles
Size US 5 (3.75mm) needles, 32" (80cm) circular needle

Notions

Stitch markers
Stitch holders or waste yarn
Blunt tapestry/yarn needle

Gauge

19 sts and 26 rnds = 4" (10cm) over St st with size US 7 (4.5mm) needles
If we ask really nice, will you check your gauge?

Techniques

KITCHENER STITCH (OR GRAFTING OR WEAVING): In other words, you're joining two sets of live stitches without leaving a seam. Great tutorials are online at www.KnittingHelp.com (video) and www. Knitty.com. You'll need a tapestry needle for this.

THREE-NEEDLE BIND-OFF: Divide stitches evenly on two needles. Hold both needles in left hand with right sides together and needles parallel. Using a third needle in your right hand, knit together the first stitch from both needles. *Knit together the next stitch from both needles. Lift first stitch on right needle over top of second stitch, then off the needle—1 stitch remains on right needle; repeat from * until all stitches have been bound off. Fasten off remaining stitch on right needle.

WORKING SHORT ROWS: On right-side rows, knit to where you need to turn, bring the yarn to the right side, slip the next stitch purlwise, bring the yarn back to the wrong side, slip the stitch back to the left needle, then turn (wrap & turn; w&t). On wrong-side rows, purl to where you need to turn, bring yarn to right side of work, slip the next stitch purlwise, bring the yarn to back to the wrong side, slip the stitch back to the left needle, then turn (wrap & turn; w&t).

PICKING UP AND WORKING WRAPS: On right-side rows, knit to the wrapped stitch, lift the wrap up and over the stitch, knit both wrap and stitch together through the back of the loops so the wrap falls to the wrong side. On wrong-side rows, purl to the wrapped stitch, lift the wrap up from the right side and over the stitch, purl both wrap and the stitch together.

Abbreviations

beg begin(ning) • **BO** bind off
cont continu(e)(ing) • **dec** decrease
dpn(s) double-pointed needle(s)
inc increase • **k** knit
k2tog knit 2 stitches together (1 stitch decreased)
k3tog knit 3 stitches together (2 stitches decreased)
ndl(s) needle(s) • **p** purl • **pm** place marker
rem remain • **rep** repeat • **rnd(s)** round(s)
RS right side(s)
sk2p slip 1 stitch, knit 2 stitches together, pass slipped stitch over (2 stitches decreased)
Sl slip
Ssk slip, slip, knit: Slip one stitch from left needle to right needle knitwise (as if to knit), slip second stitch same way, insert left needle through front of loops on right needle, then wrap yarn around right needle. With left needle, bring loops over the yarn wrapped around the right, which will knit them together through the back of the loops (1 stitch decreased).
st(s) stitch(es) • **St st** stockinette stitch
tog together • **WS** wrong side(s)
w&t wrap and turn (see Techniques)
yo yarn over

Tips

• Markers are used to designate the beginning of rounds and where raglan shaping is to be worked. Slip all markers as you come to them.

Pattern Stitches

BOTTOM LACE PATTERN (multiple of 9 sts + 4 + 6 edge sts)

ROW 1 (WS): K3, p2, k1, *p8, k1; rep from * to last 4 sts, p1, k3.

ROW 2 (RS): K4, yo, *(ssk, yo) 3 times, k3tog, yo twice; rep from * to last 6 sts, end ssk, k4.

ROW 3: K3, p2, *p1, k1, p7; rep from * to last 5 sts, p2, k3.

ROW 4: K3,*k2tog, yo twice, (ssk, yo) twice, k3tog, yo; rep from * to last 7 sts, end k2tog, yo, k5.

ROW 5: K3, p4, *p7, k1, p1; rep from * to last 3 sts, k3.

ROW 6: K4, *k2tog, yo twice, ssk, yo, k3tog, yo, k2tog, yo; rep from * to last 6 sts, end k2tog, yo, k4.

ROW 7: K3, p3, *p7, k1, p1; rep from * to last 4 sts, p1, k3.

ROW 8: K3, k2tog, yo, *k2tog, yo twice, sk2p, (yo, k2tog) twice, yo; rep from * to last 5 sts, end k5.

ROW 9: K3, p2, *p7, k1, p1; rep from * to last 5 sts, p2, k3.

ROW 10: K4, k2tog, yo, *k2tog, yo twice, sk2p, (yo, k2tog) twice, yo; rep from * to last 4 sts, end k4.

ROW 11: K3, p1, *p7, k1, p1; rep from * to last 6 sts, p3, k3.

ROW 12: K3, k2tog, yo, *k2tog, yo twice, ssk, yo, sk2p, yo, k2tog, yo; rep from * to last 5 sts, end k5.

ROW 13: K3, p2, *p7, k1, p1, rep from * to last 5 sts, p2, k3.

ROW 14: K4, k2tog, *yo twice, (ssk, yo) twice, sk2p, yo, k2tog; rep from * to last 4 sts, end yo, k4.

ROW 15: K3, p2, *p8, k1; rep from * to last 5 sts, p2, k3.

ROW 16: K3, k2tog, *yo twice, (ssk, yo) 3 times, k3tog; rep from * to last 5 sts, end yo twice, ssk, k3.

Rep rows 1–16 for pattern.

SLEEVE LACE PATTERN (multiple of 9 sts + 4 + 4 edge sts)

ROW 1 (WS): K2, p2, k1, *p8, k1; rep from * to last 3 sts, p1, k2.

ROW 2 (RS): K3, yo, *(ssk, yo) 3 times, k3tog, yo twice; rep from * to last 5 sts, end ssk, k3.

Bottom Lace Pattern

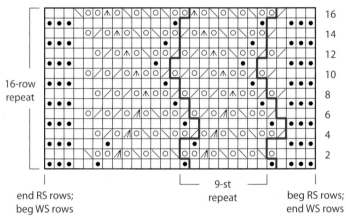

16-row repeat

end RS rows; beg WS rows

9-st repeat

beg RS rows; end WS rows

Sleeve Lace Pattern

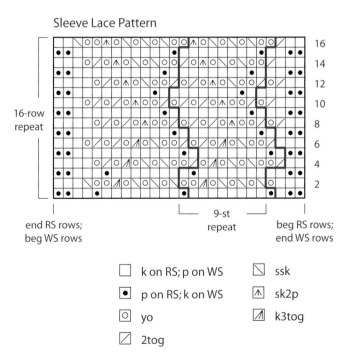

16-row repeat

end RS rows; beg WS rows

9-st repeat

beg RS rows; end WS rows

☐ k on RS; p on WS	⟍ ssk
• p on RS; k on WS	⟰ sk2p
○ yo	⟱ k3tog
⟋ 2tog	

ROW 11: K2, p1, *p7, k1, p1; rep from * to last 5 sts, p3, k2.

ROW 12: K2, k2tog, yo, *k2tog, yo twice, ssk, yo, sk2p, yo, k2tog, yo; rep from * to last 4 sts, end k4.

ROW 13: K2, p2, *p7, k1, p1; rep from * to last 4 sts, p2, k2.

ROW 14: K4, k2tog, *yo twice, (ssk, yo) twice, sk2p, yo, k2tog; rep from * to last 3 sts, end yo, k3.

ROW 15: K2, p2, *p8, k1; rep from * to last 4 sts, p2, k2.

ROW 16: K2, k2tog, *yo twice, (ssk, yo) 3 times, k3tog; rep from * to last 4 sts, end yo twice, ssk, k2.

BODY

Using middle size ndls, cast on 82 (91, 100, 109, 118) sts. K 6 rows.

ROWS 7–46: Work rows 1–16 of Bottom Lace Pattern twice, then rows 1–8 once more. Sl sts to holder and make second Bottom Lace Pattern section.

Using largest circular ndl in longer length, with RS facing, k sts from smaller ndl, pm, then k sts from

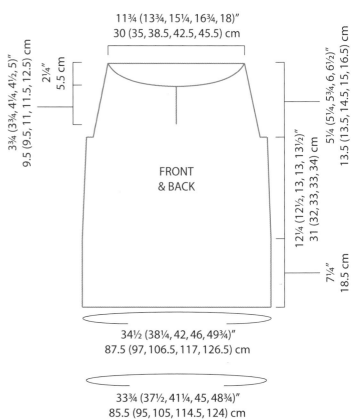

11¾ (13¾, 15¼, 16¾, 18)"
30 (35, 38.5, 42.5, 45.5) cm

2¼"
5.5 cm

3¾ (3¾, 4¼, 4½, 5)"
9.5 (9.5, 11, 11.5, 12.5) cm

5¼ (5¼, 5¾, 6, 6½)"
13.5 (13.5, 14.5, 15, 16.5) cm

FRONT
& BACK

12¼ (12½, 13, 13, 13½)"
31 (32, 33, 33, 34) cm

7¼"
18.5 cm

34½ (38¼, 42, 46, 49¾)"
87.5 (97, 106.5, 117, 126.5) cm

33¾ (37½, 41¼, 45, 48¾)"
85.5 (95, 105, 114.5, 124) cm

ROW 3: K2, p2, *p1, k1, p7; rep from * to last 4 sts, p2, k2.

ROW 4: K2, *k2tog, yo twice, (ssk, yo) twice, k3tog, yo; rep from * to last 6 sts, end k2tog, yo, k4.

ROW 5: K2, p4, *p7, k1, p1; rep from * to last 2 sts, k2.

ROW 6: K3, *k2tog, yo twice, ssk, yo, k3tog, yo, k2tog, yo; rep from * to last 5 sts, end k2tog, yo, k3.

ROW 7: K2, p3, *p7, k1, p1; rep from * to last 3 sts, p1, k2.

ROW 8: K2, k2tog, yo, *k2tog, yo twice, sk2p, (yo, k2tog) twice, yo; rep from * to last 4 sts, end k4.

ROW 9: K2, p2, *p7, k1, p1; rep from * to last 4 sts, p2, k2.

ROW 10: K3, k2tog, yo, *k2tog, yo twice, sk2p, (yo, k2tog) twice, yo; rep from * to last 3 sts, end k3.

holder—164 (182, 200, 218, 236) sts. Pm to mark beg of rnd. Join to work in the rnd.

RND 1: P3, k76 (85, 94, 103, 112), p6, k76 (85, 94, 103, 112), p3.

RND 2: K.

RNDS 3–6: Rep last 2 rnds.

RNDS 7–19: K.

RND 20 (DEC): K1, k2tog, k to 3 sts before next marker, ssk, k2, k2tog, k to last 3 sts, ssk, k1—160 (178, 196, 214, 232) sts.

SIZE S: Rnds 21–65: K.

RND 66: Rep dec rnd—156 sts.

RNDS 67–79: K.

SIZE M: Rnds 21–68: K.

RND 69: Rep dec rnd—174 sts.

RNDS 70–82: K.

SIZES L AND XL: Rnds 21–72: K.

RND 73: Rep dec rnd—192 (210) sts.

RNDS 74–85: K.

SIZE XXL: Rnds 21–75: K.

RND 76: Rep dec rnd—228 sts.

RNDS 77–89: K.

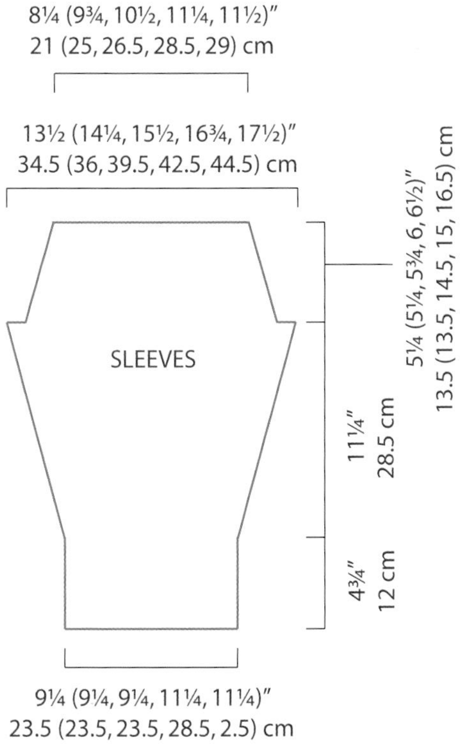

8¼ (9¾, 10½, 11¼, 11½)"
21 (25, 26.5, 28.5, 29) cm

13½ (14¼, 15½, 16¾, 17½)"
34.5 (36, 39.5, 42.5, 44.5) cm

5¼ (5¼, 5¾, 6, 6½)"
13.5 (13.5, 14.5, 15, 16.5) cm

SLEEVES

11¼"
28.5 cm

4¾"
12 cm

9¼ (9¼, 9¼, 11¼, 11¼)"
23.5 (23.5, 23.5, 28.5, 2.5) cm

ALL SIZES: Leave sts on ndl. Body should measure 19½ (19¾, 20¼, 20¼, 20¾)" [49.5 (50, 51.5, 51.5, 52.5) cm] from bottom edge.

SLEEVES (make 2)

Using middle size ndls, cast on 44 (44, 44, 53, 53) sts. K 6 rows.

ROWS 7–30: Work rows 1–16 of Sleeve Lace Pattern, then rows 1–8 once more.

Change to dpns. Pm to mark beg of rnd. Join to work in the rnd.

RND 1: K.

RND 2: P2, k to last 2 sts, p2.

RNDS 3–6: Rep last 2 rnds.

Cont St st over entire sleeve and, AT SAME TIME, inc 1 st at each end of rnd for each size as follows:

SIZE S: every 7th rnd 10 times—64 sts.

SIZE M: every 6th rnd 12 times—68 sts.

SIZE L: every 5th rnd 8 times, then every 4th rnd 7 times—74 sts.

SIZE XL: every 6th rnd 6 times, then every 5th rnd 7 times—79 sts.

SIZE XXL: every 5th rnd 8 times, then every 4th rnd 7 times—83 sts.

Work even until sleeve measures 16" (40.5cm) from bottom edge. Sl first 4 (4, 5, 5, 6) sts and last 4 (4, 5, 5, 6) sts to holder—56 (60, 64, 69, 71) sts rem on ndl.

JOIN BODY AND SLEEVES

Sl first 4 (4, 5, 5, 6) sts of body to holder or waste yarn. Using longer circular ndl, k56 (60, 64, 69, 71) sleeve sts, pm, k70 (79, 86, 95, 102) for front, sl next 8 (8, 10, 10, 12) sts to holder or waste yarn, pm, k56 (60, 64, 69, 71) sleeve sts, pm, k70 (79, 86, 95, 102) sts for back, sl rem 4 (4, 5, 5, 6) sts to holder or waste yarn with first sts of rnd—252 (278, 300, 328, 346) sts. Pm to mark beg of rnd; rnds beg at back of left sleeve.

K 5 rnds.

FRONT SLIT

RND 1: K sleeve sts and first 30 (35, 38, 43, 46) sts of front, p9, k to end.

RND 2: K.

RNDS 3 AND 4: Rep rnds 1 and 2.

RND 5: K sleeve sts and first 30 (35, 38, 43, 46) sts of front, p3, BO 3 sts, p3, k to end—249 (275, 297, 325, 343) sts. Cut yarn.

Sl sts left sleeve and left front sts from left ndl to right ndl. Working back and forth, beg rows at front edges.

SHAPE RAGLAN

ROW 1 (RS): Reattach yarn for a RS row. *K to 3 sts before marker, ssk, k2, k2tog; rep from * 3 more times, k to end—241 (267, 289, 317, 335) sts.

ROW 2: K3, p to last 3 sts, k3.

ROW 3: *K to 3 sts before marker, ssk, k2, k2tog; rep from * 3 more times, k to end—233 (259, 281, 309, 327) sts.

ROW 4: Rep row 2.

Rep rows 3 and 4, another 5 (5, 5, 6, 6) times—193 (219, 241, 261, 279) sts.

Work even for 1½ (1½, 2, 2, 2½)"/4 (4, 5, 5, 6.5) cm, ending with a WS row.

Remove front raglan markers, leaving markers for back raglan.

SHAPE BACK NECK

ROW 1 (RS): K144 (162, 178, 192, 206), w&t.

ROW 2 (WS): P96 (105, 116, 123, 134), w&t.

ROW 3: K91 (100, 111, 118, 129), w&t.

ROW 4: P86 (95, 106, 113, 124), w&t.

ROW 5: K81 (90, 101, 108, 119), w&t.

ROW 6: P76 (85, 96, 103, 114), w&t.

ROW 7: K71 (80, 91, 98, 109), w&t.

ROW 8: P66 (75, 86, 93, 104), w&t.

ROW 9: K to end, picking up wraps and working them tog with the sts they wrap.

ROW 10: K3, p to last 3 sts, picking up wraps and working them tog with the sts they wrap, k3.

ROW 11: K.

ROW 12: K3, p to last 3 sts, k3.

ROW 13: K.

ROW 14 (WS): K for turn row at top edge.

Work 5 rows of St st.

HEM

Using smallest size circular ndl and with WS facing, pick up purl bump at the top of each st, 5 rows below the turn row—you should have the same number of sts on both ndls. Hold both ndls tog, with WS tog and folded at the turn row.

Using three-needle BO, join both sets of sts and BO at the same time.

Finishing

Weave in ends. Use Kitchener stitch to join body and sleeves at underarms.

Block to measurements.

I-CORD

Using dpns, cast on 3 sts. K 1 row but do not turn. Beg working I-cord by slipping sts back to right end of ndl. *Pull yarn from end of row and k 1 row. Without turning, slide sts back to right end of ndl; rep from * until cord measures 60" (152.5cm). BO.

SMOKED JEWELS HOODED SHAWLETTE...
Designed by Sivia Harding

Beaded lace and seed stitch combine beautifully in Smoked Jewels, which you start by casting on at the bottom edge and work up to the top of the hood, where a single seam joins it all together. Shoulder shaping produces an excellent fit, and a seed-stitch border provides a lovely resting space for a shawl pin at the neck overlap.

Lisa's artisanal, hand-dyed yarn that's soft as eiderdown resonates beautifully with the pattern. The blend of pattern, color, and texture somehow took me to a magical place. ~ VICKI

Skill Level: **WING CHAIR**

Things You'll Need to Know
- Reading charts
- Lace knitting
- Knitting with beads
- Three-needle bind-off

Finished Measurements
Neck width: 15" (38cm)
Bottom width: 45½" (115.5cm)
Length at center back, from top of neck band: 15½" (39.5cm)

Yarn
Lisa Souza Hand Dyed *Baby Alpaca Sport* (100% baby alpaca); 330 yds [302m]/3.4 oz [96.4g]; 2 skeins, shown in color Silver Lake

Needles
Size US 5 (3.75mm) needle, 32" (80cm) circular needle, or size to obtain gauge
Size US 6 (4mm) needle, double-pointed needles for bind-off

Notions
Stitch markers
Two stitch holders (optional)
Blunt tapestry/yarn needle (optional)
Scrap yarn (optional)
Size US 14 steel (.60mm) crochet hook
160 size 6/0 seed beads, silver-lined crystal AB round

Gauge
22 sts and 31 rows = 4" (10cm) in lace pattern using smaller needles

23 sts and 32 rows = 4" (10cm) in seed stitch using smaller needles

What can we bribe you with to check your gauge?

Techniques

PLACING BEADS: Knit stitch as usual. Slip bead onto crochet hook; hooking last stitch on right needle, pull stitch off needle and through bead, then place stitch back on right needle. (See diagrams at right.)

THREE-NEEDLE BIND-OFF: Divide stitches evenly on two needles. Hold both needles in left hand with right sides together and needles parallel. Using a third needle in your right hand, knit together the first stitch from both needles. *Knit together the next stitch from both needles. Lift first stitch on right needle over top of second stitch, then off the needle—1 stitch remains on right needle; repeat from * until all stitches have been bound off. Fasten off remaining stitch on right needle.

Abbreviations

beg begin(ning) • **cont** continu(e)(ing) • **k** knit
k2tog knit 2 stitches together (1 stitch decreased)
m1 make 1: With tip of left needle, lift the strand of yarn between the last stitch worked and the next stitch by inserting the needle from front to back, then knit through the back of the loop to twist it (1 stitch increased).
m1p make 1 purlwise: With tip of left needle, lift the strand of yarn between the last stitch worked and the next stitch by inserting the needle from back to front, then knit through the front of the loop to twist it (1 stitch increased).
ndl(s) needle(s) • **p** purl • **pm** place marker
rem remain • **rep** repeat • **RS** right side(s)
s2kp slip 2 stitches together knitwise, knit 1 stitch, pass slipped stitches over (2 stitches decreased)
sk2p slip 1 stitch knitwise, knit 2 stitches together, pass slipped stitches over (2 stitches decreased)
sl slip
ssk slip, slip, knit: Slip one stitch from left needle

to right needle knitwise (as if to knit), slip second stitch same way, insert left needle through front of loops on right needle, then wrap yarn around right needle. With left needle, bring loops over the yarn wrapped around the right, which will knit them together through the back of the loops (1 stitch decreased).

st(s) stitch(es) • **tog** together

WS wrong side(s) • **yo** yarn over

Tips

• Lace patterns are presented in chart form only.
• Beads are added with a crochet hook as you work.
• It may be helpful to place additional stitch markers between repeats of the lace pattern while working Side Panel Charts A and B. Using markers of different sizes and/or colors than the markers at the end/beginning of the side panels will make it easier to differentiate where the sections begin and end.
• Stitch markers are used to separate pattern areas; slip markers as you come to them.

PLACING BEADS — STEP BY STEP

STEP 1: Slide the bead onto a crochet hook.
STEP 2: Insert the hook into the stitch loop where the bead will sit, making sure that the hook is facing you.
STEP 3: Pull the stitch loop through the bead.
STEP 4: Replace the beaded stitch onto the needle, if necessary.

Pattern Stitch

SEED STITCH (multiple of 2 sts)

ROW 1: *K1, p1; rep from * to end.
ROW 2: K the p sts and p the k sts from the previous row.
Rep rows 1–2 for pattern.

LOWER EDGE

Using smaller circular ndl, cast on 211 sts. Work back and forth in Seed St for 5 rows.
NEXT ROW (WS): Work Seed St over first 5 sts, p to last 5 sts, work Seed St to end.

Border Chart A

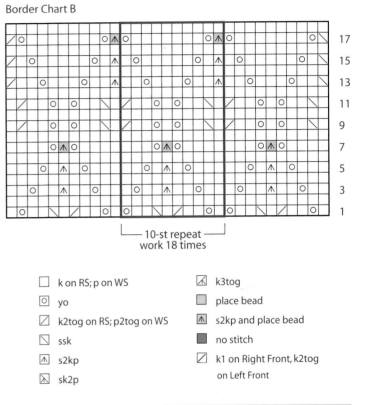

Border Chart B

□ k on RS; p on WS	☒ k3tog
⊙ yo	▨ place bead
╱ k2tog on RS; p2tog on WS	s2kp and place bead
╲ ssk	■ no stitch
⋀ s2kp	╱ k1 on Right Front, k2tog on Left Front
⋋ sk2p	

NEXT ROW (RS): Work Seed St over first 5 sts, work row 1 of Border Chart A over next 200 sts, work last st of chart, work Seed St to end.
NEXT ROW: Work Seed St over first 5 sts, p to last 5 sts, work Seed St to end.
Cont chart as established, placing 21 beads every other RS row as indicated on chart, and working a total of 8 rows.
NEXT ROW (RS): Work Seed St over first 5 sts, work row 1 of Border Chart B over next 201 sts as follows: first 10 sts of chart over next 10 sts, 10-st rep 18 times, then last 11 sts of chart over next 11 sts, work Seed St to end.
NEXT ROW: Work Seed St over first 5 sts, p to last 5 sts, work Seed St to end.
Cont chart as established through row 17.
ROW 18 (WS): Work Seed St over first 5 sts, pm, p81, pm, p40, pm, p80, pm, work in Seed St to end.

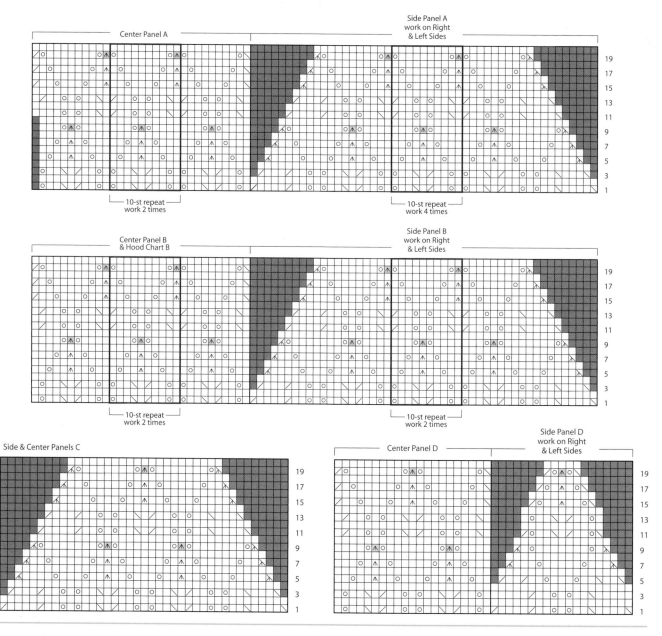

Center Panel A

Side Panel A
work on Right & Left Sides

10-st repeat
work 2 times

10-st repeat
work 4 times

Center Panel B & Hood Chart B

Side Panel B
work on Right & Left Sides

10-st repeat
work 2 times

10-st repeat
work 2 times

Side & Center Panels C

Center Panel D

Side Panel D
work on Right & Left Sides

BODY

NEXT ROW (RS): Work Seed St over first 5 sts, row 1 of Side Panel A over right front, Center Panel A over center sts, Side Panel A over left front, work Seed St to end—208 sts.

NEXT ROW (WS): Work Seed St over first 5 sts, p to last 5 sts, work Seed St to end.

Cont charts as established through row 20—173 sts.

NEXT ROW (RS): Work Seed St over first 5 sts, row 1 of Side Panel B over right front, Center Panel B over center sts, Side Panel B over left front, work Seed St to end—169 sts.

NEXT ROW (WS): Work Seed St over first 5 sts, p to last 5 sts, work Seed St to end.

Cont charts as established through row 20—133 sts.

NEXT ROW (RS): Work Seed St over first 5 sts, row 1

of Panel C over each section, work Seed St to end—127 sts.

NEXT ROW (WS): Work Seed St over first 5 sts, p to last 5 sts, work Seed St to end.

Cont chart as established through row 20 and, AT SAME TIME, m1p before first marker and after last marker every RS row, and m1 before first marker and after last marker every WS row—105 sts, with 21 sts in Seed St at each end; work increased sts in Seed St.

NEXT ROW (RS): Work Seed St over first 21 sts, row 1 of Side Panel D over right front, Center Panel D over center sts, Side Panel D over left front, work Seed St to end—101 sts.

NEXT ROW (WS): Work Seed St over first 21 sts, p to last 21 sts, work Seed St to end.

Cont charts as established through row 20—73 sts. Piece should measure about 14¼" (36cm) from beg.

NECKBAND

Work 7 rows of Seed St over all sts, removing all markers.

NEXT ROW (WS): Work Seed St over first 26 sts, pm, p21, pm, work Seed St to end.

HOOD

NEXT ROW (RS): Work Seed St over first 26 sts, row 1 of Hood Chart A to marker, work Seed St to end—75 sts.

NEXT ROW (WS): Work Seed St over first 26 sts, p to last 26 sts, work Seed St to end.

Cont chart as established through row 20—93 sts.

NEXT ROW (RS): Work Seed St over first 26 sts, row 1 of Hood Chart B to marker, work Seed St to end.

NEXT ROW (WS): Work Seed St over first 26 sts, p to last 26 sts, work Seed St to end.

Cont chart as established through row 20. Piece should measure about 10¼" (26cm) from top of neckband.

NEXT ROW (RS): Work Seed St over first 26 sts, row 1 of Hood Chart C to marker, work Seed St to end—89 sts.

NEXT ROW (WS): Work Seed St over first 26 sts, p to last 26 sts, work Seed St to end.

Cont chart as established through row 18—56 sts. Sl rem sts to holders, or thread a blunt tapestry/yarn needle with a piece of scrap yarn and thread sts onto scrap yarn.

Finishing

Immerse piece in lukewarm water and wet thoroughly. Squeeze out excess water; do not wring. Roll piece in towel and blot dry.

Pin out to finished measurements, pulling bottom edge gently into scallops as shown, if desired.

When completely dry, sl sts for top of hood to ndls, evenly dividing sts over 2 ndls. Holding ndls with RS tog, use three-needle bind-off to bind off all sts. Weave ends.

Block hood seam by dampening seam. Lay hood over the side of a plastic bottle, with bottom of bottle at lace portion. Allow to dry completely.

Hood Chart A

Hood Chart C

Become a Barefoot Sock Knitter

or How to Attain Instant Pleasure While Creating a Selfless Gift

THE BAREFOOT SOCK KNITTER

A FABLE BY VICKI STIEFEL

A day or two past yesterday, there lived a woman named Kate who was a poet and a scholar and a translator of foreign words. And while her marriage lacked children, it brimmed full of love. She wore fluffy print skirts and gypsy blouses and rubber flip-flops. She painted her lips red, her toes purple, and her hair raven black. She wore cat glasses from the early '60s, so on days it didn't drizzle, which were few, she could see the waves of Puget Sound from high on her hill in Seattle.

Because Kate adored the smell of sage, she'd often cleanse her home with a smudge stick. Unfortunately, Chicka-dee Knit Shop next door wasn't quite as enthusiastic about the smell. In fact, on those occasions when Kate burned sage, the yarn store's customers complained about the store harboring a pothead. Kate got secret chuckles out of that conceit. However, Beth, the yarn shop owner, did not.

One late October day, Kate breezed out of her home for a vigorous walk. When her cell vibrated, she was tempted to ignore it. She had a bad feeling. But it was impossible for her to not answer a vibrating phone.

33

"Kate here."

"We need 100 pair of socks for Meadowspring Charities," said her friend. "Can you help?"

"Of course," Kate said.

Sigh. "I'm so relieved. I didn't think you knit, and so . . . "

Kate frowned. "I don't knit. So what? I'll buy some nice ones."

"Thanks, but we promised hand-knit. It's not the same, you know. A gift of the hand is special."

"Oh." Fate had pinched Kate's butt.

It took Kate three days to pull open the yarn shop's door. Beth, a Talbot's gal if ever there was one, frowned when she saw her newest customer. The two were yin and yang about most everything.

Expecting a rebuke, Kate nonetheless forged ahead. "I need to learn to knit."

Beth folded her hands. "Of course."

"How much?"

Beth smiled. "A bargain. No more sage, and I'll teach you for free."

An epithet burned Kate's tongue. Instead, she stalked out.

But a day later, simmering with frustration, she returned to the shop. The women eyed each other across a bin of colorful alpaca and Noro.

"Here's the deal," Kate said with buckets of false bravado. "I'll burn the sage only late at night, once you're closed."

Beth crossed her arms. "Once a week."

Kate tapped her flip-flopped toes and sighed. "Deal."

She figured knitting had to be easier than this.

A week later, Kate again trudged over to Beth's carrying her yarn, her wands (she refused to call them needles), and a huge knitting bag of frustration.

"Relax," Beth said. "Have fun with it."

Kate held up a mangled sock. "Fun? I hate this. I used to be a nice person. Now? I even snap at old Mrs. Wilmott."

"Dear me." Beth ran her assured hands over Kate's frustrated ones. She massaged Kate's hands gently, carefully, until she felt them relax. "See? Calm. Smooth. Joyful."

The pair locked eyes, Beth's blue holding Kate's gold-brown.

Kate stuffed her paraphernalia back into her bag. "I'll keep practicing."

Another week passed, and Kate tromped back to the yarn store.

"Look." She held up something that looked suspiciously like the beginnings of a sock.

"Nice!" Beth said. "Um, how come the tips of your fingers have Band-Aids?"

Kate wiggled her fingers. "Didn't want to get blood on the sock. I'm starting to like this knitting stuff."

Kate didn't realize she was an extremist, but she was. When her passions caught fire, she was unstoppable. She practiced and practiced, and soon she was knitting socks like a pro. As the November air turned tart and crisp, she knit 20 pairs of socks for the Meadowspring charity.

Now I've done my duty, she thought. She wiggled her toes. Time to make a pair for me. *Wheeee!*

She chose an artisanal self-striping, watermelon sock yarn and a new pattern called Watermelon Vine Socks. She smiled. Her toes would be cozy this winter.

As she was casting on, her Buddha-bellied husband leaned into the room. "Are those for me?"

She patted his beard and smiled. "How did you guess?"

He chuckled. "You know how much I love watermelon."

Days later, his pleasure was palpable as he slid the watermelon socks onto his size 12 feet. "Oh, my. I love these, baby."

They made love naked—except for his watermelon socks.

And so Kate began to knit socks for all her siblings and her cousins and her friends. Her trusty mailman would get a pair of black-and-white self-stripers, while her best friend would wear a purple pair with a frill on the cuff. As her enthusiasm grew, Kate knit on and on and on, the colors of the rainbow moving smoothly across her needles.

As the days cooled further, she knit and knit and her Christmas list shrank and shrank. Finally, she found herself binding off the toe of her beloved John's second Christmas sock. She was done with her gifts.

She wiggled her toes. They were naked and looking rather blue. But she was no longer content to wear store-bought socks. Two days 'til Christmas. She had time. She could do it. She could knit one more pair for herself.

Kate sighed as she sat in front of her woodstove and rocked. And as she cast on, she thought of the many, many pairs of socks she'd knit for those in need and those she loved.

She was about to join the round when her vibrating phone interrupted her reverie. As always, she was tempted not to answer. As always, she had to do it.

"Kate here," she said.

"Hello, dear."

It was her Meadowspring Charities friend. "Is everything OK with the socks?"

"Absolutely. We've got the 100 pairs all wrapped and ready for the homeless for Christmas. Your contribution was enormous."

Pleasure suffused her soul. "I'm so glad I could help. I'm still knitting socks, you know. I'm addicted."

Kate's friend laughed. "So I've heard. I have a special request. We're two pair short. I'm knitting one, and I was wondering if . . ."

"Of course."

Gifting ...

Lisa: Knitting socks does more than warm the toes. There's an instant pleasure creating them. It's a lovely thing to knit socks as a gift. They take such time and care.

Vicki: Our Barefoot Sock Knitter is a metaphor for the gifts we, as knitters, give of ourselves to others. With every sock a knitter crafts as a gift, a part of herself is transferred to the sock, a most intimate garment.

Lisa: The socks become her instant pleasure and a selfless gift. The Secret is just that— instant pleasure coupled with a selfless gift. It's not often something like that comes along. Yes, as the yarn runs through her fingers, there is a quiet mantra that attaches to the stitches.

Vicki: It's doubly wonderful when the yarn is hand-dyed or hand-spun. Then you have the care of the dyer or spinner added to the essence of the knitter or crocheter.

Lisa: Of course, we used socks because of their intimacy, but anything will do—a hat, a shawl, a scarf, anything.

Vicki: We, the creator, get such joy from the creation. That's a huge part of the secret. It's not just the gift, but the creation itself.

Lisa: It's the bond that forms between the giver and the recipient, a bond that's reinforced whenever the receiver drapes the shawl, pulls on the sock, or touches the pillow.

Vicki: Something magic happens, doesn't it?

Lisa: You bet it does. And that's cool.

Knitters are Givers

Knitters love to knit for charity. There are many, many wonderful charitable organizations to knit for, spanning causes from abused women to shelter animals to premies.

Some favorites of ours:

PROJECT LINUS:
www.ProjectLinus.org
AFGHANS FOR AFGHANS:
www.AfghansForAfghans.org
RED SCARF PROJECT:
www.Orphan.org
THE SHIPS PROJECT:
www.TheShipsProject.com
THE MOTHER BEAR PROJECT:
www.MotherBearProject.org

More information can be found at:

www.KnittingForCharity.org
www.Knitting-Love.com/
charity-knitting-animals.
html

Knitters, crocheters, and fiber lovers are also supporters of Tricoteuses Sans Frontières (Knitters Without Borders), an offshoot of Médecins Sans Frontières (Doctors Without Borders). From December of 2004 to February of 2010, Knitters Without Borders raised a staggering $1,000,110 for Médecins Sans Frontières. (www.YarnHarlot.ca/blog/tsffaq.html)

Christmas morning, Kate slid John's presents beneath the tree. She'd bought him books and a painting and a crank flashlight. She'd put his new socks at the bottom of the pile.

Each gift they exchanged brought smiles and kisses and applause. She finally handed John his last gift. When he held up the gorgeous cashmere/merino socks she'd knit him, he grinned.

He kissed her hard and long, and when they parted, he waved a hand. "Now you open yours, babe."

She tore the paper off a huge box and tugged off the lid. Inside, resting on a bed of green tissue paper, lay a pair of beautiful red socks. She cautiously lifted them from the box. They were soft as goose down and they were hand-knit.

"Oh, John, they're beautiful. Who . . . ?"

He kissed her fingers. "I saw the way things were going. I knew you'd never make yourself a pair."

"I guess I'll always be the barefoot sock knitter."

"Not anymore you won't." From behind his back, he pulled out a quartet of double points with a gaily colored sock resting on the needles. "Men can knit, too, my sweet."

She laughed and hugged him. She was the barefoot sock knitter no more.

THE END . . .

The Barefoot Sock Knitter lives . . . in us . . . in you . . . in all those knitters who've crafted gifts for husbands and daughters, cousins and friends; for the grieving widow and the orphaned girl; for the destitute at Christmas and the abused in the shelter; for the chemo patient and the newborn and the elderly. Few things are more rewarding than being a Barefoot Sock Knitter.

TAKE A LOOK AT

Heifer International supplies animals—including sheep, llama, goats, and even a "knitting basket" of four wool-producing animals—to those in need of sustainable support around the world. *Clara Parkes'* Knitter's Review supports Heifer International (www.Heifer.org).

Two terrific books on knitting for charity are:

Knitting for Peace: Make the World a Better Place One Stitch at a Time, by Betty Christiansen (STC Craft/A Melanie Falick Book, 2006)
Knit Along with Debbie Macomber: Charity Guide for Knitters, by Debbie Macomber (Leisure Arts, Inc., 2009)

WATERMELON VINE SOCKS ...
Designed by Marian Hester

I'm crazy about these socks. The first time I saw them, I wanted to knit them. I thought, *They look delicious. What a great gift!*

I love that the pattern uses a hearty yarn and that the little vines add interest without detracting from the self-striping watermelon motif.

The watermelon yarn itself, spun at a small eco-friendly mill, is 100 percent Suffolk wool yarn from sheep raised on Manitoulin Island, Ontario, Canada. Lanolin-rich Suffolk wool does not felt easily, so the socks are machine-washable and-dryable. Suffolk wool is a dense, lofty wool and will become much softer and puffier after laundering. The color Natural also becomes much whiter.

The socks are cozy and warm and make a perfect gift for anyone, including a Barefoot Sock Knitter whose heart is large and whose feet get chilly. ~ VICKI

Skill Level: WING CHAIR

Things You'll Need to Know
• Kitchener stitch
• Knitting in the round on double-pointed needles
• Decreasing two stitches at a time

Size
One size fits most adults.

Finished Measurements
Leg circumference, after washing: 9" (23cm)
Foot circumference, after washing: 8½" (21.5cm)

Yarn
Freshisle Fibers *Suffolk Wool* (100% Suffolk wool); 200 yds [183m]/4 oz [110g] hank; worsted/medium weight {4}.
COLOR A: 1 hank. **COLOR B:** 1 hank, shown in colors Natural (A) and Self-Striping Watermelon (B)

Needles
Size US 4 (3.5mm) set of 4 or 5 double-pointed needles, or size to obtain gauge

Notions
Stitch markers (optional)
Blunt tapestry/yarn needle
Small length of waste yarn

Gauge
20 sts and 35 rows = 4" (10cm) in stockinette
21 sts and 34 rnds = 4" (10cm) in pattern
To check gauge or not to check gauge, that is the question.—*Hamlet*, by W. Shakespeare

Abbreviations
beg begin(ning) • **cont** continu(e)(ing) • **dec** decrease • **dpn(s)** double-pointed needle(s) • **k** knit **k2tog** knit 2 stitches together (1 stitch decreased)

ndl(s) needle(s) • p purl • pm place marker
rem remain(ing) • rep repeat • rnd rnd
sk2p slip 1 stitch knitwise, knit 2 stitches together, pass slipped stitch over decrease stitch (2 stitches decreased)
ssk slip, slip, knit: Slip one stitch from left needle to right needle, knitwise (as if to knit), slip second stitch same way, insert left needle through front of loops on right needle, then wrap yarn around right needle. With left needle, bring loops over the yarn wrapped around the right, which will knit them together through the back of the loops (1 stitch decreased). • st(s) stitch(es) • yo yarn over

Tips

• When working the leg with the watermelon yarn, try to end the leg on row 3 with the natural repeat of the self-striping watermelon yarn. This may help to maintain the stripes and make a smoother transition to the heel.
• Stitch count varies, so count stitches at the end of row 4 to check.
• For different sizes, increase or decrease width of the sock by adding or subtracting 1 or more stitch(es) between the lace "vines."

Techniques

KITCHENER STITCH (OR GRAFTING OR WEAVING):
In other words, you're joining two sets of live stitches without leaving a seam. Great tutorials are online at www.KnittingHelp.com (video) and www.Knitty.com. You'll need a tapestry needle for this.

CUFF

With Color A, cast on 44 sts and divide on three ndls with 11 sts on ndl 1, 21 sts on ndl 2, and 12 sts on ndl 3.
Join to work in the rnd, being careful not to twist sts; pm for beg of rnd.
Beg k3, p1 rib and work for about 1" (2.5cm) or desired length.
K 1 rnd. Cut yarn, leaving a tail about 6" (15cm) long for weaving in later.
Join Color B.

LEG

RND 1: NDL 1: K7, yo, k2tog, k2;
NDL 2: K9, yo, k3, yo, k9;
NDL 3: K2, k2tog, yo, k8—46 sts.
RND 2: K.
RND 3: NDL 1: K7, k2tog, yo, k2;
NDL 2: K10, sk2p, k10;
NDL 3: K2, yo, k2tog, k8—44 sts.
RND 4: K.
Rep these 4 rnds until leg measures 3½" (9cm), or desired length from bottom of rib, ending with rnd 3.
NEXT RND: K all sts on ndls 1 and 2; with waste yarn, k sts on ndls 3 and 1; drop waste yarn. Return to beg of ndl 3 and pick up color B. Knit across ndls 3 and 1. Mark new beg of rnd at side edge of foot; ndl 1 is now the top of sock with 21 sts, ndl 2 has 12 sts, and ndl 3 has 11 sts.

FOOT

Cont with color B for foot.
RND 1: NDL 1: K2, yo, k2tog, k5, yo, k3, yo, k5, k2tog, yo, k2;
NDLS 2 AND 3: K—46 sts.
RND 2: K.
RND 3: NDL 1: K2, k2tog, yo, k6, sk2p, k6, yo, k2tog, k2;
NDLS 2 AND 3: K—44 sts.
RND 4: K.
Rep last 4 rnds until foot measures about 3¾" (9.5cm) short of desired length, ending with rnd 4; the heel will require about 2½" (6.5cm) of length, and the toe will require about 1¼" (3cm) of length. Cut yarn, leaving a tail about 6" (15cm) for weaving in later.

TOE

Slip 1 st from beg of ndl 3 to end of ndl 1—22 sts on ndl 1, and 11 sts each on ndls 2 and 3.

NEXT RND: (Ndl 1) Kl, ssk, k to last 3 stitches on ndl, k2tog, k1;

(Ndl 2) K1, ssk, knit to end of ndl;

(Ndl 3) Knit to last 3 sts on ndl, end k2tog, k1—40 sts.

K 1 rnd even.

Rep last 2 rnds 5 more times—20 sts rem; 10 sts on ndl 1, and 5 sts each on ndls 2 and 3. Slip sts from ndl 2 to ndl 3. Graft stitches tog using Kitchener st.

HEEL

Carefully remove waste yarn—22 sts on top edge and 23 sts on bottom edge.

Sl sts to dpns with 22 sts on ndl 1, 11 sts on ndl 2, and 12 sts on ndl 3—45 sts.

Join color A and k across ndl 1, pick up and k2 at corner of opening with ndl 2, k sts on ndl 2, k sts on ndl 3, and pick up and k2 at other end of opening—49 sts; 22 sts on ndl 1, 13 sts on ndl 2, and 14 sts on ndl 3.

Join to work in the rnd and mark beg of rnd. K 1 rnd even.

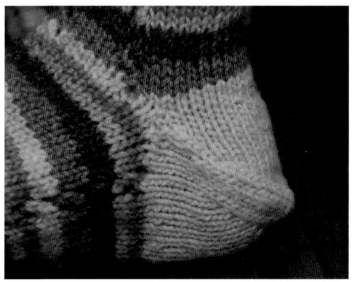

NEXT RND: NDL 1: K;

NDL 2: K1, ssk, k to end of ndl;

NDL 3: K to last 3 sts on ndl, end k2tog, k1—47 sts. K 1 rnd even. Rep last 2 rnds once more—45 sts.

NEXT RND: NDLS 1 AND 2: K;

NDL 3: K to last 3 sts on ndl, end k2tog, k1—44 sts; 22 sts on ndl 1 and 11 sts each on ndls 2 and 3.

If a deeper heel is desired, k 1 or 2 rnds even.

NEXT RND: NDL 1: Kl, ssk, k to last 3 stitches on ndl, k2tog, k1;

NDL 2: k1, ssk, k to end of ndl;

NDL 3: K to last 3 sts on ndl, end k2tog, k1—40 sts. K 1 rnd even.

Rep last 2 rnds 5 more times—20 sts rem; 10 sts on ndl 1 and 5 sts each on ndls 2 and 3. Sl sts from ndl 2 to ndl 3.

Graft stitches together using Kitchener stitch. Block to finish.

INSIDE-OUT HAT ...
Designed by Janice Kang

How cute is this Inside-Out Hat? The fact that it's reversible and extra warm because of the two layers makes it utterly practical. Aesthetically, the peekaboo lace shows off the inner hat's color. This is one cozy piece of knitting, and since it's sized for both kids and adults, it makes an ideal parent/child combo gift.

 Skill Level: **WING CHAIR**

Things You'll Need to Know
• How to work in the round on circular and double-pointed needles
• Reading charts
• How to pick up stitches
• Knitting through the back of the loop
• Three-needle bind-off

Sizes
Kid's S (6–12 months) and M (18–24 months), and Adult S (M, L)
Instructions are given for Kid's S (M) sizes and Adult S (M, L) sizes. When only one number is given and no size is mentioned, that number applies to all sizes. For Adult sizes, when two numbers are given, they apply to S (L) sizes.

Finished Measurements
Kid's circumference, relaxed: 16 (17¼)" [40.5 (44) cm]
Adult circumference, relaxed: 19½ (21, 22½)" [49.5 (53.5, 57)cm]

Yarn
KID'S HAT: Mission Falls *136 Merino Superwash* (100% merino wool); 136 yds [124 m]/ 1¾ oz [50g]; sport weight/fine [2].
COLOR A: 1 ball; **COLOR B:** 1 ball, shown in colors Rhubarb # 0534 (A) and Macaw #027 (B)
ADULT HAT: Lion Brand *LB Collection Organic Wool* (100% organic wool; 185 yds [170m]/3½ oz [100g];

worsted weight/medium [4].
COLOR A: 1 hank; **COLOR B:** 1 hank, shown in colors Natural #481-098 (A) and Toffee #481-124 (B)

Needles
KID'S HAT: Size US 7 (4.5mm) needles, 16" (40cm) circular needle or set of 4 or 5 double-pointed needles
Size US 6 (4.0mm) needles, 16" (40cm) circular needle and set of 4 or 5 double-pointed needles, or size needed to obtain gauge
ADULT HAT: Size US 10½ (6.5mm) needles, 16" (40cm) circular needle or set of 4 or 5 double-pointed needles
Size US 9 (5.5mm) needles, 16" (40cm) circular needle and 1 set of 4 or 5 double-pointed needles, or size needed to obtain gauge

Notions

7 stitch markers
Blunt tapestry/yarn needle

Gauge

KID'S HAT: 21 sts and 25 rnds using smaller needles
= 4" (10cm) in stockinette
ADULT HAT: 16 sts and 20 rnds using smaller needles
= 4" (10cm) in stockinette
We're working on a magical gauge checker. Until we've
invented it, please check the gauge yourself. Thank you.

Techniques

THREE-NEEDLE BIND-OFF: Divide stitches evenly on
two needles. Hold both needles in left hand with
right sides together and needles parallel. Using a
third needle in your right hand, knit together the
first stitch from both needles. *Knit together the
next stitch from both needles. Lift first stitch on
right needle over top of second stitch, then off the
needle—1 stitch remains on right needle; repeat
from * until all stitches have been bound off. Fasten
off remaining stitch on right needle.

Abbreviations

beg begin(ning)
dpn(s) double pointed needle(s) • **k** knit
k2tog knit 2 stitches together (1 stitch decreased)
ndl(s) needle(s) • **pm** place marker
rem remain(ing) • **rep** repeat
rnd(s) round(s) • **RS** right side(s)
sl 1 wyif slip 1 stitch knitwise with yarn in front
s2kp insert needle into next 2 sts as if to knit 2
together and slip them together to the right needle,
knit 1, pass the 2 slipped stitches over the knit
stitch (2 stitches decreased)
ssk slip, slip, knit: Slip one stitch from left needle
to right needle, knitwise (as if to knit), slip second
stitch same way, insert left needle through front of
loops on right needle, then wrap yarn around right
needle. With left needle, bring loops over the yarn
wrapped around the right, which will knit them
together through the back of the loops (1 stitch
decreased).
st(s) stitches • **St st** stockinette stitch

tbl through the back of the loop(s)
tog together • **WS** wrong side(s)
yo yarn over to make 1 stitch

Tips

• While working the Garter Band, do not cut color
A or color B; carry the unused yarn up the side of the
band.
• Use a different type or color of marker to denote
the beginning of the round.
• Once you finish the decreases for the color A
hat (the "second hat") you won't have access to the

wrong side, so weave in all ends before starting the decreases for the color A hat.

• Because of the double thickness, the inner dimensions of the hat will be slightly smaller than the outer dimensions.

• Slip all stitches purlwise unless otherwise instructed.

• Stitch markers are used to indicate where to slip stitches and decrease; slip markers as you come to them.

KID'S HAT

Using larger ndls and A, cast on 13 sts.

ROW 1 (RS): K7, pm, k6.

ROW 2 AND ALL WS ROWS: With last color used, k to marker, sl1 wyif, k to end.

ROW 3: Join B. Using B, k.

ROW 5: Using A, k.

ROW 7: Using B, k all sts.

ROW 8: With B, k to marker, sl1 wyif, k to end.
Rep rows 5–8 another 26 (28) more times–56 (60) garter ridges.

JOINING: Using size 6 (4mm) dpn, pick up and k13 sts along cast-on edge. With RS tog and B, use three-needle bind-off to join, leaving the last loop on right needle. Do not cut A or B.

COLOR B HAT

Change to smaller dpns or circular ndl. With B and RS facing, pick up and k3 sts for every 2 garter ridges as follows: *1 st in B ridge, 1 st in A ridge, 1 st before next B ridge and k tbl, rep from * to end, ending with 1 st in A ridge—84 (90) sts. Join to work in the rnd, pm for beg of rnd.
K 3 rnds.

RND 4: *Work row 1 of A, pm, k14 (15), pm, rep from * 2 more times; 6 markers with 14 (15) sts between markers.

RND 5: *Work row 2 of A, k14 (15); rep from * 2 more times.

Work as established, to end of chart.
K even until hat measures 4½ (5)" [11.5 (13)cm] from center of garter band.

NOTE: Weave in all ends before starting crown.

CROWN

If using circular ndl, change to dpns when work is too small to fit comfortably on circular ndl.

SET-UP RND [SIZE S ONLY]: *K5, k2tog, pm, k to marker, remove marker; rep from * to end of rnd, leaving beg of rnd marker—78 sts.

SET-UP RND [SIZE M ONLY]: *K5, k2tog, pm, k1, ssk, k5, remove marker; rep from * to end of rnd, leaving beg of rnd marker—78 sts.

ALL SIZES

RND 1: K.

RND 2: *K to 2 sts before marker, k2tog, k1, ssk, rep from * 5 more times, k to end—66 sts.

Rep last 2 rnds 3 more times—30 sts rem.

NEXT RND: *K2tog, remove marker, k1, ssk, rep from * to end—18 sts.

NEXT RND: S2kp 6 times—6 sts.

Cut yarn, leaving a tail about 6" (15 cm) long. Use blunt tapestry/yarn needle to thread end through rem sts. Pull tight and weave in end.

COLOR A HAT

Using smaller circular ndl, color A, and with RS facing, beg at three-needle bind-off of garter band, pick up and k1 st before the A ridge and k tbl, 1 st in A ridge, 1 st in B ridge, rep from * to end—84 (90) sts.

Join to work in the rnd, pm for beg of rnd.

Beg St st and work until hat measures 4½ (5)" [11.5 (13)cm] from center of garter band.

NOTE: Weave in all ends before starting crown.

CROWN

Change to dpns when work is to small to fit comfortably on cir ndl.

SET-UP RND [SIZE S ONLY]: *K5, k2tog, pm; rep from * to end of rnd—78 sts.

SET-UP RND [SIZE M ONLY]: *K5, k2tog, pm, k1, ssk, k5; rep from * to end of rnd—78 sts.

Complete color A crown same as color B crown.

Push the color B hat into the color A hat and secure the tops of the 2 hats tog as you weave in the end at the top of the A hat.

ADULT HAT

GARTER BAND

Using larger ndls and A, cast on 13 sts.

ROW 1 (RS): K7, pm, k6.

ROW 2 AND ALL WS ROWS: With last color used, k to marker, sl1 wyif, k to end.

ROW 3: Join B. Using B, k.

ROW 5: Using A, k.

ROW 7: Using B, k all sts.

ROW 8: With B, k to marker, sl1 wyif, k to end.

Rep rows 5–8 another 24 (26, 28) more times—52 (56, 60) garter ridges.

JOINING: Using smaller dpn, pick up and k13 sts along cast on edge. With RS tog and B, use three-needle bind-off to join, leaving the last loop on right needle. Do not cut A or B.

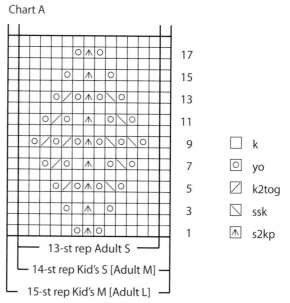

Chart A

				O	∧	O						17
			O		∧		O					15
		O	/	O	∧	O	\				13
	O	/	O		∧		O	\	O		11
O	/	O	/	O	∧	O	\	O	\	O	9

□ k
○ yo
╱ k2tog
╲ ssk
∧ s2kp

— 13-st rep Adult S —
— 14-st rep Kid's S [Adult M] —
— 15-st rep Kid's M [Adult L] —

COLOR B HAT

Change to smaller circular ndl. Slip rem st from dpn to circular ndl, with B and RS facing, pick up and k3 sts for every 2 garter ridges as follows: *1 st in B ridge, 1 st in A ridge, 1 st before next B ridge and k tbl, rep from * to end, ending with 1 st in A ridge—78 (84, 90) sts.

Join to work in the rnd, pm for beg of rnd.

K 3 rnds.

RND 4: *Work row 1 of chart A, pm, k13 (14, 15), pm, rep from * 2 more times; 6 markers with 13 (14, 15) sts between markers.

RND 5: K.

RND 6: *Work next row of chart A, k13 [14, 15]; rep from * 2 more times.

Rep rnds 2 and 3, to end of chart.

K even until hat measures 5½ (6, 6½)" [14 (15, 16.5)cm] from center of garter band.

CROWN

Change to dpns when work is too small to fit comfortably on circular ndl.

SET-UP RND [SIZES S (L)]: *K4 (5), k2tog, pm, k1, ssk, k4 (5), remove marker; rep from * to end of rnd, leaving beg of rnd marker—66 (78) sts.

SET-UP RND [SIZE M ONLY]: *K5, k2tog, pm, k to marker, remove marker; rep from * to end of rnd, leaving beg of rnd marker—78 sts.

ALL SIZES:

RND 1: K.

RND 2: *K to 2 sts before marker, k2tog, k1, ssk, rep

from * 5 more times, k to end—54 (66, 66) sts.

Rep last 2 rnds 2 (3, 3) more times—30 sts rem.

NEXT RND: *K2tog, remove marker, k1, ssk, rep from * to end—18 sts.

NEXT RND: S2kp 6 times—6 sts.

Cut yarn, leaving a tail about 6" (15cm) long. Use blunt tapestry/yarn needle to thread end through rem sts. Pull tight and weave in end.

COLOR A HAT

Using smaller circular ndl, A, and with RS facing, beg at three-needle bind-off of garter band, pick up and k1 st before the A ridge and k tbl, 1 st in A ridge, 1 st in B ridge, rep from * to end—78 (84, 90) sts.

Join to work in the rnd, pm for beg of rnd.

Beg St st and work until hat measures 5½ (6, 6½)" [14 (15, 16.5)cm] from center of garter band.

NOTE: Weave in all ends before starting crown.

CROWN

Change to dpns when work is too small to fit comfortably on circular ndl.

SET-UP RND [SIZES S (L)]: *K4 (5), k2tog, pm, k1, ssk, k4 (5); rep from * to end of rnd—66 (78) sts.

SET-UP RND [SIZE M ONLY]: *K5, k2tog, pm; rep from * to end of rnd—78 sts.

Complete color A crown same as color B crown.

Push the color B hat into the color A hat and secure the tops of the 2 hats tog as you weave in the end at the top of the color A hat.

VINTAGE QUILT SOCKS ...
Designed by Judy Sumner • Knit by Tami Sutter

These socks are big favorites with anyone who has made them or received them as gifts. To the pattern's advantage, Judy used the springy quality of the yarn, allowing this texture to rule the roost. The patterning stops before the foot enters the shoe, making for a cozy fit. Choose a different color, and it is great for women or men. ~ LISA

 Skill Level: WING CHAIR

Things You'll Need to Know
- Kitchener stitch
- Picking up stitches
- Knitting in the round on double-pointed needles

Sizes
One size fits most adults

Finished Measurements
Leg circumference: 7¼" (18.5cm)
Foot circumference: 7¼" (18.5cm)

Yarn
Lisa Souza *Hand Dyed Hardtwist Merino Petite* (100% merino superwash wool); 500 yds [457m]/3½ oz [100g]; sock weight/superfine [1]; 1 skein, shown in color Foxglove

Needles
Size US 1 (2.25mm) set of 5 double-pointed needles, or size needed to obtain gauge

Notions
Blunt tapestry/yarn needle

Gauge
33½ sts and 50 rnds = 4" (10cm) in stockinette
Each diamond = 2½" (6.5cm)
Go ahead, knit a giant, unwearable sock. Either that, or check your gauge.

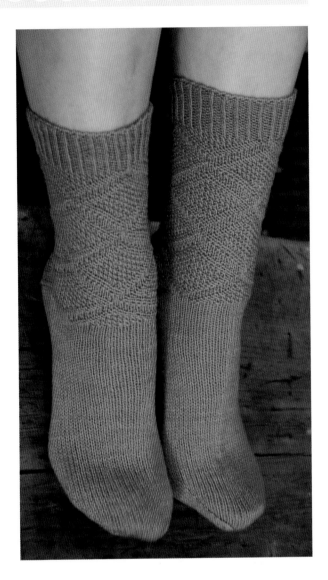

Techniques
KITCHENER STITCH (OR GRAFTING OR WEAVING):
In other words, you're joining two sets of live stitches without leaving a seam. Great tutorials are online at www.KnittingHelp.com (video) and www.Knitty.com. You'll need a tapestry needle for this.
MAKE 1: With tip of left needle, lift the strand of yarn between the last stitch worked and the next stitch by inserting the needle from front to back, then knit through the back of the loop to twist it (1 stitch increased).

Pattern Stitch

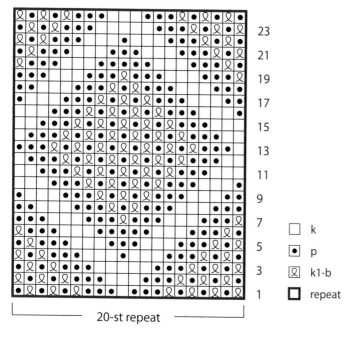

20-st repeat

☐	k
•	p
ℚ	k1-b
☐	repeat

Abbreviations

beg begin(ning) • **cont** continue

dec decreas(e)(ing) • **dpn(s)** double pointed needle(s) • **k** knit

k1-b knit 1 stitch through the back of the loop to twist it

k2tog knit 2 stitches together (1 stitch decreased)

m1 make 1 stitch • **ndl(s)** needle(s) • **p** purl

p2tog purl 2 stitches together (1 stitch decreased)

rem remain(ing) • **rep** repeat • **rnd(s)** round(s)

RS right side(s) • **sl** slip

skp slip, knit, pass: slip 1 stitch knitwise, knit 1 stitch, pass slipped stitch over top of knit stitch and off right needle (1 stitch decreased)

st(s) stitch(es) • **St st** stockinette stitch

tog together • **WS** wrong side(s)

Tip

• Work the top of the sock on three needles in order to work the pattern more easily. Once the heel flap has been completed, change to four (plus the working needle) so that it is easy to see which stitches will be the top (instep) and which will be the back/bottom of the sock.

Pattern Stitch (multiple of 20 sts)

RND 1: *(K1-b, p1) 4 times, p2, k1, p3, (k1-b, p1) 3 times; rep from * to end.

RND 2: *(P1, k1-b) 3 times, p3, k3, p3, (k1-b, p1) twice, k1-b; rep from * to end.

RND 3: *(K1-b, p1) 3 times, p2, k5, p3, (k1-b, p1) twice; rep from * to end.

RND 4: *(P1, k1-b) twice, p3, k3, p1, k3, p3, k1-b, p1, k1-b; rep from * to end.

RND 5: *(K1-b, p1) twice, p2, (k3, p3) twice, k1-b, p1; rep from * to end.

RND 6: *P1, k1-b, p3, k3, p5, k3, p3, k1-b; rep from * to end.

RND 7: *(K1-b, p3, k3, p3) twice; rep from * to end.

RND 8: *P3, k3, p3, (k1-b, p1) twice, p2, k3, p2; rep from * to end.

RND 9: *P2, k3, p3, (k1-b, p1) 3 times, p2, k3, p1; rep from * to end.

RND 10: *P1, k3, p3, (k1-b, p1) 4 times, p2, k3; rep from * to end.

RND 11: *K3, p3, (k1-b, p1) 5 times, p2, k2; rep from * to end.

RND 12: *K2, p3, (k1-b, p1) 6 times, p2, k1; rep from * to end.

RND 13: *K1, p3, (k1-b, p1) 7 times, p2; rep from * to end.

RND 14: Rep rnd 12.

RND 15: Rep rnd 11.

RND 16: Rep rnd 10.

RND 17: Rep rnd 9.

RND 18: Rep rnd 8.

RND 19: Rep rnd 7.

RND 20: Rep rnd 6.

RND 21: Rep rnd 5.

RND 22: Rep rnd 4.

RND 23: Rep rnd 3.

RND 24: Rep rnd 2.

Rep rnds 1–24 for pattern.

CUFF

Cast on 60 sts. Distribute sts evenly on three ndls with 20 sts on each ndl. Join to work in the rnd, being careful not to twist sts.

Work k1-b, p1 rib for 1½" (4cm).

Work Pattern St rnds 1–24 twice, then work rnds
1–12 once more.

SET-UP FOR HEEL FLAP:

NEXT RND, k15, place rem 5 sts from ndl 1 on ndl 2,
then turn.

Sl 1 st, p14 sts, then p15 from next ndl, and place
rem 5 sts from left ndl on ndl 2—30 sts on ndl 1
for heel flap. Rearrange sts on ndl 2 so there are 15
instep sts each on ndls 2 and 3.

HEEL FLAP

ROW 1 (RS): *Sl 1, k1; rep from * to end, turn.

ROW 2 (WS): Sl 1, p to end, turn.

Rep these 2 rows 11 more times, ending with
a WS row.

TURNING THE HEEL

ROW 1 (RS): Sl 1, k16, skp, k1, turn.

ROW 2 (WS): Sl 1, p5, p2tog, p1, turn.

ROW 3: Sl 1, k6, skp, k1, turn.

ROW 4: Sl 1, p7, p2tog, p1, turn.

Cont in this manner, working 1 more st before
dec on each row until all sts have been worked—
18 sts rem.

GUSSETS

NEXT ROW, k heel sts, pick up and k13 sts along side
of heel flap, m1 in loop between heel flap and instep
ndl, k across instep ndls, m1 in loop between instep
ndl and heel flap, pick up and k13 sts along rem side
of heel flap—76 sts.

Divide sts on 4 dpns; heel sts, m1, and gusset sts on
ndls 1 and 4, and instep sts on ndls 2 and 3.

Join to work in the rnd, beg rnds at center under
foot.

RND 1: NDL 1: K to last 2 sts, k tog the m1 st and
gusset st;

NDLS 2 AND 3: K;

NDL 4: Skp, then k to end—74 sts.

NEXT RND (DEC): NDL 1: K to last 3 sts, skp, k1;

NDLS 2 AND 3: K;

NDL 4: K1, k2tog, k to end—72 sts.

K 1 rnd even. Rep these 2 rnds 5 more times, then
dec rnd once more—60 sts rem, with 15 each on
ndls 1 and 4.

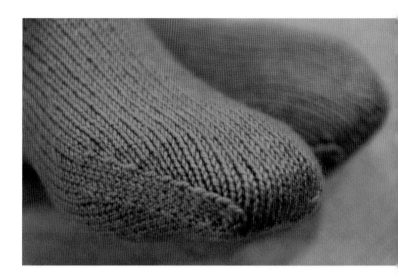

FOOT

Work even in St st until foot is 1½" (4cm) short of
desired length from back of heel.

TOE

NEXT RND (DEC): NDL 1: K to last 3 sts, skp, k1;

NDL 2: K1, k2tog, k to end of ndl;

NDL 3: K to last 3 sts, skp, k1;

NDL 4: K1, k2tog, k to end of rnd—56 sts.

K 2 rnds even.

Rep these 3 rnds twice more, then dec every other
rnd 3 times—36 sts. Dec every rnd 4 times—20 sts
rem. Sl sts from ndl 4 to ndl 1, and sts from ndl 2
to ndl 3.

Graft toe using Kitchener stitch. Block to finished
measurements.

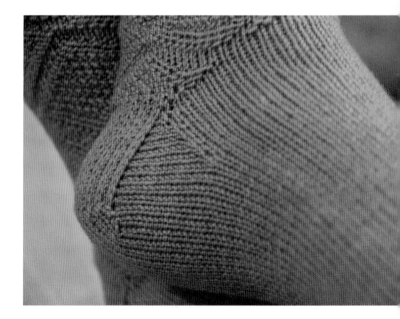

Take the Color Leap of Faith

or How to Gain Sure-footedness in the Color Jungle

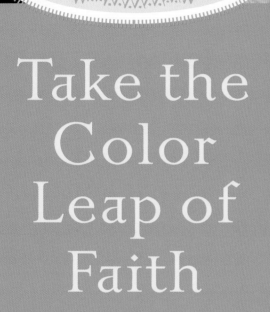

We All Love Color! Gosh, how we love color! Yet it scares the heck out of us. Do you . . .

- knit with the same colors over and over and over?
- knit only with the colors shown in a pattern?
- consistently pick black or gray or beige for a project?
- get terrified when the time comes to choose colors for a project?
- feel overwhelmed by the riot of color choices as you stand before a wall of yarn at your local yarn store (or LYS)?

If so, take heart, take hold, and be bold with your color creativity.

When it comes to color, children are born with no fear. Only as they're socialized at school do children learn to conform and to curb their creative color flow. As an adult, it's a challenge to unlearn that school programming. Perhaps now is the time to reawaken and trust your color instincts. Go ahead—ask that inner child to come out to play!

Kaffe Fassett taught knitters to dump out their yarn stash and see how the reds, the blues, the oranges, the purples they'd chosen naturally complemented one another. The genius of artist-teacher Fassett is that he reached out to those adults who had lost their colorful vision of the world. He taught legions to happily

MY STITCHES FELL OFF MY NEEDLE! NOW WHAT???

PANIC! NO, WE'RE KIDDING. BUT MOST PEOPLE DO JUST THAT. SO, YOU'VE DROPPED A PILE OF STITCHES, NOW YOU:

BREATHE DEEPLY AND RELAX, AS ALL GOOD LAIDBACK KNITTERS SHOULD.

THEN, SLIP THE STITCHES BACK ONTO THE NEEDLE IN THE ORDER THEY FELL OFF.

BUT ONE IS DROPPING DOWN FARTHER!!!

BREATHE, REMEMBER? GRAB AN OPENABLE STITCH MARKER OR SAFETY PIN, AND SECURE IT TO THE RUNAWAY STITCH. THEN, LATER, WHEN YOU'RE AGAIN COMPOSED, YOU CAN WEAVE THAT STITCH UP THE "LADDER" USING A CROCHET HOOK AND PLACE IT BACK ON THE NEEDLE.

ONCE IT'S BACK ON AND YOU BEGIN KNITTING AGAIN, GO SLOWLY, SO YOU CAN CHECK IF YOU'VE PUT ALL THE LOOPS ON IN THE SAME DIRECTION.

PEACE.

jump into the world of knitting with color, to create previously unimagined combinations that somehow naturally worked.

Ah, nature. . . . Imagine the blue in blueberries, the red of a cardinal, the azure of the Aegean Sea, the orange in a sunset. How about the gray bark of a beech tree or the brown of spring earth or the yellow of lemon peel? Picture the green of a palm leaf, the purple of a plum, the golden of amber. Nature's creations are riotous, subtle, shocking, calming. They're a feast, one meant to nourish the Laid Back Knitter.

When looking at a sample garment, do you ever wish that the designer had made it in another color? Do you have a favorite hue that you are not seeing represented in ready-to-wear? Whether you Google "color chart" online or peruse your LYS's dazzling wall of color, begin with a visual baseline when contemplating color for your next project.

Do you love the design of that little shrug shown in bright red but can't imagine yourself wearing that particular shade? What color makes your mouth water or triggers a grin? This is where you can begin to feed your soul. Have you always loved lime green or purple? This is your inner self, asking for permission to have some fun! Remember, there are no mistakes with color, just glorious choices.

Some of us are born with the artist's Eye, but most feel we must be taught color sense. Perhaps you just need some tools or crib notes (see "Color, Color Everywhere ..." on following page). Use a color wheel to help you visualize color relationships. Rings of color swatches work, too. Do you go for the cool colors of blue, green, and purple, or would you rather sizzle in the heat of yellow, red, and orange? Go low tech by gleaning bits and pieces from nature, medium tech by gathering paint chips from the hardware store, or high tech with a whizbang application for your iPhone, such as myPantone. Whatever you do, however you experiment, relax, have fun, and become playful again.

LISA, THE ARTIST

How can an artist explain the moment she first begins to observe the world in a way that translates to paper or canvas or fiber? For me, it was probably at the age of 4, with the aid of the cardboard from my dad's freshly laundered shirts and a child's tin of watercolor paint. At each point in my life, the creative palette would change—from the enamel tray used for my art-college watercolor class to the tray of my grandma's cedar chest, which housed my array of fine embroidery floss, arranged by colors and hues for the work that I did with mixed-media painting and embroidery. The medium did not matter, because color is color is color. And for me, color is always thrilling; color is Life.

I began to dye fiber for spinning in the mid-1980s because it seemed to be the natural progression of the craft. Whether ecru-or natural-colored fleece, I experimented by pouring and squirting color into my dye pots to create deep,

rich color changes that would entertain me as I spun for hours and hours and then knitted that colorful yarn into unique garments. What I learned working with dyed-in-the-wool yarn helped me years later to understand what I wanted to create in hand-dyed, mill-spun yarn. It was a quest to reproduce the look of that dye process, introduced at the core of the yarn. It began at a sheep shearing.

The physical palette can change from crayons to watercolor, beads to embroidery floss. But my color sense comes from within. I study nature and have found that my recent move to the foothills of the Sierras and the change of environment gave me a new perspective and renewed excitement for what I do. ~ LISA

Color, Color Everywhere . . . But What Does It All Mean?

Why does everyone talk about the color wheel? It simplifies, that's why. The color wheel represents a visual map of color.

PRIMARY COLORS: Red, blue, yellow.

SECONDARY COLORS: These come about by mixing primary colors—red and yellow make orange; yellow and blue make green; blue and red make violet. Hence, orange, green, and violet are secondary colors.

HUE: A hue family is a single hue (pure color) plus all its variations. Think lime green, khaki green, grass green, etc.

VALUE: How dark or light is the color?

SATURATION: How bright or dull is the color?

TINT: If you add white to a color, it makes the color less saturated and lighter.

SHADE: If you add black to a color, it makes the color less saturated and darker.

TONE: If you add gray to a color, it decreases the color's saturation but maintains its value.

ANALOGOUS COLORS sit next to each other on the color wheel. They share a common color.

COMPLEMENTARY COLORS sit opposite each other on the color wheel.

Another way to observe color theory is to take a stroll in nature.

Nature's colors: Alive and incomparable

TAKE A PHOTO . . . SEE WHAT COLOR CAN DO

Photographing your knitting can really help with your color choices. It allows you to step back and really see what might work and what might tank.

You say: I stink at photographing my knitting!

We say: Easily fixable with a few tips.

Here's how:

• **TAKE IT OUTDOORS:** Natural light is the best. Can't get outside? Go to a window where natural light spills inside. Try to avoid using a flash.

• **TIMING:** The early morning or late afternoon will allow you to capture the best images—no harsh shadows to ruin your photo.

• **GET STABLE:** Rest your arm on a tree trunk, a rock, or use a tripod. No blurs for you.

• **BACKGROUND:** Look for something simple, appealing, and natural. A rock, grass, a wood floor, even snow. If your yarn is variegated, don't use a busy background. You'll get mush.

• **WANT STITCH DEFINITION?** Use your macro setting if you have one.

• **FILL THE FRAME:** Avoid cropping. If you fill the frame with your image, you won't have to crop. If you must crop, do it with a simple imaging application.

• **BAG THE DIGITAL ZOOM:** Optical zoom is great, but digital zoom degrades the photo. You'll get what's called pixilation and/or noise. Not nice.

• **EMBELLISH:** Place your work next to a flower, a leaf, a rock, a porcelain cup, your dog—something interesting that complements the knitting. It'll add texture and depth to your photo.

With flickr, Ravelry, Facebook, Twitter, and MySpace, abundant opportunities exist for you to show off your knitting online, whether it's a work in progress or finished item.

MEMORIES TAB CARDIGAN ...
Designed by Brenda Patipa

Color, color, everywhere. Brenda and I threw colorful yarn down on the floor as we searched through my stash of yarns to create this riot of color. You can create any number of color combinations by going through the little balls of leftover yarn in your stash. Choose a main color and let your imagination soar. We bet that you and your friends will have fun swapping bits and bobs from past projects. Each little flag will be a tangible memory!
~ LISA

 Skill Level: **DINING CHAIR**

Things You'll Need to Know
• Short row shaping
• Knitting together stitches from two needles
• Making buttonholes
• Cable cast-on

Sizes
S (M, L, XL)
Instructions are given for size S, with larger sizes in parentheses. When only one number is given and no size is mentioned, that number applies to all sizes.

Finished Measurements
Bust: 36 (40, 44, 48)" [91.5 (101.5, 112, 122)cm]
Length: 22¾ (23½, 24¼, 25)" [56 (59.5, 61.5, 63.5)cm]

Yarn
Lisa Souza's *Hand Dyed Blue Faced Leicester Worsted* (100% wool); 250 yds [229m]/4 oz [113.5g]; worsted/medium weight [4].) 5 (6, 6, 7) skeins, shown in color Poiple (MC)
Assorted Lisa Souza yarns and colors, total of 250 (271, 290, 312) yds [229 (248, 265, 285)ml, is needed for tabs:
Blue Faced Leicester Sport (100% wool), shown in colors Electra and St. Valentine

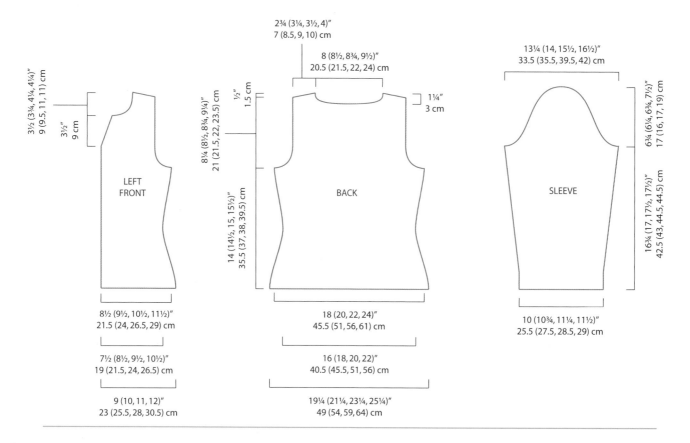

Blue Faced Leicester Worsted (100% wool), shown in color Emerald City

Super Sport (100% superfine superwash merino wool), shown in color Bruise

Glacier (100% silk), shown in color Silver Lake

Kid (90% kid mohair, 10% nylon), shown in color Elektra

Baby Alpaca Sport (100% baby alpaca), shown in color Aww-Tum

El Dorado (70% kid mohair, 30% silk), shown in color Poiple

Fat Bunny (60% angora, 20% merino wool, 20% nylon), shown in color Garnet

Handspun (50% cashmere, 50% merino), shown in color Tudor

Handspun (100% blue faced leicester), shown in color Aww-Tum

Needles

Size US 6 (4mm) needles, 32" (80cm) circular needle, and set of 5 double-pointed needles, or size needed to obtain gauge

Size US 6 (4mm) needle, 60" (152 cm) circular needle for button band (optional)

Notions

Removable stitch markers

Stitch holders, large safety pins, or spare needles to hold tabs

Three to five ¾" (19cm) buttons

Gauge

20 sts and 26 rows = 4" (10cm) in stockinette

You know what happens if you don't check your gauge? Exactly!

Techniques

WORKING SHORT ROWS: On right-side rows, knit to where you need to turn, bring the yarn to the right side, slip the next stitch purlwise, bring the yarn back to the wrong side, slip the stitch back to the left needle, then turn (wrap & turn; w&t). On wrong-side rows, purl to where you need to turn, bring yarn to right side of work, slip the next stitch purlwise, bring the yarn to back to the wrong side, slip the stitch back to the left needle, then turn (wrap & turn; w&t).

PICKING UP AND WORKING WRAPS: On right-side rows, knit to the wrapped stitch, lift the wrap up and over the stitch, knit both wrap and stitch together through the back of the loops so the wrap falls to the wrong side. On wrong-side rows, purl to the wrapped stitch, lift the wrap up from the right side and over the stitch, purl both wrap and stitch together.

ONE-ROW BUTTONHOLES: Bring yarn to front of work, slip 1 purlwise, then bring yarn to back of work. * Slip next stitch from left needle and pass first slipped stitch over second stitch and off needle to bind off 1 stitch; repeat from * until required number of stitches for buttonhole have been bound off. Slip the last bound-off stitch back to left needle and turn. Use cable cast-on and cast on 1 more stitch than was bound off, then turn. Slip the first stitch from left needle and pass the extra cast-on stitch over the slipped stitch.

CABLE CAST-ON: An easy cast-on, once you're clear how it works. Keep it loose, or you'll get into trouble. Start with a slip knot. Knit into the slip knot, leaving the stitch on the left needle. *Knit into the gap between the two stitches on the left needle. Place the knitted stitch that's now on the right needle onto the left needle. And so on. Thanks to www.KnittingHelp.com for the info. (Seeing the video of this cast-on makes all the difference.)

Abbreviations

beg begin(ning) • **BO** bind off

cont continu(e)(ing) • **dec** decrease

dpn(s) double-pointed needle(s)

inc increase • **k** knit

k2tog knit 2 stitches together (1 stitch decreased)

m1 make 1: With tip of left needle, lift the strand of yarn between the last stitch worked and the next stitch by inserting the needle from front to back, then knit through the back of the loop to twist it (1 stitch increased).

MC main color • **ndl(s)** needle(s) • **p** purl

rem remain(ning) • **rep** repeat

RS right side(s) • **s1** slip

ssk slip, slip, knit: Slip one stitch from left needle to right needle, knitwise (as if to knit), slip second stitch same way, insert left needle through front of loops on right needle, then wrap yarn around right needle. With left needle, bring loops over the yarn wrapped around the right, which will knit them together through the back of the loops (1 stitch decreased). • **st(s)** stitch(es) • **St st** stockinette stitch • **tog** together • **w&t** wrap and turn (see techniques) **WS** wrong side(s)

Tips

• Each tab uses approximately 2 yards (1.8m) of yarn, and there are about 120 (130, 140, 150) tabs on this sweater. Yarn weights vary, but all were knit using size US 6 (4mm) needles. You'll need to use 2 strands for some thinner yarns.

• Widths of the tabs vary depending on the yarn used, but all are about 1" (2.5cm) long.

• Weave in the cast-on tails of the tabs while you knit, eliminating the need to do it all later. To weave in as you knit, hold both the tail and the working end of the yarn together as you knit. When you reach the last stitch, bring the yarn to the back of the work between the last 2 stitches, then slip the last stitch and turn.

• As you continue to make tabs, slip tabs of the same yarn and color to the same needles or stitch holders. This way, as you need to add tabs to the sweater, you have easy access to one of any color and yarn.

• All shaping for the armholes, neck, and shoulders are done by working short rows, then binding off after the short rows are complete. This creates a smooth edge, so you don't have the stair step edge you get when binding off traditionally.

TABS

Make 120 (130, 140, 150) tabs; more or fewer may be needed depending on your knitting gauge and resulting width of tabs.

With dpns, cast on 6–9 sts as desired. Work back and forth.

ROW 1: K to last st, weaving in tail as you work, sl last st.

ROW 2: K first st, k to last st, weaving in rem tail as you work, sl last st.

Cont with working strand only until tab measures about 1" (2.5cm). Cut yarn, leaving a 7" (18cm) tail. Sl sts to holder.

POCKET LINING (make 2)

Using dpns and MC, cast on 20 (22, 24, 26) sts. Working back and forth, work 4" (10cm) of St st. Sl sts for pocket to holder.

BACK

Using circular ndl and MC, cast on 96 (106, 116, 126) sts. Working back and forth, k 4 rows.

NEXT ROW (RS, ATTACH TABS): K1, sl sts for 1 tab to dpn and hold in front of work, *with both MC and yarn from tab held tog, k tog 1 st of tab and next st of body; rep from * until tab is attached. Cont attaching tabs across row to last st, end k1. Work 3 rows of St st.

NEXT ROW: K1, attach tabs across row as before to last st, end k1.

Rep last 4 rows once more. P 1 row.

WAIST SHAPING

NEXT ROW (RS): K1, ssk, k to last 3 sts, k2tog, k1—94 (104, 114, 124) sts.

Work 3 rows even. Rep these 4 rows 6 more times, then dec row once more—80 (90, 100, 110) sts. Work 7 (9, 9, 11) rows even.

NEXT ROW (RS): K1, m1, k to last st, m1, k1—82 (92, 102, 112) sts.

Work 5 rows even. Rep these 6 rows 3 more times, then inc row once more—90 (100, 110, 120) sts. Work even until piece measures 14 (14½, 15, 15½)" [35.5 (37, 38, 39.5)cm] from cast-on edge, end with a WS row.

SHAPE ARMHOLES

ROW 1: (RS): K85 (95, 105, 115), w&t.

ROW 2: (WS): P80 (90, 100, 110), w&t.

ROW 3: K77 (87, 96, 107), w&t.

ROW 4: P74 (84, 92, 102), w&t.

ROW 5: K73 (81, 89, 99), w&t.

ROW 6: P72 (78, 86, 96), w&t.

ROW 7: K71 (77, 84, 93), w&t.

ROW 8: P70 (76, 82, 90), w&t.

ROW 9: K69 (75, 81, 89), w&t.

ROW 10: P68 (74, 80, 88), w&t.

ROW 11: K to end, picking up wraps and knitting them tog with the sts they wrapped.

BO 11 (13, 15, 16) sts at beg of next 2 rows, picking up wraps and working them tog with the sts they wrapped—68 (74, 80, 88) sts.

Work even until armhole measures 7¼ (7½, 7¾, 8¼)" [18.5 (19, 19.5, 21)cm], end with a WS row.

RIGHT SHOULDER AND NECK SHAPING

ROW 1 (RS): K25 (27, 29, 31), w&t.

ROWS 2, 4, 6, AND 8 (WS): P.

ROW 3: K21 (23, 25, 27), w&t.

ROW 5: K18 (20, 22, 24), w&t.

ROW 7: K16 (18, 20, 22), w&t.

ROW 9: K14 (16, 18, 20), w&t.

ROW 10: P7 (8, 9, 10), w&t.

ROW 11: K to end, picking up wraps and knitting them tog with the sts they wrapped.

LEFT SHOULDER AND NECK SHAPING

ROW 1: (WS): P25 (27, 29, 31), w&t.

ROWS 2, 4, 6, AND 8 (WS): K.

ROW 3: P21 (23, 25, 27), w&t.

ROW 5: P18 (20, 22, 24), w&t.

ROW 7: P16 (18, 20, 22), w&t.

ROW 9: P14 (16, 18, 20), w&t.

ROW 10: K7 (8, 9, 10), w&t.

ROW 11: P7 (8, 9, 10), w&t.

ROW 12: K14 (16, 18, 20).

ROW 13: BO purlwise, picking up wraps and purling them tog with the sts they wrapped.

RIGHT FRONT

Using circular ndl and MC, cast on 45 (50, 55, 60) sts. Working back and forth, k 4 rows.

Attach a row of tabs in same manner as back.

Work 3 rows of St st.

Rep last 4 rows once more, then attach another row of tabs.

P 1 row.

WAIST SHAPING

NEXT ROW (RS): K to last 3 sts, k2tog, k1—44 (49, 54, 59) sts.

Work 3 rows even. Rep these 4 rows 6 more times, then dec row once more—37 (42, 47, 52) sts.

Work 1 row even.

INSERT POCKET

Sl pocket sts to dpn.

K8 (9, 11, 12) sts of front, with RS facing and pocket lining sts held in back of front piece, k first st of pocket lining tog with next st of right front, sl next 18 (20, 22, 24) sts of front to holder, k pocket sts from dpn, then k to end.

Work 5 (7, 7, 9) rows even.

NEXT ROW (RS): K to last st, m1, k1—38 (43, 48, 53) sts.

Work 5 rows even. Rep these 6 rows 3 more times, then inc row once more—42 (47, 52, 57) sts.

Work even until piece measures 14 (14½, 15, 15½)" [35.5 (37, 38, 39.5)cm] from cast-on edge, end with a WS row.

SHAPE ARMHOLE

ROW 1 (RS): K37 (42, 47, 52), w&t.

ROWS 2, 4, 6, 8, AND 10 (WS): P.

ROW 3: K34 (39, 43, 47), w&t.

ROW 5: K33 (36, 40, 44), w&t.

ROW 7: K32 (35, 38, 42), w&t.

ROW 9: K31 (34, 37, 41), w&t.

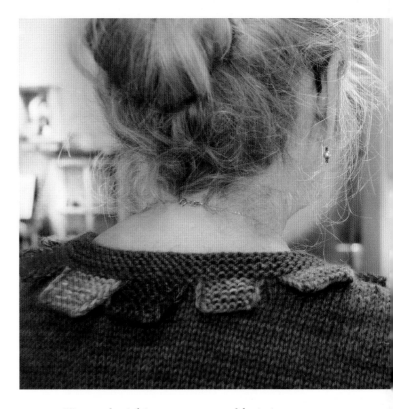

ROW 11: K to end, picking up wraps and knitting them tog with the sts they wrapped.

ROW 12: BO 11 (13, 15, 16) sts purlwise, p to end—31 (34, 37, 41) sts.

SHAPE RIGHT NECK EDGE

NEXT ROW (RS): K1, ssk, k to end—30 (33, 36, 40) sts.

Work 3 rows even. Rep last 4 rows 5 times more, then k 1 more row—25 (28, 31, 35) sts.

ROW 23 (WS): P21 (23, 26, 30), w&t.

ROWS 24 AND 26: K.

ROW 25: P18 (20, 23, 26), w&t.

ROW 27: P16 (18, 20, 23), w&t.

ROW 28: K, picking up wraps and knitting them tog with the sts they wrapped, and AT SAME TIME, bind off the first 11 (12, 13, 15) sts—14 (16, 18, 20) sts.

Work even until armhole measures same as back to shoulder, end with a WS row.

NEXT ROW (RS): K7 (8, 9, 10), w&t.

NEXT ROW (WS): P.

BO all sts, picking up wrap and knitting it tog with the st it wrapped.

LEFT FRONT

Using circular ndl and MC, cast on 45 (50, 55, 60) sts. Work back and forth, k 4 rows.

Attach a row of tabs in same manner as back.

Work 3 rows of St st.

Rep last 4 rows once more, then attach another row of tabs.

P 1 row.

WAIST SHAPING

NEXT ROW (RS): K1, ssk, k to end—44 (49, 54, 59) sts.

Work 3 rows even. Rep these 4 rows 6 more times, then dec row once more—37 (42, 47, 52) sts.

Work 1 row even.

INSERT POCKET

Sl pocket sts to dpn.

K9 (11, 12, 14) sts of front, with RS facing and pocket lining sts held in back of front piece, k first st of pocket lining tog with next st of right front, sl next 18 (20, 22, 24) sts of front to holder, k pocket sts from dpn, then k to end.

Work 5 (7, 7, 9) rows even.

NEXT ROW (RS): K1, m1, k to end—38 (43, 48, 53) sts.

Work 5 rows even. Rep these 6 rows 3 more times,

then inc row once more—42 (47, 52, 57) sts.

Work even until piece measures 14 (14½, 15, 15½)" [35.5 (37, 38, 39.5)cm] from cast-on edge, end with a RS row.

SHAPE ARMHOLE

ROW 1 (WS): P37 (42, 47, 52), w&t.

ROWS 2, 4, 6, 8, AND 10 (RS): K.

ROW 3: P34 (39, 43, 47), w&t.

ROW 5: P33 (36, 40, 44), w&t.

ROW 7: P32 (35, 38, 42), w&t.

ROW 9: P31 (34, 37, 41), w&t.

ROW 11: P to end, picking up wraps and purling them tog with the sts they wrapped.

ROW 12: BO 11 (13, 15, 16) sts knitwise, k to end— 31 (34, 37, 41) sts.

Work 1 row even.

SHAPE LEFT NECK EDGE

NEXT ROW (RS): K to last 3 sts, k2tog, k1—30 (33, 36, 40) sts.

Work 3 rows even. Rep last 4 rows 5 times more— 25 (28, 31, 35) sts.

ROW 23 (RS): K21 (23, 26, 30), w&t.

ROWS 24 AND 26: P.

ROW 25: K18 (20, 23, 26), w&t.

ROW 27: K16 (18, 20, 23), w&t.

ROW 28: P picking up wraps and purling them tog with the sts they wrapped, and AT SAME TIME, bind off the first 11 (12, 13, 15) sts—14 (16, 18, 20) sts.

Work even until armhole measures same as back to shoulder, end with a RS row.

NEXT ROW (WS): P7 (8, 9, 10), w&t.

NEXT ROW (RS): K.

BO all sts, picking up wrap and purling it tog with the st it wrapped.

SLEEVES (make 2)

Using circular ndl and MC, cast on 50 (54, 56, 58) sts. Working back and forth, k 4 rows.

Attach a row of tabs in same manner as back.

Work 3 rows of St st.

Rep last 4 rows once more, then attach another row of tabs.

P 1 row.

NEXT ROW (RS): K1, m1, k to last st, m1, k1—52 (56, 58, 60) sts.

Work 11 (11, 7, 7) rows even. Rep last 12 (12, 8, 8) rows 6 (6, 4, 6) more times, then rep inc row once more—66 (70, 68, 74) sts.

SIZES L AND XL: Work 9 rows even. Rep inc row. Rep last 10 rows 4 (3) times more—78 (82) sts.

ALL SIZES: Work even until sleeve measures 16¾ (17, 17½, 17½)" [42.5 (43, 44.5, 44.5)cm] from cast-on edge, end with a WS row.

SHAPE CAP

ROW 1 (RS): K61 (65, 73, 77), w&t.

ROW 2 (WS): P56 (60, 68, 72), w&t.

ROW 3: K53 (57, 64, 68), w&t.

ROW 4: P50 (54, 60, 64), w&t.

ROW 5: K49 (51, 57, 61), w&t.

ROW 6: P48 (48, 54, 58), w&t.

ROW 7: K47 (47, 52, 55), w&t.

ROW 8: P46 (46, 50, 52), w&t.

ROW 9: K45 (45, 49, 51), w&t.

ROW 10: P44 (44, 48, 50), w&t.

ROW 11: K to end, picking up wraps and knitting them tog with the sts they wrapped.

Bind off 11 (13, 15, 16) sts at beg of next 2 rows, picking up wraps and working them tog with the sts they wrapped—44 (44, 48, 50) sts.

Work 10 (8, 8, 14) rows even.

NEXT ROW (RS): K1, ssk, k to last 3 sts, k2tog, k1—42 (42, 46, 48) sts.

Work 1 row even. Rep these 2 rows 5 (5, 6, 6) more times—32 (32, 34, 36) sts.

NEXT ROW (RS): K30 (30, 32, 34), w&t.

NEXT ROW (WS): P28 (28, 30, 32), w&t.

NEXT ROW: K26 (26, 28, 30), w&t.

NEXT ROW: P24 (24, 26, 28), w&t.

NEXT ROW: K21 (22, 24, 26), w&t.

NEXT ROW: P18 (20, 22, 24), w&t.

NEXT ROW: K15 (17, 19, 21), w&t.

NEXT ROW: P12 (14, 16, 18), w&t.

NEXT ROW: K to end, picking up wraps and knitting them tog with the sts they wrapped.

NEXT ROW: P to end, picking up wraps and purling them tog with the sts they wrapped.

BO all sts knitwise.

POCKET TRIM

Choose 3 tabs for pocket edge, making smaller tabs if needed.

Sl sts for one pocket to dpn.

With RS facing and holding ndl with tabs in front of work, attach tabs to front as before.

Work 1" (2.5cm) of garter st, end with a WS row.

Bind off knitwise on RS.

Neatly sew ends of garter st band to front.

Complete rem pocket trim in same manner.

Finishing

Weave in ends. Block to finished measurements.

Sew body tog at shoulders and sides. Sew sleeves tog along underarm edges.

Sew sleeves into armholes.

FRONT BAND

Place markers on both sides of front for placement of buttons and buttonholes; place top markers at the bottom of V-neck shaping, then evenly space rem markers as desired, keeping bottom markers above pockets.

Using circular ndl and MC, and with RS facing, beg at lower edge of right front, pick up and k2 sts for every 3 rows along vertical edges, and 1 st in each st along edges of front and back neck shaped with short rows.

Pm at corners of front neck shaping and bottom of V-neck.

Cut yarn, leaving a tail to weave in.

Work back and forth, beg with a RS row.

ROW 1: K, joining tabs as desired along neck and front edges.

ROW 2: K and m1 at both markers at bottom of V-neck, and m1 on both sides of both markers at corners of front neck.

K 2 rows even.

ROW 5: Rep row 2 and work buttonholes, each over 2 sts on right front where marked.

K 3 rows even.

Bind off knitwise. Weave in rem ends.

Sew buttons to left front at markers.

MAYFAIR RUFFLES BAG ...
Designed by Holly Haynes

Felting is one of those things that I've seen work time and again, yet with each object I felt, I'm again stunned by the process and its results. From the years-ago moment I held my hideously Barbie-sized Villager sweater —courtesy of Mom—to the day I photographed Holly's beautifully sculpted and ruffled bag, felting has fostered my awe in the magic of nature. By using a deep, saturated color for Holly's bag, you'll achieve a real Pow! effect. ~ VICKI

 Skill Level: RECLINER

Things You'll Need to Know
- How to knit an I-cord
- Mirrored decreases
- Increasing stitches by knitting into the front and back of the loop
- Picking up stitches

Size
Approximately 6½" (16.5cm) high x 11½" (29cm) long after felting

Yarn
Brown Sheep *Lamb's Pride Worsted* (85% mohair, 15% wool); 190 yds [174m]/4 oz [113g] skein; worsted weight/medium [4]; 2 skeins, shown in color Fuchsia M23

Needles
Size US 13 (9mm), 16"–24" (40–60cm) long circular needle
Size US 15 (10mm), 16"–24" (40–60cm) long circular and double-pointed needles, or size needed to obtain gauge

Notions
Stitch markers
Removable stitch marker
Zippered pillowcase

SHOUT COLOR CATCHERS® (available in the U.S. and Canada; similar products are available in other countries)
Pins
Sewing needle and thread or embroidery floss
Buttons (optional)
Magnetic snap (optional)
Beaded chain (optional)

Gauge
10 sts and 12 rows using larger needles before felting = 4" (10cm) over stockinette
Checking the gauge is a pain. We know. But just pretend it's fun.

Techniques
THREE-NEEDLE BIND-OFF: Divide stitches evenly on two needles. Hold both needles in left hand with right sides together and needles parallel. Using a third needle in your right hand, knit together the first stitch from both needles. *Knit together the next stitch from both needles. Lift first stitch on right needle over top of second stitch, then off the needle—1 stitch remains on right needle; repeat from * until all stitches have been bound off. Fasten off remaining stitch on right needle.

I-CORD: Cast on required number of stitches. Knit 1 row and do not turn. Slip stitches back to right end of needle. *Pull yarn from end of row and knit 1 row. Without turning, slide stitches back to right end of needle; repeat from*.

Abbreviations
beg begin(ning) • **BO** bind off • **cir** circular
cont continu(e)(ing) • **dec** decrease(s)
inc increase(s) • **k** knit
k2tog knit 2 stitches together (1 stitch decreased)
kfb knit into the front loop, then through the back loop of the same stitch (1 stitch increased)
ndl(s) needle(s) • **rem** remain(ing) • **rep** repeat

rnd(s) round(s) • RS right side(s)
skp slip 1 stitch knitwise, knit 1 stitch, pass slipped stitch over knit stitch (1 stitch decreased)
st(s) stitch(es) • St st stockinette stitch
tog together • WS wrong side(s)

Tips

• Stitch markers are used to indicate the beginning and center of rounds; slip markers as you come to them.
• The final size of this bag will vary depending on the yarn, the number of times the pieces are washed, and the water temperature used. Knitting and felting a swatch is highly recommended.
• Carefully check the pieces after each wash cycle for desired size and felted consistency; once they have begun to felt, things will go quickly. Once the pieces have felted, there is only a small amount of stretching that can be done, so it's important to keep a close watch on the process. The bag shown was washed in 130°F (54°C) water.
• The strap may not felt at the same speed as the bag, so it's recommended to felt both pieces before attaching the strap.

BAG BODY

Using smaller cir ndl and 1 strand of yarn, cast on 70 sts. Join to work in the rnd, making sure not to twist sts; mark beg of rnd.

RND 1: K35, place center marker, then k to end.

RND 2: P.

Change to larger cir ndl. K 4 rnds.

RND 7: Kfb, k33, kfb twice, k33, kfb—74 sts. K 3 rnds even.

RND 11: Kfb, k35, kfb twice, k35, kfb—78 sts.
Cont inc every 4th rnd 4 more times, with 2 more sts between inc each time—94 sts. Work 2 rnds even.

RND 30: K1, skp, k to 3 sts before center marker, k2tog, k2, skp, k to last 3 sts, k2tog, k1—90 sts. K 1 rnd even.

RND 32: K1, skp, k to 3 sts before center marker, k2tog, k2, skp, k to last 3 sts, k2tog, k1—86 sts.
Rep last rnd once more—82 sts. K1 rnd even.

RNDS 35–37: K1, skp, k to 3 sts before center marker, k2tog, k2, skp, k to last 3 sts, k2tog, k1—70 sts.
K 1 rnd even. Rep dec rnd once—66 sts.
Rep last 2 rows once more—62 sts.
Bind off. Sew bottom of bag tog.

OPTION: Instead of binding off, distribute sts evenly over two needles so that beg of rnd and center of rnd are at sides of bag's body. Turn bag with WS out and bind off sts using three-needle BO.

FLAP

Using removable marker and with RS facing, mark center st on back edge of bag.

Using larger cir ndl and 2 strands of yarn held tog, beg 15 sts before marker and pick up and k31 sts along top back edge of bag's body.

Working back and forth, k 2 rows.

ROW 3, AND ALL OTHER ODD-NUMBERED ROWS THROUGH ROW 23: P.

ROW 4: K1, skp, k to last 3 sts, k2tog, k1—29 sts.

Rep last 2 rows 5 more times—19 sts.

ROW 16: K1, skp, k1, k2tog, k to last 6 sts, (k2tog, k1) twice—15 sts.

ROW 18: K1, skp, k to last 3 sts, k2tog, k1—13 sts.

ROW 20: K1, skp, k1, k2tog, k to last 6 sts, (k2tog, k1) twice—9 sts.

ROW 22: K1, skp, k3, k2tog, k1—7 sts.

ROW 24: K1, skp, k1, k2tog, k1—5 sts.

ROW 25: K2tog, k1, k2tog—3 sts.

ROW 26: K3tog.

Cut yarn, and leave a tail about 6" [15cm] long. Thread tail through rem st. Weave in ends.

FLAP EDGING

Using smaller cir ndl, 1 strand of yarn, and with RS facing, pick up and k27 sts along one side edge of flap, 2 sts in point, then 27 sts along rem side of flap—56 sts.

Working back and forth, kfb in each st across row—112 sts.

K 1 row, then work 8 rows of St st.

Bind off loosely in St st.

I-CORD STRAP

Using larger ndls and 2 strands of yarn held tog, cast on 4 sts.

Work I-cord as directed above until cord measures 50" (127cm) long.

Bind off.

FELTING

Place bag and strap into a zippered pillowcase (strap may be felted separately if desired), and add some type of color absorbent, which traps loose dyes in the wash (SHOUT COLOR CATCHER® works well). Close pillowcase. Place pillowcase into washing machine with heavy items. Add ¼ cup (about 60ml) of vinegar and soap (1 tablespoon [about 15ml] for front-loading machines and ¼ cup [about 60ml] for top-loading washing machines) to wash cycle each time. Set machine to hot wash/cold rinse cycle. Check bag after each wash cycle to determine size and change COLOR CATCHER® as needed.

The process may take 3 or 4 cycles to achieve desired felting; the strap may need to be put through only 2 cycles, so make sure to check both bag and strap each time. Watch carefully while washing.

Finishing

When pieces have reached desired size, remove from washer. Stretch and pull into shape as needed. You may need to finger-shape the ruffle around the edge of the flap for desired fullness.

Stuff the bag with plastic grocery bags to give it shape. Straighten the strap to make sure it will dry straight. Allow all pieces to air-dry completely.

ATTACHING STRAP

Pin ends of strap to inside of bag, placing ends about ¾" (2cm) below top edge at sides.

Using matching thread, sew each end of strap to inside of bag, taking care not to twist strap.

A button can be added to the outside of the flap, and a magnetic snap used on the underside if desired. Sew the magnetic snap pieces to small pieces of ribbon, then sew the ribbon to the front of the bag and the back of the flap.

AUDREY'S ELFIN LEAVES ...
Designed by Audrey F. Clarke

Few do color better than Mr. Eisaku Noro, creator of Noro Yarns. The yarn we use here—Noro Kureyon—is especially legendary for its stunning color changes. Mr. Noro's artistry encompasses his belief in the purity and preservation of nature. He oversees everything, from the color choices and dye process to using only fiber from animals raised in chemical-free and humane conditions. Our kind of man and our kind of yarn.

Audrey Clarke designed and knit the marvelous Audrey's Elfin Leaves. Sadly, Audrey passed away before our book was complete. And so we dedicate this page in loving memory of Audrey Filion Clarke.

Skill Level: **DINING CHAIR**

Things You Need to Know
• Cable cast-on
• Attaching a border as you knit
• Simple lace knitting
• Simple crochet

Finished Measurements
Width: 6" (15cm)
Length: 83" (211cm)

Yarn
Noro *Kureyon Sock* (70% wool, 30% nylon); 462 yds [422m]/3½ oz [100g]; sock/superfine weight [1]; 2 skeins, shown in color Lime, Hot Pink, Orange #95

Needles
Size US 4 (3.5mm) needles, 32" (80cm) circular needle, or size needed to obtain gauge
Size D/3 (3mm) crochet hook

Notions
Blunt tapestry/yarn needle (optional)
Size US 4 (3.5mm) spare double-pointed needle (optional)

Gauge
15 sts = 4" (10cm) in garter
Border = about 1¾" (4.5cm) wide
Eenie, meenie, miney, gauge. OK, we can't think of any rhymes, but if you check your gauge, maybe you can.

Techniques
CABLE CAST-ON: An easy cast-on, once you're clear how it works. Keep it loose, or you'll get into trouble. Start with a slip knot. Knit into the slip knot, leaving the stitch on the left needle. *Knit into the gap between the two stitches on the left needle. Place the knitted stitch that's now on the right needle onto the left needle. And so on. Thanks to www. KnittingHelp.com for the info. (Seeing the video of this cast-on makes all the difference.)

ATTACHING BORDER AS YOU KNIT: This is worked along an edge with either live stitches or loops along the edges. Every other row, as you work back toward

the main part of the piece, knit the last border stitch together with the next live stitch or edge loop, then turn. Slip the first stitch, then work to the outer edge of the border.

TURNING CORNERS: To turn the corner, you'll need to work extra rows before and after the corner for the border to lie flat. When you reach the last stitch of one side edge, work the joining row as before, then turn. Slip the first stitch and work to the outer edge of the border. On the next joining row, instead of working into the next edge stitch or loop, knit the last border stitch together with the previous edge loop or live stitch, then turn. Slip the first stitch and work back to the outer edge of the border—4 rows have been worked into 1 stitch. Repeat these 4 rows with the first edge loop along the next side edge.

PICOT: *Chain 5, slip stitch in last single crochet; repeat from * twice more—3 chain loop picots made.

Abbreviations

beg begin(ning) • **BO** bind off • **k** knit
kfb knit into the front loop, then through the back loop of the same stitch (1 stitch increased)
k2tog knit 2 stitches together (1 stitch decreased)
ndl(s) needle(s) • **p** purl
rem remain • **rep** repeat
RS right side(s) • **sc** single crochet
sk2p slip 1 stitch knitwise, knit 2 stitches together, pass slipped stitches over (2 stitches decreased)
sl slip • **Sl st** slip stitch
ssk slip, slip, knit: Slip one stitch from left needle to right needle, knitwise (as if to knit), slip second stitch same way, insert left needle through front of loops on right needle, then wrap yarn around right needle. With left needle, bring loops over the yarn wrapped around the right, which will knit them together through the back of the loops (1 stitch decreased).
st(s) stitch(es) • **tog** together • **WS** wrong side(s)
wyb with yarn in back • **yo** yarn over

Scallop Leaf Border

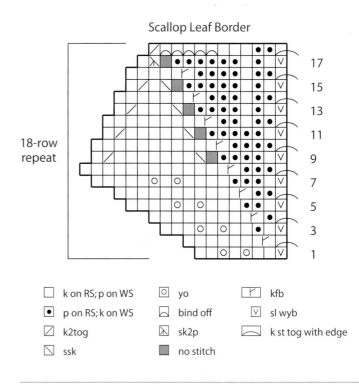

18-row repeat

☐ k on RS; p on WS	◉ yo
• p on RS; k on WS	◸ bind off
◩ k2tog	◪ sk2p
◺ ssk	▨ no stitch
⌐ kfb	
V sl wyb	
◡ k st tog with edge	

Pattern Stitch

SCALLOP LEAF BORDER (beg with 6 sts)
ROW 1 (RS): Sl 1, k2, yo, k1, yo, k2—8 sts.
ROW 2 (WS): P6, kfb, k last st tog with edge—9 sts.
ROW 3: Sl 1, k1, p1, k2, yo, k1, yo, k3—11 sts.
ROW 4: P8, kfb, k1, k last st tog with edge—12 sts.
ROW 5: Sl 1, k1, p2, k3, yo, k1, yo, k4—14 sts.
ROW 6: P10, kfb, k2, k last st tog with edge—15 sts.
ROW 7: Sl 1, k1, p3, k4, yo, k1, yo, k5—17 sts.
ROW 8: P12, kfb, k3, k last st tog with edge—18 sts.
ROW 9: Sl 1, k1, p4, ssk, k7, k2tog, k1—16 sts.
ROW 10: P10, kfb, k4, k last st tog with edge—17 sts.
ROW 11: Sl 1, k1, p5, ssk, k5, k2tog, k1—15 sts.
ROW 12: P8, kfb, k2, p1, k2, k last st tog with edge—16 sts.
ROW 13: Sl 1, k1, p1, k1, p4, ssk, k3, k2tog, k1—14 sts.
ROW 14: P6, kfb, k3, p1, k2, k last st tog with edge—15 sts.
ROW 15: Sl 1, k1, p1, k1, p5, ssk, k1, k2tog, k1—13 sts.
ROW 16: P4, kfb, k4, p1, k2, k last st tog with edge—14 sts.
ROW 17: Sl 1, k1, p1, k1, p6, sk2p, k1—12 sts.

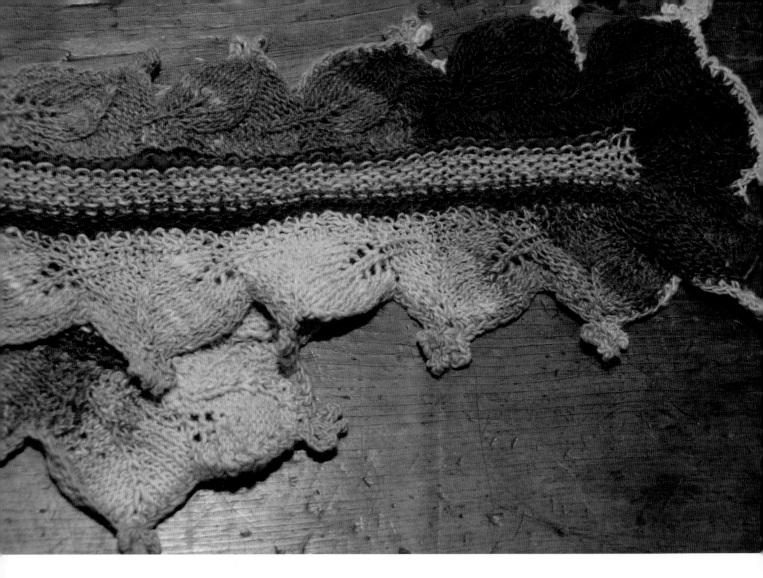

ROW 18: P2tog, BO 5 sts, k1, p1, k2, k last st tog with edge—6 sts.

Rep rows 1—18 for pattern.

CENTER STRIP

With circular ndl, cast on 300 sts.

Working back and forth, k 14 rows; do not cut yarn.

LEAF BORDER

Using cable cast-on method, cast on 6 sts at end of last row.

SET-UP ROW (WS): P5, k last border st tog with first st of center strip, then turn.

Beg Scallop Leaf Border, working last st of every WS row tog with next st along edge of center strip, and working 2 WS rows into each corner.

After working last live st on long edge, pick up 22 loops along short edge, 300 loops of cast-on edge, then 22 loops along rem short edge, and join border as you work, making sure to work 4 rows at each corner st, working to last st of second short edge.

End with a complete rep of pattern. BO rem 6 sts. You should have 72 reps of Scallop Leaf around all edges of scarf. Sew last bound-off edge to cable cast-on edge to join ends of border.

If desired, do not bind off. With spare needle, pick up 6 loops along cable cast-on edge.

Hold ends with RS tog and join using three-needle BO.

PICOT EDGE

Beg at bound-off edge of a leaf and work 1 sc in each st, *make picot in point of leaf, work 14 sc along side edge of same leaf and top of next leaf; rep from * to last leaf, make picot in point of leaf, then work 8 sc along side of last leaf.

Join with a sl st to first sc. Fasten off.

Finishing

Weave in ends. Block to finished measurements.

PERFECT HARMONY SOCKS ...
Designed by Judy Sumner • Knit by Tami Sutter

How do you look at a skein of rich hand-painted yarn and imagine a pattern that will stand up to the business of the colors? Judy Sumner has been doing just that for a couple of artisan dyers for years. The pattern work in Perfect Harmony enhances the color movement and makes this a great sock for men or women.

Skill Level: **WING CHAIR**

Things You'll Need to Know
- Kitchener stitch
- Picking up stitches
- Working in the round on double-pointed needles
- Twisting stitches without a cable needle

Sizes
One size fits most adults

Finished Measurements
Leg circumference: 6½" (16.5cm)
Foot circumference: 8" (20.5cm)

Yarn
Lisa Souza *Hand Dyed Hardtwist Merino Petite* (100% merino superwash wool); 500 yds [457m]/3½ oz [100g] skein; sock weight/superfine [1]; 1 skein, shown in color Aww-tum

Needles
Size US 1 (2.25mm) set of 5 double-pointed needles, or size needed to obtain gauge

Notions
Blunt tapestry/yarn needle

Gauge
32 sts and 45 rnds = 4" (10cm) over stockinette
12-st diamond = 1¼" (3cm) wide
"Do the Swatchy, Swatchy!" sung to "Do the Hokey Pokey!"

Techniques
KITCHENER STITCH (OR GRAFTING OR WEAVING): In other words, you're joining two sets of live stitches without leaving a seam. Great tutorials are online at www.KnittingHelp.com (video) and www.Knitty. com. You'll need a tapestry needle for this.

TWISTING STITCHES WITHOUT A CABLE NEEDLE: To twist stitches so the one on top slants to the left, knit in the back of the second stitch on left needle, then knit first and second stitches together through the back of the loops and slip both stitches from left needle (LT). To twist stitches so the one on top slants to the right, knit 2 stitches together, then knit the first stitch again and slip both stitches from left needle (RT).

Abbreviations:
beg begin(ning) • **cont** continue
dec decreas(e)(ing) • **dpn(s)** double pointed needle(s) • **k** knit
k1-b knit 1 stitch through the back of the loop to twist it
k2tog knit 2 stitches together (1 stitch decreased)
LT left twist

Rib Pattern

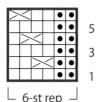

L— 6-st rep —J

Diamond Pattern

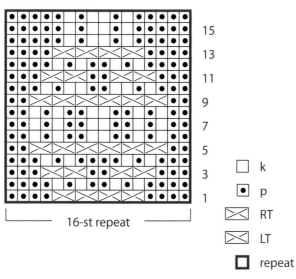

L— 16-st repeat —J

□ k
⊡ p
⧖ RT
⧗ LT
□ repeat

m1 make 1: With tip of left needle, lift the strand of yarn between the last stitch worked and the next stitch by inserting the needle in from front to back, then knit through the back of the loop to twist it (1 stitch increased).

ndl(s) needle(s) • **p** purl

p2tog purl 2 stitches together (1 stitch decreased)

rem remain(ing) • **rep** repeat

rnd(s) round(s) • **RS** right side(s)

RT knit 2 stitches together but do not remove from left needle, knit the first stitch again, then slip both stitches from left needle

skp slip, knit, pass: Slip 1 stitch knitwise, knit 1 stitch, pass slipped stitch over top of knit stitch and off right needle (1 stitch decreased).

Sl slip • **st(s)** stitch(es) • **St st** stockinette stitch

tog together • **WS** wrong side(s)

RIB PATTERN (multiple of 6 sts)

RNDS 1, 3, AND 5: *P2, k4; rep from * to end.

RND 2: *P2, LT, k2; rep from * to end.

RND 4: *P2, k1, LT, k1; rep from * to end.

RND 6: *P2, k2, LT; rep from * to end.

Rep rnds 1–6 for pattern.

DIAMOND PATTERN (multiple of 16 sts)

RND 1: *P4, RT twice, LT twice, p4; rep from * to end.

RND 2: *P4, k1, p1, k1, p2, k1, p1, k1, p4; rep from * to end.

RND 3: *P3, RT twice, p2, LT twice, p3; rep from * to end.

RND 4: *P3, k1, p1, k1, p4, k1, p1, k1, p3: rep from * to end.

RND 5: *P2, RT twice, LT, RT, LT twice, p2; rep from * to end.

RNDS 6–8: *P2, k1, p1, k1, p2, k2, p2, k1, p1, k1, p2; rep from * to end.

RND 9: *P2, LT twice, RT, LT, RT twice, p2; rep from * to end.

RND 10: *P3, k1, p1, k2, p2, k2, p1, k1, p3; rep from * to end.

RND 11: *P3, LT twice, p2, RT twice, p3; rep from * to end.

RND 12: Rep rnd 2.

RND 13: *P4, LT twice, RT twice, p4; rep from * to end.

RND 14–16: *P5, k1, p1, k2, p1, k1, p5; rep from * to end.

Rep rnds 1–16 for pattern.

LEG

Cast on 72 sts. Distribute sts evenly on 4 ndls with 18 sts on each ndl. Join to work in the rnd, being careful not to twist sts.

Work 6-rnd rep of Rib Pattern 3 times.

NEXT RND, *p2tog, k4, p2, k4, p2tog, k4; rep from * to end—64 sts.

WORK RNDS 2–16 of Diamond Pattern, rnds 1–16 twice, then rnds 1–15 once more.

SET UP FOR HEEL FLAP: Work rnd 16 on ndl 1, then turn.

Sl 1 st, p sts from ndl 1 and ndl 4. Sl all heel sts to same ndl.

HEEL FLAP

ROW 1 (RS): *Sl 1, k1; rep from * to end, turn.

ROW 2 (WS): Sl 1, p to end, turn.

Rep these 2 rows 10 more times, ending with a WS row.

TURNING THE HEEL

ROW 1: Sl 1, k17, skp, k1, turn.

ROW 2: Sl 1, p5, p2tog, p1, turn.

ROW 3: Sl 1, k6, skp, k1, turn.

ROW 4: Sl 1, p7, p2tog, p1, turn.

Cont in this manner, working 1 more st before dec on each row until all sts have been worked, ending last 2 rows with dec before turning—18 sts rem. K across and begin gussets.

GUSSETS

Next row, k heel sts, pick up and k13 sts along side of heel flap, m1 in loop between heel flap and instep ndl, k sts across instep ndls, m1 in loop between instep ndl and heel flap, pick up and k13 sts along rem side of heel flap—78 sts.

Divide sts on 4 dpns: heel sts, m1 and gusset sts on ndls 1 and 4, and instep sts on ndls 2 and 3.

Join to work in the rnd, beg rnds at center under foot.

RND 1: NDL 1: K to last 2 sts, k tog the m1 st and gusset st;

NDLS 2 AND 3: K;

NDL 4: Skp, then k to end—76 sts.

NEXT RND (DEC): NDL 1: K to last 3 sts, skp, k1;

NDLS 2 AND 3: K;

NDL 4: K1, k2tog, k to end—74 sts.

K 1 rnd even. Rep these 2 rnds 4 more times, then dec rnd once more—64 sts rem, with 16 each on ndls 1 and 4.

FOOT

Work even in St st until foot is 1½" (4cm) short of desired length from back of heel.

TOE

NEXT RND (DEC): NDL 1: K to last 3 sts, skp, k1;

NDL 2: K1, k2tog, k to end of ndl;

NDL 3: K to last 3 sts, skp, k1;

NDL 4: K1, k2tog, k to end of rnd—60 sts.

K 2 rnds even.

Rep these 3 rnds twice more, then dec every other rnd 3 times—36 sts.

Dec every rnd 5 times—20 sts rem.

Slip sts from ndl 4 to ndl 1, and sts from ndl 2 to ndl 3.

Graft toe using Kitchener stitch. Block to finished measurements.

See the Souls of Fibers

and Become a More Confident and Happier Knitter

FIBER, FIBER, FIBER!

A friend, a member of our Laidback Knitters Ravelry group, posed this question: "About a week ago, I finished the most adorable poncho. I knit it with bulky-weight, 100 percent alpaca. I wore it every day. And it's growing. It's getting longer and longer and longer! What did I do wrong?!"

What, indeed, did she do wrong?

First off, "wrong" is a nasty word. We'd rather think of her *faux pas* as a result of a lack of education, and education is easily obtainable in the fiber world. She knit her big, heavy poncho with pure alpaca, an incredibly wonderful fiber that's soft and sweet and a joy to use. The problem: Alpaca has little memory compared with wool from sheep. And so the poor, forgetful fiber, if knit up into a large heavy garment or afghan, can grow and grow and grow. Had she knit her poncho with an alpaca-wool blend, she would have retained alpaca's softness and gained wool's marvelous memory. Ah, well, we live. We learn. It's only knitting, after all, and with knitting, we can always put things right.

So . . . for our fifth secret we say: Know and Understand the Souls of Fibers.

Can we teach you everything there is to know about fibers? No way. Not in these

pages, at least. Can we set you on the path to not merely understanding fibers but reveling in them? We sure can.

A few fiber gurus exist in the knitting world. Two stars that shine the brightest are *Linda Cortright* and *Clara Parkes*.

A MEETING WITH WILD LINDA

When I pull up to Linda Cortright's hilltop aerie, I'm surrounded by trees and ledge. The scent of earth and animal and flowers perfumes the air. A door's flung open—and out lopes Linda, her long legs gobbling the earth. It's easy to picture her striding across the Argentinean pampas, scaling Himalayan mountains, or surfing through Alaskan snow. Linda's a woman of the world, a truly international soul, who not only is the architect and builder and essence of *Wild Fibers* magazine but a passionate advocate for all creatures—particularly those that bear fiber.

She reaches me far sooner than I reach her, and her embrace warms me.

All too soon, blackflies halo our faces.

"C'mon in," says Linda, and we rush inside and slam the door.

A vast picture window encompasses one wall of Linda's comfy living room, dotted with cushy chairs and artifacts from her travels around the world. Linda's fiber journey has taken her from a Main Line childhood to an all-girls' boarding school to an upper-crust college to a promo job at CBS. Her fiber conversion began slowly. The noise of the world grew so powerful, she needed a "cave" of sorts to collect her thoughts. She found one in semi-rural Maine. There, she began collecting goats. Not any goats, not Linda, but cashmere goats with painted faces and fluffy coats. And she began to learn fiber. I mean, really learn, down to the souls of the creatures growing the fleece.

"What are those?" Linda gestures at the grocery bags I've put on the floor.

"Carrots," I say.

"C'mon."

Outside, through a gate, up a rock-tumbled grassy slope, I spot my first cashmere goat. Spectacular—black and white and gray faces; long coats draped over a puffy undercoat; wild, unbridled horns; glistening eyes of blue. Linda's flock is wary, as only animals concerned with predation can be. The pasture smells delicious—inviting and healthy.

We tempt Linda's flock with carrots, and they instantly approach her. It's obvious that Linda knows and loves these beasts, and vice versa. Me? Time elapses. When one goat finally takes the carrot from my fingers, her warm breath brushes the back of my hand. That these animals produce such glorious fiber seems miraculous.

Their cashmere fluffiness is everywhere—wafting from horns, draped from a tree, caught on a shed door. It's as if their fiber trails are salutes to Linda, a woman who leads the charge to save the wild-fibered beasts around the world.

Linda's written about alpaca and camels, musk-ox and Navajo-Churro sheep, yak and guanaco and buffalo. She's traveled from the Gobi to Swaziland to Texas, from the Andes to the Arctic to Tibet and back again, learning the truth of the many beasts that feed us fibers. She's been a knitter and spinner, a writer and photographer, an advocate for change and an early adopter of living lightly on this earth.

Linda's *Wild Fibers* has given her the opportunity to teach, to lecture, and to rabble-rouse. Most especially, Linda is a tireless advocate for the beasts that walk our Earth, both the domesticated kind and the wild-and-woolly ones. *Linda Cortright* is wild. Linda Cortright is fearless. Linda Cortright is the change she wishes to see in others. (www.WildFibersMagazine.com)

LET'S TALK A FEW FIBER TERMS . . .

LOFT—no, not the SoHo kind, but rather the fluffiness. Then there's CRIMP, or curliness. Finally, FINENESS = complicated definition: fiber diameter; simple definition: how soft does it feel?

There's more, lots more. Remember, this is a tasting, not a meal.

When we say "warm," we mean the fiber will keep you warm; when we say "cool" the fiber will allow you to cool off.

PROTEIN FIBERS—FIBERS FROM CRITTERS

ANGORA FIBER: angora rabbit; warm and impossibly soft; low memory. If properly spun, it won't shed much; German, French and English angora bunnies are the best known. Slippy-slidey for socks—not good—but for a loose-fitting cami or a frothy scarf, perfection. A personal favorite of Vicki's. Angora "halos" beautifully. Wraith-like (see Chapter 8).

POSSUM FIBER: possum, marsupial; extremely soft underhairs. Warm; low memory; fur, must be blended with wool. Mostly from New Zealand. Why? That's another story. FYI, possums are not opossums but distant cousins. How odd is that? Soft and warm and knittable for sweaters, socks (with nylon), afghans, just about anything, given that it's always mixed with wool. Pettable.

SILK FIBER: caterpillar, from a cocoon secretion (TMI?!). Warm and cool, slick and lustrous; no memory; sourced mostly from China, Japan, India. On its own? A scarf, a short skirt, a shawl, a necklace— luminescent and elegant. Combined with wool, the yarn glows, and the wool increases silk's usability for garments.

WOOL FIBER: sheep; wide spectrum of softness, depending on breed, care, feeding, and processing; anywhere from creamy soft to bristly rough; lots of memory; warm; great water-shedding properties;

ANIMAL SPIRITS

I've thought a lot about why certain fibers matter to me and why I feel they should matter to our readers. When you can choose alpaca over llama, why even bother with the latter? Because you're not simply engaged with a product— the yarn—but with the yarn's source, too.

The llama is a very different beast from the alpaca. The llama guards, whereas the alpaca is the guardee. When I knit with camel, I see the Gobi Desert and an immense and ancient creature capable of carrying a human for miles and miles. When I knit with cashmere, I see the fluff draped on the goats and the Mongolian goatherds who watch their flocks. When I knit with yak and musk-ox, I get chilly as I picture these giant, primeval beasts dusted with snow.

Some First Nations believe we assume an animal's spirit properties when we wear its pelts or skins. Somehow, that makes sense to me, as I feel a connection to the Earth and to the creature when I knit with animal fiber. And that matters to me. ~ VICKI

"FROGGING" is **ripping it out.** Get it: *ribbit.*

flammability—self-extinguishing; incredibly hard-working fiber; sheep are found worldwide. Perfect for knitting almost anything unless it's a summer-style garment; feltable. Wool runs the gamut from buttery to itchy. Be sure to feel before buying dozens of skeins for a sweater. Arguably the all-around perfect fiber.

MOHAIR FIBER: angora goat; hairy and fuzzy; warm; medium elasticity; can be itchy; go for the Kid Mohair, which isn't itchy. Mohair goats are found worldwide. A mohair blend is perfect shawl or hat material. Mohair can glow, too.

CASHMERE FIBER: cashmere goat, the Tiffany of fiber; very warm; medium elasticity; go gently with it. Cashmere goats predominantly found in Mongolia, Tibet, China, as well as locally raised. Great cashmere floats, almost untouched by gravity. Be careful to choose a good and reputable brand. Just like Fool's Gold, Fool's Cashmere is fake. Artisanal can be lovely. If Vicki had to choose one fiber to knit with, cashmere would be it. A cashmere hat, scarf, or sweater approaches the divine.

CAMELIDA—FIBERS NAMED FOR THEIR CRITTERS

ALPACA: warm, very soft, medium to low elasticity. Alpacas are originally South American but are now found in Europe and the United States. An alpaca sweater can turn into a sweathouse, yet it's a great fiber for kids' clothes, accessories, and when blended with wool, sweaters, too.

GUANACO: a llama relative, some domesticated; rare, expensive, soft.

VICUNA: extremely rare; very expensive; heaven on needles and to wear.

LLAMA: warm, not as soft as alpaca, but can be lower-priced; when spun with wool, llama makes for hearty sweaters and hats. Artisanal llama found at fiber fests often has an interesting texture.

CAMEL: warm, can be hairy, medium-to-low elasticity; most camels are Middle Eastern; gorgeous caramel color; another earthy yarn. Hand-spun used as a fundraiser for the Snow Leopard Trust (www. SnowLeopard.org). A wonderful fiber for a pillow or a toy or sizzling socks when combined with wool and nylon. BTW, camelids spit, so don't tick them off.

BOVINE FIBERS—YES, THEY'RE SORT OF LIKE COWS

YAK: somewhat rare, warm, low elasticity; originally found in the Himalayas, Mongolia, but now also Colorado-raised. Hearty and mellow. When mixed with various yarns, yak becomes a deeply satisfying knit. Shawls, sweaters, hats—yak can do it all.

QIVIUT OR QIVIUK: Arctic musk-ox; some memory, warmer, more expensive, and finer than cashmere; native to Canada, Greenland,

WHAT'S ORGANIC FIBER?

That is one tough question. Here's the URL for the Organic Trade Association's Organic Standards for Fiber, both plant and animal: www.OTA.com/ AmericanOrganicStandards- forFiber.html

We obtained a copy of this 49-page document. Yes, 49 pages. Quite specific. But if you Google "organic standards for fiber" you'll find a raft of info. Unlike "natural," you can't just put "organic" on a label and have it fly.

FYI, companies use the term "natural" a lot. What does "natural" mean, anyway? Not much. While "organic" is a regulated term, "natural" is generic and unregulated. With "green" being so "in," companies tend to *exaggerate* the "naturalness" of a product. Keep an eye out.

Alaska; laceweight heaven. A frothy cowl, an airy scarf, a wispy shawl—perfection.

BUFFALO: bison; soft, cloudy, retains warmth, little memory. Found in the U.S. Make a pair of fingered mitts for a fella in buffalo. He'll love 'em.

ASK YOUR-
SELF, WITH
A PARTICULAR
YARN . . .

★ ONCE KNIT, HOW DOES
THE FABRIC FLOW? DOES
IT DRAPE? IS IT BOUNCY?
FUZZY? CURLY?

★ DOES THE FIBER "BLOOM,"
MEANING ACQUIRE A
HALO?

★ WILL THE PIECE BE WORN
CLOSE TO YOUR SKIN? IS IT
ITCHY?

★ WHAT WORDS COME TO
MIND WHEN THINKING
OF A PARTICULAR FIBER?
BUMPY? COZY? SILKY?

★ DOES THE FIBER'S TEXTURE
ENHANCE THE DESIGN?
DETRACT FROM IT?

★ IF YOU WANT GREAT STITCH
DEFINITION, WILL YOUR
CHOSEN YARN SHOW IT?

★ IF THE ITEM IS TO BE WORN
OFTEN, HAVE YOU CHOSEN
AN APPROPRIATELY TOUGH
FIBER OR A WEAK ONE?

OTHER CRITTERS

DOG: various; often spun for the animal's owner; little memory, sometimes spun with wool; hot; soft.

FOX: very rare; little memory; usually spun with wool.

MINK, CHINCHILLA, and other specialty yarns are "fur" and spun with wool, often merino wool.

CELLULOSE FIBERS, AKA PLANTS

COTTON: from the cotton plant; cool, no memory; left matte (natural state) or mercerized (a process that makes it shiny); breathable. Infinitely versatile—so much so, everything from T-shirts to dishcloths to basket liners have been knit up in cotton yarn. To explore the yarn, knit up a motif dishcloth. Hundreds of themed dishcloth patterns are online.

LINEN: flax plant; cool, no elasticity; stiff, but softens on washing; great breathability and durability; a super yarn if you're looking for drape. It knits a beautiful loose-fit top, a window curtain, a slinky shawl.

HEMP—hemp plant; much like linen, can be rough; no memory (and, no, you can't smoke it). It'll knit up a wonderful dish towel and, when combined with wool, it gains elasticity, so it makes a fine sweater.

TRANSFORMED CELLULOSE FIBERS

Modal, acetate, Lyocell (Tencel), seaweed, corn, soy, and other names for transformed cellulose are cool fibers with no memory and offer a variety of pluses and minuses. These fibers are reconstituted in some way.

RAYON: reconstituted tree pulp. Cool, slinky, no elasticity, great drape. Breathable and dense. Beware the stretching monster that can bite your pure rayon knit projects.

BAMBOO: breathable, great drape, cool, can split. Much like rayon.

SYNTHETIC FIBERS

NYLON: strong, made using petrochemicals, stretchy. The strength and stretchy business is what makes a small dose of nylon great for sock yarns.

POLYESTER: similar to nylon.

ACRYLIC: Think of it as a long, stringy LP record. In other words, acrylic is made up of approximately 85 to 90 percent vinyl. The balance of the yarn creates the texture and feel. This is one tough yarn, which is why it's so popular for wash-and-wear items.

For an in-depth understanding of all types of yarn, read *The Knitter's Book of Yarns* and *The Knitter's Book of Wool* by Clara Parkes.

IS THERE A PERFECT KNITTING BAG?

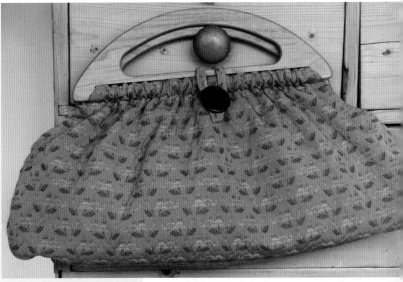

Obsessed with finding the perfect knitting bag? I admit it: I am. So we've surveyed more than 14 purveyors of knitting bags. We've polled knitter friends, who've raved about some of the bags; others just look heavenly. Lisa and I both drool over photos. All are interesting in a variety of ways. Many offer accessory bags, too.

• ATENTI BAGS: $$$; tapestry; gorgeous. If I could test-run one bag, the Atenti Doctor Bag would be it. (www.AtentiBags.blogspot.com)

• BAGSMITH: $$; highly functional canvas. I have one, and this stand-up bag works great. (www.Bagsmith.com)

• BE SWEET: $$$; beautiful; proceeds aid the South African women who make them—I love that. (www.BeSweetProducts.com)

• DELLA Q: $$; glamorous silk and fabrics; pretty. The little silk pouches are almost edible! (www.DellaQ.com)

• GREEN MOUNTAIN: $$$; exquisite, hand-crafted bags. I'm lucky to own one. (www.GreenMountainKnittingBags.com)

• JORDANA PAIGE: $$; vegan leather. The functionality and hip styling really make these bags sing. (www.JordanaPaige.com)

• LANTERN MOON: $ to $$; huge array of fabrics; proceeds aid the Vietnamese women who make them. (www.LanternMoon.com)

• LEXIE BARNES: $$$; stunning and functional; waxed canvas. Urbane bags with punch. The Lady B rocks it. (www.LexieBarnes.com)

• NAMASTE BAGS: $$; colorful, durable vegan leather. Stylish and well priced. Lisa owns a purple one and loves it. (www.Namasteinc.com)

• NANTUCKET DITTY BAGG: $$; reversible, convertible tool bag. A serious bag for serious knitters. (www.NantucketBagg.com)

• OFFHAND DESIGNS: $$$; luxurious, tapestry bags. I lust after these. (I know, I have a real problem with my lusts!) (www.OffhandDesigns.com)

• TOM BIHN KNITTING BAGS: $$; great organization and hearty; a workaholic of a bag. (www.tombihn.com)

• WOOLY BULLY: $$; adorable, fun, gorgeous fabrics, designed for knitters. (www.WoolyBully.com)

• GOKNIT POUCH: $; for sock knitters everywhere. (www.KnowKnits.com)

• Both of us use various totes, also. We need more than one bag, as we have more than one project going at a time. How about you? ~ VICKI

WILD LINDA'S CAMISOLE ...
Designed by Linda Cortright • Knit by Elizabeth Risch

We've knit up Linda's light and airy camisole with a yarn that combines two beautiful protein fibers: merino wool and silk. Having the fiber fit the garment or accessory is such a plus. As you start knitting, and as the pattern and fiber begin to work together, the item will take shape in incredibly satisfying ways.

 Skill Level: **DINING CHAIR**

Things You'll Need to Know
- Three-needle bind-off
- Simple lace knitting
- Reading charts

Sizes
XS (S, M, L)
Shown in size XS.
Instructions are given for size XS, with larger sizes in parentheses. When only one number is given, it applies to all sizes.

Finished Measurements
Bust: 28 (32, 36, 40)" [71 (81.5, 91.5, 101.5)cm]
Length: 17 (17¾, 18½, 19¼)" [43 (45, 47, 49)cm]

Yarn
Lisa Souza *Hand Dyed Petal* (50% merino wool/50% silk); 667 yds [610m]/51/3 [151g]; fingering/super-fine weight [1]; 1 (1, 1, 1) skein, shown in color Mother of Pearl

Needles
Size US 3 (3.25mm) needles and double-pointed needles for shoulder bind-off, or size needed to obtain gauge

Notions
Stitch holders
Blunt tapestry/yarn needle

Gauge
30 sts and 38 rows = 4" (10cm) in stockinette;
32 sts and 40 rows = 4" (10cm) in Spiral Lace
Linda says a yak will come eat you if you don't check gauge. Of course, we think yaks are herbivores. *Hummm.*

Techniques
THREE-NEEDLE BIND-OFF: Divide stitches evenly on two needles. Hold both needles in left hand with right sides together and needles parallel. Using a third needle in your right hand, knit together the first stitch from both needles. *Knit together the next stitch from both needles. Lift first stitch on right needle over top of second stitch, then off the needle—1 stitch remains on right needle; repeat from * until all stitches have been bound off. Fasten off remaining stitch on right needle.

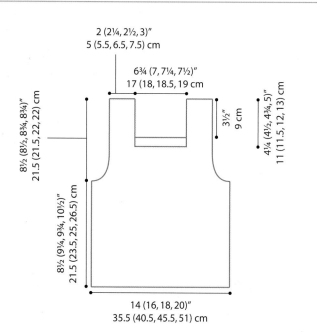

2 (2¼, 2½, 3)"
5 (5.5, 6.5, 7.5) cm

6¾ (7, 7¼, 7½)"
17 (18, 18.5, 19 cm)

3½"
9 cm

4¼ (4½, 4¾, 5)"
11 (11.5, 12, 13) cm

8½ (8½, 8¾, 8¾)"
21.5 (21.5, 22, 22) cm

8½ (9¼, 9¾, 10½)"
21.5 (23.5, 25, 26.5) cm

14 (16, 18, 20)"
35.5 (40.5, 45.5, 51) cm

Abbreviations

beg begin(ning) • **BO** bind off
cont continu(e)(ing) • **dec** decrease(s)
dpn(s) double-pointed needle(s)
k2tog knit 2 stitches together (1 stitch decreased) • **ndl(s)** needle(s) • **p** purl
pm place marker • **p4tog** purl 4 stitches together • **rem** remain(ing)
rep repeat • **RS** right side(s) • **sl** slip
ssk slip, slip, knit: Slip one stitch from left needle to right needle, knitwise (as if to knit), slip second stitch same way; insert left needle through front of loops on right needle, then wrap yarn around right needle. With left needle, bring loops over the yarn wrapped around the right, which will knit them together through the back of the loops (1 stitch decreased). • **St st** stockinette stitch
tbl through the back of the loop(s)
tog together • **WS** wrong side(s)
wyf with yarn in front
wyb with yarn in back • **yo** yarn over

Tip

• The pattern can be easily adjusted for individual length preferences by adding more rows between the top of the Grand Eyelet Lace and the armholes, as well as working an extra 4 rows of the Grand Eyelet Lace pattern.

Pattern Stitches

SLIP STITCH MESH (multiple of 2 sts + 2)
ROW 1 (RS): P.
ROW 2 (WS): K.
ROW 3: K1, *k1, sl 1 wyb; rep from * to last st, k1.
ROW 4: K1, *sl 1 wyf, k1; rep from * to last st, k1.
ROW 5: K1,* yo, k2tog; rep from * to last st, k1.
ROW 6: P.

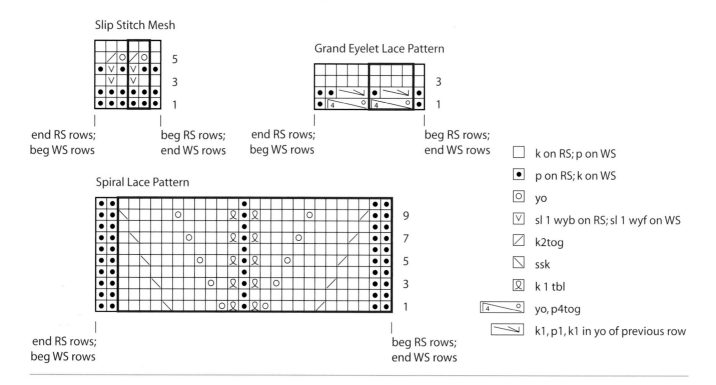

Slip Stitch Mesh

5
3
1

end RS rows;
beg WS rows

beg RS rows;
end WS rows

Grand Eyelet Lace Pattern

3
1

end RS rows;
beg WS rows

beg RS rows;
end WS rows

Spiral Lace Pattern

9
7
5
3
1

end RS rows;
beg WS rows

beg RS rows;
end WS rows

☐ k on RS; p on WS

● p on RS; k on WS

Ⓞ yo

Ⅴ sl 1 wyb on RS; sl 1 wyf on WS

╱ k2tog

╲ ssk

Ⓠ k 1 tbl

4 ─── ᵒ yo, p4tog

╲──── k1, p1, k1 in yo of previous row

GRAND EYELET LACE PATTERN

(multiple of 4 sts + 2)

ROW 1: P1, *yo, p4tog; rep from * to last st, p1.

ROW 2: K1, *k1, (k1, p1, k1) into yo of previous row, rep from * to last st, k1.

ROW 3: K loosely.

ROW 4: P.

SPIRAL LACE PATTERN

(multiple of 25 sts + 2)

ROW 1 (RS): *P2, k4, k2tog, k4, yo, k1 tbl, p1, k1 tbl, yo, k4, ssk, k4; rep from * to last 2 sts, p2.

ROW 2 AND FOLLOWING WS ROWS: K2, *p11, k1, p11, k2; rep from * to end of row.

ROW 3: *P2, k3, k2tog, k4, yo, k1, k1 tbl, p1, k1 tbl, k1, yo, k4, ssk, k3, rep from * to last 2 sts, p2.

ROW 5: *P2, k2, k2tog, k4, yo, k2, k1 tbl, p1, k1 tbl, k2, yo, k4, ssk, k2, rep from * to last 2 sts, p2.

ROW 7: *P2, k1, k2tog, k4, yo, k3, k1 tbl, p1, k1 tbl, k3, yo, k4, ssk, k1, rep from * to last 2 sts, p2.

ROW 9: *P2, k2tog, k4, yo, k4, k1 tbl, p1, k1 tbl, k4, yo, k4, ssk; rep from * to last 2 sts, p2.

ROW 10: Rep row 2.

Rep rows 1–10 for pattern.

BACK

Cast on 112 (128, 144, 160) sts.

K 5 rows. Beg with a RS row and work 8 (10, 10, 12) rows in St st.

Work the 4 rows of Grand Eyelet Lace.

Work St st until piece measures about 2¾ (3½, 4, 4¾)" [7 (9, 10, 12)cm] from bottom, end with a WS row.

Work the 6 rows of Slip Stitch Mesh.

NEXT ROW (RS): K5 (13, 8, 4), pm, work row 1 of Spiral Lace Pattern over next 102 (102, 127, 152) sts, pm, k5 (13, 9, 4).

NEXT ROW: P5 (13, 8, 4), work row 2 of Spiral Lace Pattern over next 102 (102, 127, 152) sts, p5 (13, 8, 4).

Cont as established until piece measures 8½ (9¼, 9¾, 10½)" [21.5 (23.5, 25, 26.5)cm] from bottom.

ARMHOLES

BIND OFF 4 (5, 6, 7) sts at beg of next 2 rows, 3 sts at beg of next 2 rows, then 2 sts at beg of next 4 (4, 4, 6) row—90 (104, 118, 128) sts.

Dec 1 st at each end of every RS row 5 (9, 13, 13) times—80 (86, 92, 102)) sts.

AT SAME TIME, when 6 (6, 7, 7) reps of Spiral Lace have been completed, work the 6 rows of Slip Stitch Mesh.

Work 10 rows of St st. Rep these 16 rows to end.

AT SAME TIME, when piece measures 13½ (14¼, 15, 15¾)" [34.5 (36, 38, 40)cm] from bottom, end with a WS row.

NECK

NEXT ROW (RS), k15 (17, 19, 22), attach second ball of yarn and bind off next 50 (52, 54, 58) sts, k rem 15 (17, 19, 22) sts.

Work even in pattern until armhole measures 8½ (8½, 8¾, 8¾)" [21.5 (221.5, 22, 22)cm].

Place sts on holders.

FRONT

Work front same as back until piece measures 12¾ (13¼, 13¾, 14¼)" [32.5 (33.5, 35, 36)cm] from bottom.

NECK

NEXT ROW (RS), k15 (17, 19, 22), attach second ball of yarn and bind off next 50 (52, 54, 58) sts, k rem 15 (17, 19, 22) sts.

Work even in pattern until armhole measures 8½ (8½, 8¾, 8¾)" [21.5 (221.5, 22, 22)cm].

Place sts on holders.

Finishing

Block pieces to measurements.

Sl sts for left front shoulder to a dpn, and sts for left back shoulder to another dpn. Holding ndls with RS tog, use three-needle bind-off to bind off all sts. Join right shoulder in same manner. Sew side seams. Weave in ends.

Rumi Maki, an Incan martial art, is divided into five levels. Three of the levels share their names with beloved fiber animals: Llama, Alpaca, and Vicuña.

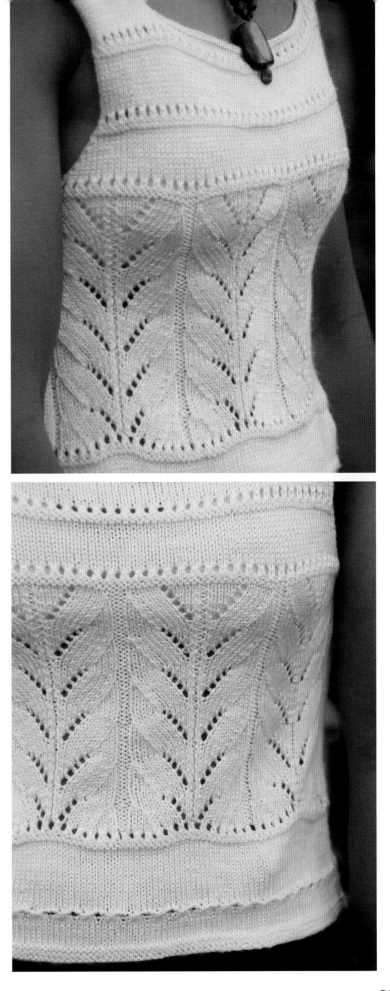

ROMI'S GEMS ...
Designed by Rosemary (Romi) Hill

We love Romi's idea of creating a "scarf necklace"—a sort of cross between a necklace and a scarf—to be worn as a decoration. Her inspiration was an incredible yarn with a fine strand of stainless steel running through it. As light and airy as it is, the yarn also creates a surprisingly strong piece that can be molded and shaped with your fingers into lovely organic shapes.

In this case, in particular, the fiber is as important as the pattern.

Skill Level: WING CHAIR

Things You'll Need to Know
- Lace knitting
- Knitting with beads
- Provisional cast-on
- Reading charts and "no stitch"

Finished Measurements
Measurements taken after finger-blocking.
Width: 2" (5cm)
Length: 47" (119.5cm)

Yarn
Habu Textiles, *A-148 1/17.6* wool/stainless steel (75% wool, 25% stainless steel); 547 yds [492m]/1 oz [28.5g]; lace/superfine weight [1]; 150 yards (137.2m), shown in color Terra Cotta #45

Needles
Size US 0 (2mm) steel double-pointed needles, or size needed to obtain gauge

Notions
50 size 6/0 seed beads, gold
Size US 8 steel (.90mm) crochet hook, or size small enough to fit through holes in beads
Size C/2 (2.75mm) crochet hook for provisional cast-on
Sewing needle
Smooth waste yarn for provisional cast-on

Gauge
40 sts and 40 rows = 4" (10cm) in stockinette
NOTE: Gauge given is approximate; correct gauge is not critical for this project. Finger-block your lace swatch before measuring gauge.

Techniques
PLACING BEADS: Knit stitch as usual. Slip bead onto crochet hook; hooking last stitch on right needle and pull stitch off needle and through bead, then place stitch back on right needle. (See Placing Beads—Step by Step, page 29.)

PROVISIONAL CAST-ON: Choose a smooth yarn of similar weight to the item. Cast on the number of stitches as normal, knit one row in the waste yarn, then start knitting with the actual yarn. When you remove the waste yarn, unravel it one stitch at a time and pop that stitch onto the needle.

Abbreviations
beg begin • **dpn(s)** double-pointed needle(s)
k knit • **k2tog** knit 2 stitches together (1 stitch decreased)
k3tog knit 3 stitches together (right-leaning double decrease) • **p** purl
pb place bead • **psso** pass slipped stitch over
rem remain(s) • **RS** right side(s)
sk2p slip 1 stitch, knit 2 stitches together, pass slipped stitch over (left-leaning double decrease)
sl slip • **ssk** slip, slip, knit: Slip one stitch from left needle to right needle, knitwise (as if to knit), slip second stitch same way, insert left needle through front of loops on right needle, then wrap yarn around right needle. With left needle, bring loops over the yarn wrapped around the right, which will knit them together through the back of the loops (1 stitch decreased). **st(s)** stitch(es) • **WS** wrong side(s)

Tips

• Beads are not prestrung but are added as the scarf is knit. As shown (detail page 84), the scarf uses beads that have holes large enough to accommodate a very small crochet hook.

• As you knit, block the piece by pulling it into shape with your fingers.

Pattern Stitches

BEADED END

SET-UP ROW: K.

ROW 1: K6, k3tog, yo, k1, yo, p2, yo, k1, yo, sk2p, k6.

ROWS 2, 4, 6, 8: P10, k2, p10.

ROW 3: K4, k3tog, (k1, yo) twice, k1, p2, (k1, yo) twice, k1, sk2p, k4.

ROW 5: K2, k3tog, k2, yo, k1, yo, k2, p2, k2, yo, k1, yo, k2, sk2p, k2.

ROW 7: K3tog, k3, yo, pb, yo, k3, p2, k3, yo, pb, yo, k3, sk2p.

Rep rows 1–8 nine more times.

LEAF END

ROW 1: Ssk, k8, yo, k2tog, yo, k8, k2tog–21 sts.

ROW 2 AND OTHER EVEN-NUMBERED ROWS: P.

ROW 3: Ssk, k5, k2tog, k1, yo, pb, yo, k1, ssk, k5, k2tog–19 sts.

Leaf End

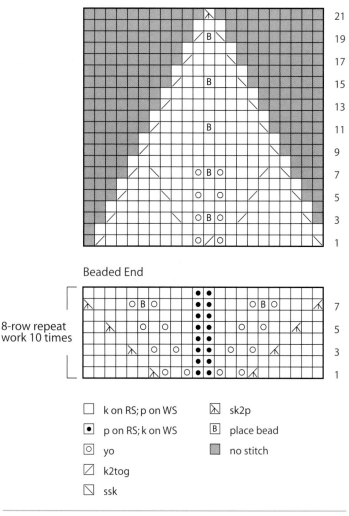

Beaded End

8-row repeat
work 10 times

	k on RS; p on WS		sk2p
•	p on RS; k on WS	B	place bead
O	yo		no stitch
⟋	k2tog		
⟍	ssk		

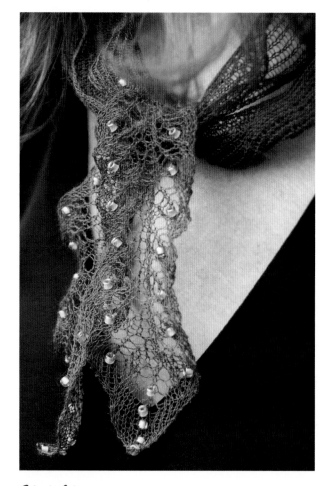

Finishing

Weave in ends. Finger-block, stretching and smoothing leaves into organic shapes.

ROW 5: Ssk, k3, k2tog, k2, yo, k1, yo, k2, ssk, k3, k2tog—17 sts.

ROW 7: Ssk, k1, k2tog, k3, yo, pb, yo, k3, ssk, k1, k2tog—15 sts.

ROW 9: Ssk, k11, k2tog—13 sts.

ROW 11: Ssk, k4, pb, k4, k2tog—11 sts.

ROW 13: Ssk, k7, k2tog—9 sts.

ROW 15: Ssk, k2, pb, k2, k2tog—7 sts.

ROW 17: Ssk, k3, k2tog—5 sts.

ROW 19: Ssk, pb, k2tog—3 sts.

ROW 21: Sk2p—1 st rem.

Fasten off.

Using waste yarn and crochet hook, cast on 22 sts provisionally. Sl sts to dpn. Switch to working yarn. Work Beaded End, then Leaf End.

Remove provisional cast-on and pick up 22 sts. Beg St st and work for 33" (84cm), finger-blocking to desired measurements as you work. End with a WS row. Work Beaded End from row 1, then Leaf End.

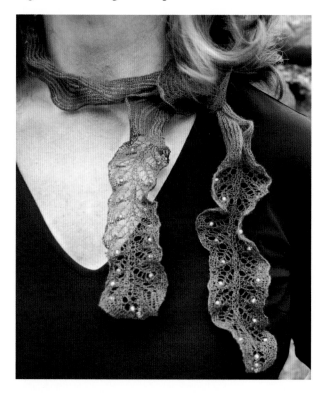

TABLE TALK PLACE MATS ...
Designed by Rosemary (Romi) Hill

Shetland Hap Shawls represent tradition, wearability, and aesthetics rolled into one garment. These cheerful place mats are an homage to that tradition, worked in a decidedly nontraditional fiber—linen—and intended for home use. The linen plant fiber will soften with time, yet it's eminently durable and perfect for place mats. Enjoy using them on a sunny morning for breakfast, or, worked in more subdued colors, for a lovely dinner.

 Skill Level: **DINING CHAIR**

Things You'll Need to Know
- Lace knitting
- Knitting in the round
- Provisional cast-on
- Picking up stitches

Finished Measurements
Width: 17½" (44.5cm)
Length: 12" (30.5cm)

Yarn
Louet North America *Euroflax Fine Lace Weight* (110% linen); 1,160 yds [1,061m]/3½ oz [100g]; lace/fine weight [2]; **MC:** 1 cone, shown in Terra Cotta #47; **CC:** 1 cone, shown in Crabapple #27

Needles
Size US 2 (2.75mm) needles, 16" (40cm) circular needle, or size needed to obtain gauge

Notions
Size US C/2 (2.75mm) crochet hook
Smooth waste yarn for provisional cast-on
Sewing needle

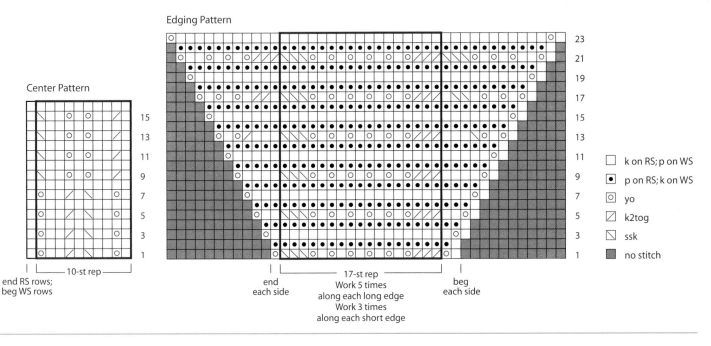

Edging Pattern

Center Pattern

		23
		21
		19
		17
		15
		13
		11
		9
		7
		5
		3
		1

☐ k on RS; p on WS

• p on RS; k on WS

o yo

⟋ k2tog

⟍ ssk

▨ no stitch

end RS rows;
beg WS rows

⊢—— 10-st rep ——⊣

end
each side

17-st rep
Work 5 times
along each long edge
Work 3 times
along each short edge

beg
each side

Gauge

30 sts and 40 rows = 4" (10cm) in stockinette

30 sts and 48 rows = 4" (10cm) in Center Pattern

NOTE: Gauge given is approximate; correct gauge is not critical for this project. Block your swatch before measuring gauge.

Techniques

PROVISIONAL CAST-ON: Choose a smooth yarn of similar weight to the item. Cast on the number of stitches as normal, knit one row in the waste yarn, then start knitting your item with the actual yarn. When you remove the waste yarn, unravel the waste yarn one stitch at a time and pop that stitch onto the needle.

Abbreviations

beg begin(ning) • **CC** contrast color
cont continu(e)(ing) • **k** knit • **k2tog** knit 2 stitches together (1 stitch decreased) • **MC** main color •
ndl(s) needle(s) • **p** purl • **pm** place marker • **rem** remain • **rep** repeat • **rnd(s)** round(s) • **RS** right side(s) • **sl** slip • **ssk** slip, slip, knit: Slip one stitch from left needle to right needle, knitwise (as if to knit), slip second stitch same way, insert left needle through front of loops on right needle, then wrap yarn around right needle. With left needle, bring loops over the yarn wrapped around the right, which will knit them together through the back of the loops (1 stitch decreased).
st(s) stitch(es) • **WS** wrong side(s) • **Yo** yarn over

Tips

• Stitch markers are used to indicate corners; slip markers as you come to them.

• Markers may be used between pattern repeats to help you keep your place. Make sure to use markers of a different size and color than the corner and beginning-of-round markers.

• The chart for the Edging Pattern shows only ¼ of the pattern; to work the edging, work the chart along each side of the place mat.

Pattern Stitches

CENTER PATTERN (multiple of 10 sts + 1)

ROWS 1, 3, 5, AND 7 (RS): *K1, yo, k2, ssk, k1, k2tog, k2, yo; rep from * to last st, k1.

ROW 2 AND ALL OTHER WS ROWS: P.

ROWS 9, 11, 13, AND 15: *K1, k2tog, k2, yo, k1, yo, k2, ssk; rep from * to last st, k1.

ROW 16: P.

Rep rows 1–16 for pattern.

EDGING PATTERN (multiple of 17 + corner sts)

RND 1: *K1, yo, [(k2tog) 3 times, (yo, k1) 5 times, yo, (ssk) 3 times] 5 times, yo, k1, yo, [(k2tog) 3 times, (yo, k1) 5 times, yo, (ssk) 3 times] 3 times, yo; rep from * once more—8 sts increased.

RND 2 AND ALL EVEN-NUMBERED RNDS: *K1, p to next marker; rep from * to end.

RNDS 3, 7, 11, 15, 19, AND 23: *K1, yo, k to next marker, yo; rep from * to end—8 sts increased.

RND 5: *K1, yo, k2, [(k2tog) 3 times, (yo, k1) 5

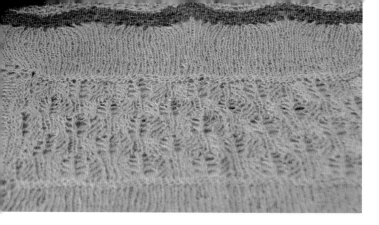
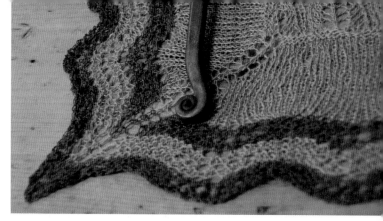

times, yo, (ssk) 3 times] 5 times, k2, yo, k1, yo, k2, [(k2tog) 3 times, (yo, k1) 5 times, yo, (ssk) 3 times] 3 times, k2, yo; rep from * once more—8 sts increased.

RND 9: *K1, yo, k4, [(k2tog) 3 times, (yo, k1) 5 times, yo, (ssk) 3 times] 5 times, k4, yo, kl, yo, k4 [(k2tog) 3 times, (yo, k1) 5 times, yo, (ssk) 3 times] 3 times, k4, yo; rep from * once more—8 sts increased.

RND 13: *(K1, yo) twice, ssk, k3, [(k2tog) 3 times, (yo, k1) 5 times, yo, (ssk) 3 times] 5 times, k3, k2tog, (yo, k1) 3 times, yo, ssk, k3, [(k2tog) 3 times, (yo, k1) 5 times, yo, (ssk) 3 times] 3 times, k3, k2tog, yo, k1, yo; rep from * once more—8 sts increased.

RND 17: *K1, (yo, k1) 3 times, (ssk) twice, k1, [(k2tog) 3 times, (yo, k1) 5 times, yo, (ssk) 3 times] 5 times, k1, (k2tog) twice, (k1, yo) 6 times, k1, (ssk) twice, k1, [(k2tog) 3 times, (yo, k1) 5 times, yo, (ssk) 3 times] 3 times, k1, (k2tog) twice, (k1, yo) 3 times; rep from * once more—8 sts increased.

ROW 21: *K1, yo, k2, (yo, k1) twice, yo, (ssk) 3 times, [(k2tog) 3 times, (yo, k1) 5 times, yo, (ssk) 3 times] 5 times, (k2tog) 3 times, (yo, k1) 3 times, (k1, yo) twice, k2, (yo, k1) twice, yo, (ssk) 3 times, [(k2tog) 3 times, (yo, k1) 5 times, yo, (ssk) 3 times] 3 times, (k2tog) 3 times, (yo, k1) 3 times, k1, yo; rep from * once more—8 sts increased.

CENTER

Using waste yarn and crochet hook, cast on 61 sts provisionally.
Sl sts to ndl. Change to MC.
SET-UP ROW: K.
ROW 1 (RS): Work 10-st rep of Center Pattern 6 times, end k1.
ROW 2 (WS): P.
Cont as established, work rows 1–16 of Center Pattern twice, then rows 1–7 once more.

STOCKINETTE BORDER SET-UP ROW

With RS facing, pm, yo, pm, pick up and k27 evenly spaced along left side of lace center, pm, yo, pm.
Remove provisional cast-on and place 61 live sts on left ndl, k61, pm, yo, pm, pick up and k27 evenly spaced along right side of lace center, pm for beg of rnd—179 sts.

RND 1: Yo, pm, p61, k1, p27 tbl, k1, p61, k1, p27 tbl—180 sts.
RND 2: [K1, yo, p to marker, yo] 4 times—188 sts.
RND 3: P.
RND 4: [K1, yo, k to next marker, yo] 4 times—196 sts.
RND 5: K.
Rep Rnds 4–5 10 times—276 sts, with 85 sts on each long edge between corner yos and 51 sts on each short edge between corner yos.

LACE EDGING

Using CC, beg Edging Pattern, working 5 17-st reps along each long side and 3 17-st reps along the short sides. Work through rnd 8, cut yarn leaving a tail to weave in. Attach MC and work rnds 9–16 of Edging Pattern. Cut yarn, leaving a tail to weave in. Attach CC and work rnds 17–23 of Edging Pattern.
NEXT RND: K2, sl sts back on left ndl, ssk, *k1, sl both sts back on left ndl, ssk; rep from * to end. Fasten off rem st.

Finishing

Weave in ends. Wet thoroughly. Squeeze out excess water; do not wring. Roll piece in towel and blot dry. Pin out to finished measurements so lace edging form scallops, as shown.

Listen as the Yarn Speaks to You

Go Roving with Roving and Glean Some Spinning Inspiration

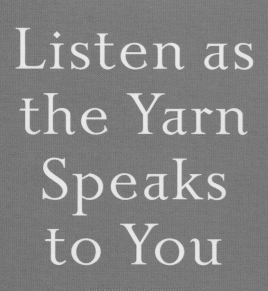

"More!" they said. "I need more!"

That cry—shouted by knitters who felt the need to delve ever deeper into the fibers and the process of the yarn they'd grown to love—was answered by the spindle and the wheel.

Thousands of knitters spin. They spin out of curiosity or because they want to create a garment start to finish. They spin because they've fallen in love with Cormo sheep or cashmere goats. They spin because they need to know the "why" of fibers. They spin because they're mesmerized by the rhythms and the texture of the process. And they spin just because of the glorious yarn they can create from the fiber they raised or the roving they chose.

To knit with a beautiful hand-spun is to knit with the sublime. Hand-spun yarn represents the convergence of fiber and human in a most transcendent way.

Whether you spin or not, the secret is to learn to hear the yarn and to understand what it tells you; to learn the subtle difference between rich, lanolin-y Shetland and ethereal angora; to recognize how hand-spun yarn can add depth and complexity to any project.

And the Secret? Knitting with hand-spun yarn is a double gift—that of the fiber and that of the spinner.

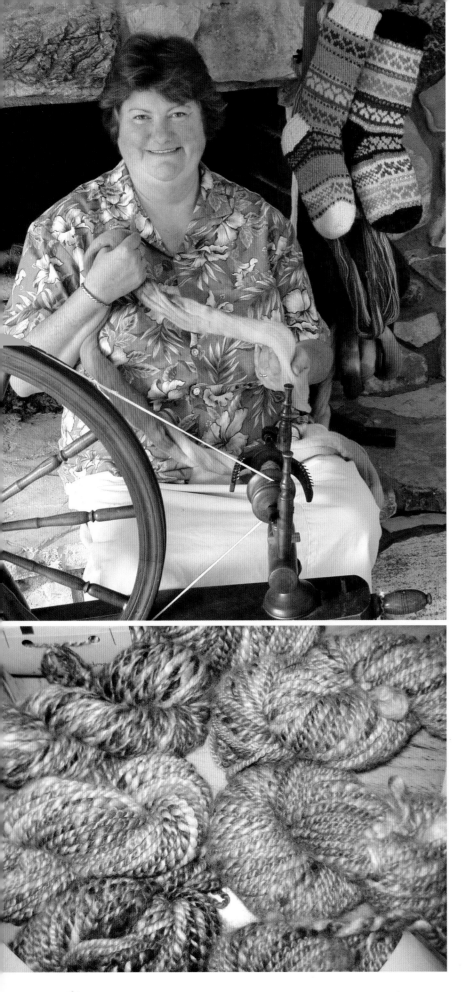

Let us introduce you to two marvelous spinners: *Trish Anderson* is the dyer/spinner who markets her wares. *Lexi Boeger* is the wild-child artist who just experiments and sets stuffy spinners free. Welcome to their worlds.

TRISH ANDERSON'S TANGLEWOOD FIBER CREATIONS

Trish Anderson had a small plan to spin beautiful yarn for an artsy yarn store while living the life of an artistic wife and mother. Her daughter, Becky, had bigger plans for Trish's talents, and when Becky graduated college, she talked Trish into growing this kernel of an idea into a full-fledged business called Tanglewood Fiber Creations.

In July of 2004, when Trish and Becky began this plan, few hand-spinners sold their yarn, let alone at a wholesale price that would allow yarn shop owners to make a profit on, as well as thrill their customers with such treasures. Spinners scoffed at Trish, thinking it was impossible to wholesale hand-dyed and hand-spun luxury yarn without losing buckets of money.

Trish stood up to her detractors by boldly shopping her wares to Lint, a yarn store in Portland, Oregon. She gave the owners an offer they could not refuse—a basket of hand-spun cashmere left on consignment. Her hand-spun was a success for Lint. Trish had found her niche market.

At Tanglewood Fiber Creations' first TNNA wholesale market, orders piled higher and higher, but the exhilaration of such success could be tempered only by the realization that Trish and Becky had to find help—and pronto.

Soon, they adopted old-fashioned, cottage-industry methods by employing spinners who worked from home. With riotous color, the finest cashmere, and a big personality, Trish Anderson made magic happen and shared her success with both her spinners and yarn shop owners.

The magic continues today, with Tanglewood Fiber's line of cashmere blends, beaded yarns, and the finest of washable wools. Read about Trish's adventures on her blog, www.SpinningMom.blogspot.com, and at www.TanglewoodFiber Creations.com.

THE WILD IMAGININGS OF LEXI BOEGER, AKA PLUCKFLUFF

Artists come the world with a different way of seeing, a special way of imagining. Add to that the support of an entrepreneurial family, and that artist can be fearless. Such is *Lexi Boeger*, aka Pluckyfluff, who hails from Placerville, a small town in the gold country of California

Daughter of the Boeger Winery family, Lexi possesses an artistic curiosity that brought her to the fiber arts through crochet. While she wasn't much of a crocheter, she fell in love with the myriad yarns available. When she ran out of a favorite yarn for a project, she discovered that it had been spun by the owner of her local yarn store, Lou of Lofty Lou's, and realized why it was unique. Intrigued by the idea of spinning her own yarn, Lexi signed up for Lou's comprehensive

I've made a bazillion garments for others over the years, and my seaming technique was like a mantra ... two running stitches and one back stitch, repeat.

The one back stitch really gives you a secure, non-puckery seam. I just made it up, but it always worked. Of course, my latest garment was made with no side seams. Ha!

Fun Stuff

You just finished a magnificent intarsia sweater for your loved one of choice. You wrap it carefully in tissue paper and present it. But something's missing. What? A neat fabric tag that says "Hand-knit by Molly" or some such sentiment. Fabric tags really personalize your knitted gifts. You can sew them on or just pin them.

We'd bet your recipient will love them as much as you do. Order online.

spinning classes, which took her from scouring a fleece through crafting yarn on both spindle and wheel. Lexi was smitten.

Pluckyfluff was born out of a second eureka moment, when Lexi began teaching her friends what she had learned. Seeing one friend's ball of lumpy, kinky yarn, her artist's eye absorbed the beauty in the irregularity and the freedom of the form. She understood the blissful uniqueness of each skein, and soon she was spinning that way herself, adding bits of color, fluff, beads, fabric, and even doll parts. She'd found her artist's voice, and her sculptural and wild art yarn found a following. Lexi had sparked a movement, one that resonated with other artists.

Lexi continues to teach, which has brought relaxed happiness to spinners who have embraced this new form that revels in artistic imperfection and untamed imagination.

Thanks to the Internet and her forward thinking, Lexi's art-yarn movement has gone global. Her Camp Pluckyfluff workshops traverse the globe, and Majacraft has even invented a spinning wheel named Wild Flyer, a wheel crafted to handle these wild yarns and Lexi's even wilder imagination.

So You Want to Learn to Spin?

First: Which method shall you choose? Either a Drop Spindle or a Wheel will get you there. Sure, everyone's seen spinning wheels. They're so ubiquitous, they're often used as a metaphor. But they're not cheap. Whereas a drop spindle will allow you to start spinning tomorrow without dropping a wad of cash.

DROP SPINDLE: Purchase for between $20 and $60. Some drop spindles are works of art.

SPINNING WHEEL: A nice wheel goes for around $350 and up. You also can spend a bit less or a whole lot more. (Ask yourself if you wish to travel with your wheel. There are traveling or fold-up wheels perfect for carrying on the road.)

Two super articles on Choosing Your First Spinning Wheel:
www.AbbysYarns.com/2008/12/choosing-your-first-spinning-wheel and www.JoyOfHandspinning.com/select-a-wheel.shtml.

So now, you've acquired your method of spinning. What's next? Fiber, of course! The stuff that dreams and yarn are made from.

Second: What type of fiber should you choose for your learning project? Sheep's wool. Why? Because it's the easiest of fibers to use and forgiving of a beginning spinner. Well, what kind of sheep?

You can pick Corriedale, Romney, Shetland, Lincoln, Sussex, merino, and on and on. What really matters is the length of the staple, meaning the length of the individual fibers. You want them long. Again, why? Because the longer the length (or staple), the easier the spinning for a beginner.

Here's a great page for discovering staple length: www.Spin-Knit-Dye.com/wool-breeds.html, or just Google "sheep staple length."

Third: What type of wool to buy? Raw fleece from sheep is big, smelly if unwashed, and usually sold in a plastic bag. You'll have to wash and otherwise prepare the fleece using special equipment to get it ready to spin. As a beginning spinner, you probably should avoid a fleece.

Your best choice is to purchase some roving (most often carded on a carding machine—the easiest to spin) or possibly clouds (washed, prepared fluff with no form—trickier to spin) at a fiber festival, online, or at your LYS. Roving and clouds are already cleaned and ready to spin.

So . . . you now have your spindle or wheel and your clean balls of fluff. You're ready to spin!

But wait: You'll need some other gear if you're using a wheel: bobbins, a niddy-noddy, an orifice hook. You've chosen a spindle? You're good to go with the spindle and the roving.

Obviously the Laidback Knitters aren't teaching you how to spin. Classes abound. So do some marvelous books. In fact, www.Knitty.com has collected a useful bibliography on spinning books. Spinning videos are all over the Web, as are some amazing spinning sites. *Spin-Off* magazine is a super resource, too. What's so fun about spinning? Many, many things, but as a knitter, you will eventually be able to custom-spin any kind of yarn you wish, from angora to cashmere to alpaca and beyond.

Finally, a word of warning! Be very, very careful, as spinning is highly addictive.

WHAT ARE WRAPS PER INCH AND WHY DO THEY MATTER?

Particularly for hand-spun yarn, spinners and knitters use wpi (wraps per inch) to determine a yarn's thickness, aka "weight." The yarn is wrapped around a special tool (although you can even use a pencil, an index card, etc.), and then the number of wraps in an inch is counted. For superior accuracy, you can count the wpi, then average out wraps in 2 or 3 inches.

LACEWEIGHT: 35wpi or more, aka 2-ply

FINGERING WEIGHT: 19–22wpi, aka 3-ply

SPORTWEIGHT: 15–18wpi, aka 4-ply

DK: 12–14wpi

WORSTED, ARAN, OR FISHERMAN: 9–11wpi

BULKY OR CHUNKY: 7–8wpi

SUPERBULKY: 6 or fewer

Anne Hennessy is a master spinner, one famed throughout New England as a spinning teacher. "By the '60s and '70s," Anne says, "spinning had nearly died out. Few spun yarn. It was a rarity. In the late '70s, I saw an ad for a spinning class. I was curious. So I took it — and fell in love. "We spinners had to reinvent the wheel."

Spinning wheels were hard to come by. "Once a year, somebody in the state [N.H.] would take orders to fill a shipping container with wheels from New Zealand. That's how you got your wheel. From that container."

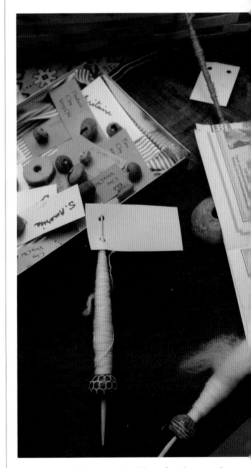

Ancient African spindle whorls, made from clay and stone

FRILLED MITTS ...
Designed by Vicki Stiefel

I love to knit mitts. This is one of those mash-up patterns that is simple to knit and produces a glam look. I used Lisa's gorgeous hand-spun cashmere-merino. It's incredibly soft, and I love its slight irregularity. Depth and texture—that's what hand-spun is all about.

 Skill Level: ROCKING CHAIR

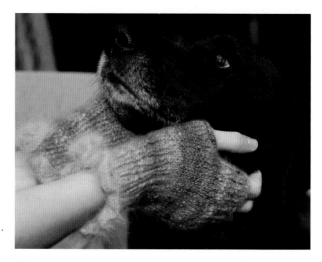

Things You'll Need to Know
• Knitting in the round with double pointed needles
• Cable cast-on

Sizes
Women's M/L (Men's M/L)

Finished Measurements
Hand circumference: 7½ (9¾)" [19 (25)cm]
Length: 7¼ (7¼)" [18.5 (18.5)cm]

Yarn
Lisa Souza *Hand Spun Cashmere Merino* Olive Tones (50% cashmere, 50% merino wool); 130 yds [119m]/3 oz [85g]; worsted/medium weight {4}; **COLOR A:** 1 (1) skein, shown in color Camoo

Valerie di Roma *Angora* (100% angora); 55 yds [50m]/⅜ oz [10g]; DK/light weight {3}; **COLOR B:** 1 (1) skein, shown in color Mustard (women's mitt only)

Needles
Sizes US 5 and 7 (3.75 and 4.5mm) double-pointed needles, or size needed to obtain gauge

Notions
Stitch markers
Blunt tapestry/yarn needle

Gauge
19 sts and 28 rnds = 4" (10cm) in stockinette on larger needles
I hate checking gauge, too. I just suck it up. Hope you do, too.

Techniques
CABLE CAST-ON: An easy cast-on, once you're clear how it works. Keep it loose, or you'll get into trouble. Start with a slip knot. Knit into the slip knot, leaving the stitch on the left needle. *Knit into the gap between the two stitches on the left needle. Place knitted stitch that's now on the right needle onto the left needle. And so on.
Thanks to www.KnittingHelp.com for the info. (Seeing the video of this cast-on makes all the difference.)

Abbreviations
beg begin(ning) • **BO** bind off
dec decrease • **dpn(s)** double-pointed needle(s)
inc increase • **k** knit
k2tog knit 2 stitches together (1 stitch decreased)
m1 make 1: With tip of left needle, lift the strand of yarn between the last stitch worked and the next stitch by inserting the needle from front to back, then knit through the back of the loop to twist it (1 stitch increased).

pm place marker • rep repeat • rnd(s) round(s)
st(s) stitch(es) • yo yarn over

Tips

• Be sure to read through the pattern first, so that you're clear on how to work the thumb gusset. It can catch you by surprise. It has me.

• For a neat and elastic edge, use the cable cast-on to cast on the stitches above the thumb opening. If you get a hole where the thumb joins the hand, sew it up using some remnants of yarn from the mitts. It won't be noticeable. Don't stress.

CUFF

Using smaller dpns and color A, cast on 36 (46) sts. Pm to mark beg of rnd. Join to work in the rnd, being careful not to twist sts.
Work 3" (7.5cm) of k1, p1 rib and inc 1 st at center of last rnd—37 (47) sts.

HAND

Change to larger dpns.
NEXT ROW: K18 (23), pm, m1, k1, m1, pm, k18 (23)—39 (49) sts. K 1 rnd even.
NEXT ROW: K18 (23), m1, k to 1 st before next marker, m1, k18 (23)—41 (51) sts. K 1 rnd even.
Rep the last 2 rnds 4 (6) more times—49 (63) sts; 13 (17) sts between markers for thumb gusset.
NEXT RND: K18 (23), BO next 13 (17) sts for thumb, k18 (23)—36 (46) sts.
NEXT RND: K18 (23), cast on 2 sts over opening, k18 (23)—38 (48) sts.

Change to smaller dpns. Work 8 rnds of k1, p1 rib. Bind off loosely in rib.
Make second mitt.

FRILLS (WOMEN'S MITT ONLY)

With smaller dpns and color B, pick up and k36 sts along cast on edge. Pm to mark beg of rnd. Join to work in the rnd.
RNDS 1 & 2: K.
RND 3: *K1, m1; rep from * to end— 72 sts.
RNDS 4 & 6: K.
RND 5: *K1, m1, k1, yo; rep from * to end—144 sts.
Bind off. Weave in ends.

As you can see below, the caramel-colored gloves are unfinished. Why? I saved them to show the difference in knitting when under stress. Look at that huge gauge change between mitts, even though I used the same needles and same yarn! ~ VICKI

RHYTHM 'N ROLL VEST ...

Designed by Lisa Souza

I've made this vest for several clients, always in hand-spun yarn. Knitters asked for the "recipe," and I began helping them to create their own vest with a few ounces of my hand-spun, whether merino, bluefaced Leicester, or cashmere. I went whole hog this time and spun up the cashmere. It is an Old Friend vest that will be a happy addition to your wardrobe for years to come, whether you spin the yarn or find a treasure at a fiber festival! ~ LISA

Skill Level: **ROCKING CHAIR**

Things You Need to Know
- Twisting stitches without a cable needle
- Picking up stitches
- Making buttonholes

Sizes
S (M/L, XL)
Instructions are given for size Small, with larger sizes in parentheses. When only one number is given and no size is mentioned, that number applies to all sizes.

Finished Measurements
Bust: 34¾ (39½, 44¼)" [88.5 (100.5, 112.5)cm]
Length: 19 (19½, 20)" [48.5 (49.5, 51)cm]

Yarn
Lisa Souza *Hand Spun Cashmere Merino 2 ply* (50% merino wool/50% cashmere); 52 yds [48m]/1 oz [28g]; chunky/bulky weight [5]; 8¼ (9, 10) oz/234 (255, 284)g, shown in color Mahogany

Needles
Size US 10 (6mm) needle, 36" (91cm) circular needle
Size US 11 (8mm) needle, 36" (91cm) circular needle, or size needed to obtain gauge

Notions
Small safety pins
Stitch holders (optional)
Blunt tapestry/yarn needle
Four ¾" (19mm) buttons

Gauge
16 sts and 22 rows = 4" (10cm) in rib pattern
You will lose definite cool points if you fail to check your gauge.

Techniques
BUTTONHOLES: Knit 2 stitches together, yarn over twice, ssk. Next row, work rib to buttonhole, work the 2 yarn overs in rib as established.

TWISTING STITCHES WITHOUT A CABLE NEEDLE (RIGHT TWIST): Knit into the front of the second stitch on the left needle, without slipping it off the needle, then knit the first stitch. Slip both stitches off the left needle.

Abbreviations
beg begin(ning) • **BO** bind off
cont continu(e)(ing) • **dec** decrease • **k** knit
k2tog knit 2 stitches together (1 stitch decreased)
ndl(s) needle(s) • **p** purl • **rem** remain(s)(ing)
rep repeat • **RS** right side(s) • **RT** right twist
ssk Slip, slip, knit: Slip one stitch from left needle to right needle, knitwise (as if to knit), slip second stitch same way; insert left needle through front of loops on right needle, then wrap yarn around right needle. With left needle, bring loops over the yarn wrapped around the right, which will knit them together through the back of the loops (1 stitch decreased).
st(s) stitch(es) • **WS** wrong side(s)

Tips
• This vest is knit in one piece to the armholes. I recommend working all three sections at the same

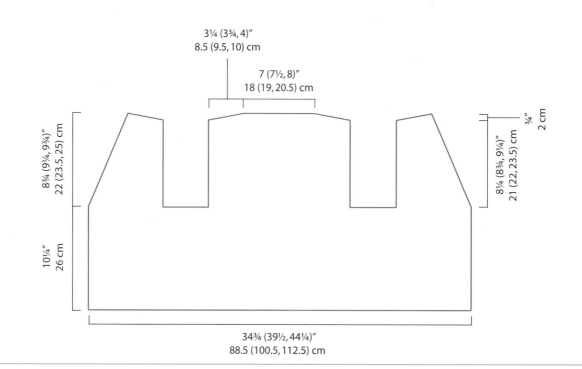

3¼ (3¾, 4)"
8.5 (9.5, 10) cm

7 (7½, 8)"
18 (19, 20.5) cm

8¾ (9¼, 9¾)"
22 (23.5, 25) cm

8¼ (8¾, 9¼)"
21 (22, 23.5) cm

¾"
2 cm

10¼"
26 cm

34¾ (39½, 44¼)"
88.5 (100.5, 112.5) cm

time, with three separate balls of yarn; this keeps everything moving along nicely with no mistakes.

• For a more deeply textured look, you can choose to leave this vest unblocked.

Pattern Stitches

TWISTED RIB (multiple of 4 sts + 2)

ROW 1 (WS): K2, *p2, k2; rep from * to end.

ROW 2 (RS): P2, *k2, p2; rep from * to end.

ROW 3: Rep row 1.

ROW 4: P2, *RT, p2; rep from * to end.

Rep rows 1–4 for pattern.

MAIN PATTERN (multiple of 8 sts + 6)

ROW 1 (RS): P2, *RT, p6; rep from * to lasts 4 sts, end RT, p2.

ROW 2 (WS): K2, *p2, k6; rep from * to last 4 sts, end p2, k2.

ROW 3: P2, *k2, p6; rep from * to last 4 sts, end k2, p2.

ROW 4: Rep row 2.

Rep rows 1–4 for pattern.

VEST

Using smaller ndls, loosely cast on 142 (158, 174) sts. Work back and forth in Twisted Rib for 2" (5cm), ending with row 3.

Change to larger ndls.

Beg Main Pattern and work until the piece measures 10" (25.5cm) from bottom, end with a RS row.

ARMHOLES

Next row, work 28 (30, 31) sts in pattern, attach another ball of yarn and BO 16 (19, 24) sts for armhole, work next 54 (60, 64) sts, attach another ball of yarn and BO 16 (19, 24) sts for armhole and then work rem 28 (30, 31) sts.

SHAPE NECK: Working each section separately, cont pattern and work 3 rows even.

NEXT ROW (WS, DEC): K1, ssk, work to last 3 sts of right front, k2tog, k1—2 sts dec.

Work 1 row even.

NEXT ROW (WS DEC): K1, ssk, work to last 3 sts of right front, k2tog, k1—2 sts dec.

Rep last 6 rows 6 more times, then rep dec row once more—13 (15, 16) sts rem on each side of front. Work even until piece measures 18¼ (18¾, 19¼)"/46.5 (47.5, 49cm) from bottom edge, ending with a WS row.

SHAPE SHOULDERS

NEXT ROW (RS): Work right front, BO the first 6 (7, 8) sts of back, then work to end of back, BO the first 6 (7, 8) sts of left front, then work to end.

NEXT ROW: Work left front, BO the first 6 (7, 8) sts of back, then work to end of back, BO the first 6 (7, 8) sts of right front, then work to end—7 (8, 8) sts rem on each front and 42 (46, 48) sts for back.

NEXT ROW: Work right front, BO the next 7 (8, 8) sts of back, then work to end of back, BO rem 7 (8, 8) sts of left front.

NEXT ROW: BO the next 7 (8, 8) sts of back, then work to end of back, BO rem 7 (8, 8) sts of right front—28 (30, 32) sts rem for back.

Bind off rem back sts.

Finishing

Sew shoulder seams together.

FRONT BAND

Using smaller ndl, beg at lower edge of right front. Pick up and k sts along front and back neck edges; pick up and *k1 in first 3 rows, skip 1 row; rep from * to top of right front, pick up 28 (30, 32) sts along back neck edge, then rep from * to lower edge of left front. Work back and forth, beg with a WS row. Work 1 row of k1, p1 rib. Mark right front for buttonholes, placing bottom marker about ¾"/2cm from bottom edge, and top marker about ½"/1.5cm from beg of neck shaping, then evenly space rem buttons in between.

BUTTONHOLE ROW

*Work rib to 2 sts before marker, k2tog, yo twice, ssk; rep from * 3 more times, then work in rib to end of row.

NEXT ROW: Work in rib, working (yo twice) in rib. Cont rib until band measures about ¾"/2cm. BO loosely in rib. Weave in ends. If desired, block piece to finished measurements.

Sew buttons to left front band under buttonholes.

Value the Partnership in Knitting

between Knitter and Designer, and Welcome the Handclasp of Two

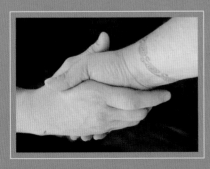

Have you ever thought of knitting as a partnership? Most of the time, it truly is. The partnership consists of the knitter and the designer coming together as a unit to create something beautiful . . . special . . . amusing . . . delightful.

A pattern is the designer saying to the knitter, "Here—I've created this design for you. Just follow a few simple rules, and you'll knit something that you love." And it's the knitter saying to the designer, "I love your work. I love your design. And most especially, I trust you, in that if I follow your instructions, if I do as I'm directed, what I create will look and fit like what is pictured in your design."

The Secret? When knitters and designers accept that joyous partnership, something marvelous grows.

How does the partnership work?

If the knitter aims to create what's pictured in the pattern, the knitter must:

- Use the yarn specified or a good substitute with similar gauge and fiber content. That includes yarn content (alpaca, silk, cotton, etc., don't have the same memory as wool; see Chapter 5), size, and twist.
- Always knit a swatch to compare your gauge to that of the designer's.

101

SPEAKING OF STITCH PATTERNS ...

WE'RE HUGE FANS OF BARBARA WALKER'S FOUR TREASURIES (PUBLISHED BY SCHOOLHOUSE PRESS). HERE'S THE WALKER TREASURY PROJECT ONLINE: WWW.THEWALKERTREASURY. WORDPRESS.COM. SEEING THESE MARVELOUS PATTERNS IN COLOR IS PRETTY TERRIFIC.

BECOME YOUR OWN PARTNER

Have you ever wanted to make something, needed a pattern, but couldn't find one? Or wanted a sweater to fit perfectly? Online you can find pattern generators. They're pretty cool. You need to subscribe to some, whereas others are free.

Knitting Fool: www.KnittingFool.com

Knitting Fiend: www.TheDietDiary.com/ knittingfiend/index.html

Knitting Software: www.KnittingSoftware.com/ sweaterwiz.htm

Just Google "knitting pattern generators," and you're there.

- Have a working knowledge of the stitches and techniques required for the pattern, which can always be practiced in your swatch.
- Pick a pattern at your skill level, which may include charts that you understand or want to learn to understand.

If the designer aims to craft a pattern the knitter will follow with satisfaction, the designer must:

- Use the same knitting terms and abbreviations throughout the pattern.
- Write a pattern that's easily comprehensible.
- Include a good representative photograph or drawing that illuminates the pattern's details for the knitter.
- Describe the pattern's realistic level of difficulty to ensure success for your knitter.

This partnership can be exciting and wonderful and can produce something magical, or it can be frustrating and nightmarish and result in something ill-fitting and ugly.

It all depends on the embrace of the partners.

A PAIR OF KNITTING DESIGN QUEENS

They snipe, they snip, they laugh, they hug, they snipe some more. On and on they talk, their banter interspersed with gauge changes and yarn colors and stitch styles. And somehow, almost impossibly, a synergy occurs and evolves into a knitting pattern only the *Queenie Sisters* could bring to life.

Tall, lean *Ellen,* the darker-haired redhead, hails from North Carolina. Now she lives just north of New York City. Short, round Danna, the lighter-haired redhead, is New York City-born and -bred, yet she lives in North Carolina.

Both appreciate the irony.

Ellen's self-taught in numerous needle arts, from macramé to sewing to knitting to needlepoint. Her voice lilts with the South, evoking languid days and steamy nights, mint juleps and cotillions. She has manners and class. She could easily pull off a Chanel suit, yet she's wearing a funky dress of fantastical design.

Knitting in fiction? Wuthering Heights, A Tale of Two Cities, Great Expectations, and Virginia Woolf's To the Lighthouse.

Danna learned to crochet at 10 from her dad's grandmother. Her voice, her manner, her stance shouts the Big Apple. Her array of hair whirls in all directions and complements the giant gold earrings, the immense purse, and the mile-long attitude. She spews terms like "Fibonacci sequence," as if non-geeks would have a clue. While she sounds like an M.I.T. professor, she looks as if she belongs on the Broadway stage.

The fact that they design together seems absurd, ridiculous, implausible. Yet as strange as their partnership appears, it works.

Not sisters by blood, they fit that term in every other way. In 1998, Ellen and her daughter were taking a knitting class at the High Point library in North Carolina. Danna was one of the teachers. Ellen and Danna began riffing almost immediately. The two are so sisterly, they often call each other The Bickersons. They not only clicked but lasted, and soon the new fast friends were talking passionately about the design and color and shape of the objects they knit.

Two years later, they dipped their toes into the knitting design world. Ask them to describe how they design together, from opposite ends of the East Coast, and they laugh and shrug. They can't. Not entirely.

THE PROCESS

They begin with a premise. They discuss stitch pattern; they swatch; they talk about gauge. More discussion. Ellen draws a picture that's formed in her mind. Danna peppers her with questions about details. The Idea, working its way toward a pattern, evolves, devolves, until something real and true and exciting coalesces. Phone calls. Tons of phone calls. Danna is responsible for the tech part of the pattern, which makes sense given her math and science background. Danna loves numbers; Ellen, shapes. Ellen's focus is artistic; Danna's mathematical.

Do you like to design? I ask them. "Depends on the week!" says Ellen.

Jump backward to 2003 . . . Having informally designed for a couple of years, the duo entered a national retailer's design competition. They won, and thus the Queenie Sisters was launched. Now they wholesale their patterns at several online knitting sites.

And from where did they get their name? According to Danna, her ancient cat, Prrrinks, acts like a queen. Somehow the cat, the bickering, the joie de vivre evolved into the Queenie Sisters. Personally, I believe they were twins separated at birth.

With the Queenie Sisters, the sum of the parts is more than the individuals together. And that's called synergy.

RIBS WITH A SIDE OF LACE ...
Designed by the Queenie Sisters

The Queenie Sisters have designed a fabulous scarf and impressive knitted coat (see photo page 100). Here is the pattern for the scarf. The complete coat pattern can be found on our Web site: www.LaidBackKnitters.com.

We've included the scarf pattern here to give you a taste of the entire order of delicious Ribs with a Side of Lace. Knit on!

 Skill Level: DINING CHAIR

Finished Measurements
Scarf 65" by 6¾" [165 cm by 17cm] at widest points

Yarn
Lisa Souza *Sierra* (50% alpaca, 30% merino wool, 20% silk); 500 yds [457m]/8 oz [227g]; heavy worsted/medium weight [4]; 1 skein or about 250 yards, shown in color Emerald City

Needles
Size US 5 (3.75mm) needles, 16" and 39" (40 and 100cm) circular needles, or size needed to obtain gauge
Size US 3 (3.25mm) needles, 39" (100cm) circular needle; second short circular needle is optional

Notions
Stitch markers
Removable stitch markers
Blunt tapestry/yarn needle
Slippery waste yarn for provisional cast-on

Gauge
31 sts and 28 rows = 4" (10cm) in Herringbone Rib using larger needles
18 sts and 30 rows = 4" (10cm) in Ellen's Favorite Lace using smaller needles

Abbreviations
Beg begin(ning) • **BO** bind off
CC contrast color • **dec** decrease • **k** knit
k2tog knit 2 stitches together (1 stitch decreased)
ndl(s) needle(s) • **p** purl • **pm** place marker
rem remain • **rep** repeat **RS** right side(s) • **sl** slip

ssk slip, slip, knit: Slip one stitch from left needle to right needle, knitwise (as if to knit), slip second stitch same way, insert left needle through front of loops on right needle, then wrap yarn around right needle, with left needle, bring loops over the yarn wrapped around the right, which will knit them together through the back of the loops (1 stitch decreased). • **st(s)** stitch(es)

s2kp slip 2 stitches together as if to knit them together, knit 1 stitch, pass slipped stitches over the last stitch knit in the order they are on the needle (2 stitches decreased)

w&t wrap and turn (see techniques)

ws wrong side(s) • **yo** yarn over

Pattern Stitches

HERRINGBONE RIB

(multiple of 6 + 2 sts, worked back and forth)

Row 1 (RS): *P2, k1, sl1, k1, yo, psso, k1; rep from * to last 2 sts, p2.

ROW 2: *K2, p4; rep from * to last 2 sts, k2.

Rep Rows 1 and 2 for pattern.

ELLEN'S FAVORITE LACE

(multiple of 7 + 4 sts)

ROW 1 (WS) AND ALL ODD-NUMBERED ROWS: Purl.

ROW 2: K3, *yo, ssk, k1, k2tog, yo, k2; rep from * to last st, k1.

ROW 4: *K2, (yo, ssk) twice, k1; rep from * to last 4 sts, k2, yo, ssk.

ROW 6: K1, *(yo, ssk) 3 times, k1: rep from * to last 3 sts, yo, ssk, k1.

ROW 8: *K2, (yo, ssk) twice, k1; rep from * to last 4 sts, k2, yo, ssk.

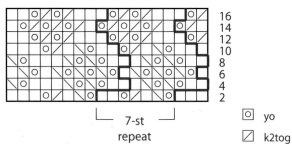

Ellen's Favorite Lace Pattern

7-st repeat

⊡	yo
╱	k2tog
╲	ssk
☐	repeat

This chart shows even-numbered rows only; all odd-numbered rows should be purled when worked back and forth, or knit when worked in the round.

ROW 10: K1, *k2, yo, ssk, k1, k2tog, yo; rep from * to last 3 sts, k3.

ROW 12: K2tog, yo, *k3, (k2tog, yo) twice; rep from * to last 2 sts, k2.

ROW 14: K1, k2tog, yo, *k1, (k2tog, yo) 3 times; rep from * to last st, k1.

ROW 16: Rep Row 12.

Rep Rows 1 – 16 for pattern.

SCARF

NOTE: If working a dec with wrapped sts, be sure to work both wraps and sts at the same time.

Using smaller ndl in longer length and CC, use provisional cast-on to cast on 284 sts.

Work back and forth, beg Ellen's Favorite Lace Pattern and short-row shaping as follows:

ROW 1: Work row 1 of pattern to last st, pm, w&t.

ROW 2: K2, *yo, ssk, k1, k2tog, yo, k2; rep from * to last st, pm, w&t.

ROW 3 AND ALL WS ROWS THROUGH ROW 19: P to 1 st before marker, s next st to wrap, remove marker, wrap slipped st and return to left ndl, pm, then turn.

ROW 4: (Yo, ssk) twice, k1, *k2, (yo, ssk) twice, k1; rep from * to 3 sts before marker, k2, sl next st to wrap, remove marker, wrap slipped st and return to left ndl, pm, then turn.

ROW 6: (Yo, ssk) twice, k1, *(yo, ssk) 3 times, k1; rep from * to 1 st before marker, w&t and move marker.

ROW 8: Yo, ssk, k1, *k2, (yo, ssk) twice, k1; rep from * to 1 st before marker, w&t and move marker.

ROW 10: K1, k2tog, yo, *k2, yo, ssk, k1, k2tog, yo; rep from * to 6 sts before marker, k2, yo, ssk, k1, w&t and move marker.

ROW 12: K1, k2tog, yo, *k3, (k2tog, yo) twice; rep from * to 4 sts before marker, k3, w&t and move marker.

ROW 14: K1, k2tog, yo, *k1, (k2tog, yo) 3 times; rep from * to 2 sts before marker, k1, w&t and move marker.

ROW 16: K1, *k3, (k2tog, yo) twice; rep from * to 2 sts before marker, k1, w&t and move marker.

ROW 18: K1, *yo, ssk, k1, k2tog, yo, k2; rep from * to 7 sts before marker, yo, ssk, k1, k2tog, yo, k1, w&t and move marker.

ROW 20: K1, yo, ssk, k1, *k2, (yo, ssk) twice, k1; rep from * to 2 sts before marker, k1, w&t and move marker.

ROWS 21, 23, AND 25: P to 2 sts before marker, w&t and move marker. (NOTE: For rnds 21–26, you'll need to slip an extra st in order to move the marker; return that st to left ndl before wrapping.)

ROW 22: Yo, ssk, k1, *(yo, ssk) 3 times, k1; rep from * to 7 sts before marker, (yo, ssk) twice, w&t and move marker.

ROW 24: *K2, (yo, ssk) twice, k1; rep from * to 6 sts before marker, k2, yo, ssk, w&t and move marker.

ROW 26: K1, yo, ssk, k1, k2tog, yo, *k2, yo, ssk, k1, k2tog, yo; rep from * to 3 sts before marker, k1, w&t and move marker.

ROWS 27, 29, AND 31: P to 3 sts before marker, w&t and move marker. (NOTE: For rnds 21–26, you'll need to slip an extra 2 sts in order to move the marker; return those sts to left ndl before wrapping.)

ROW 28: (K2tog, yo) twice, *k3, (k2tog, yo) twice; rep from * to 7 sts before marker, k4, w&t and move marker.

ROW 30: K2tog, yo, *k1, (k2tog, yo) 3 times; rep from * to 3 sts before marker, w&t and move marker.

ROW 32: K1, (k2tog, yo) twice, *k3, (k2tog, yo) twice; rep from * to 8 sts before marker, k3, k2tog, yo, w&t and move marker.

ROW 33: P to end of row, removing marker and working wraps tog with the sts they wrap.

ROW 34: K3, *(yo, ssk, k1, k2tog, yo, k2); rep from * to end of row, removing marker and working wraps tog with the sts they wrap.

ROW 35: P. Do not cut yarn.

SCARF EDGING

Change to larger circular ndl in longer length. Work along entire edge and work 5 rows of Herringbone Rib.

NEXT ROW (WS): BO knitwise.

Carefully remove provisional cast-on and sl sts to smaller circular ndl in longer length. Change to larger circular ndl in longer length. With RS facing, join CC and work 5 rows of Herringbone Rib.

NEXT ROW: BO knitwise.

MITERED CORNERS (make 2)

Using larger circular ndl in shorter length, CC and with RS facing, beg at outer edge of one corner and pick up and k6 sts along end of one edging, 1 st at inner corner, then 6 sts along end of other edging—13 sts. Pick up row counts as first row.

ROW 2 (WS): K.

ROW 3 (RS): K5, s2kp, k5—11 sts.

ROW 4: K.

ROW 5: K4, s2kp, k4—9 sts.

ROW 6: K.

ROW 7: K3, s2kp, k3—7 sts.

ROW 8: K.

ROW 9: K2, s2kp, k2—5 sts.

ROW 10: K.

ROW 11: K1, s2kp, k1—3 sts.

ROW 12: K.

ROW 13: S2kp. Fasten off rem st.

Finishing

Work in ends. Block to measurements.

NORAH'S SCARF FOR BILL ...
Designed by Norah Gaughan

Norah and her scarf represent everything that's wonderful about the partnership between the knitter and the designer. Norah not only loves knitters; she also loves the process of knitting. She's passionate about designing, a truth reflected in her incredible design aesthetic. She genuinely welcomes the handclasp of two.

 Skill Level: **ROCKING CHAIR**

Things You'll Need to Know
• Cables
• Reading charts

Finished Measurements
Width: 7½" (19cm)
Length: 56" (142cm)

Yarn
Berroco *Blackstone Tweed* (65% wool, 25% super-kid mohair, 10% angora rabbit hair); 130 yds [119m]/1¾ oz [50g]; worsted/medium weight [4]; 4 balls, shown in color Plum Island #2637

Needles
Size US 7 (4.5mm) needles, or size needed to obtain gauge

Notions
Cable needle

Gauge
18 sts and 25 rows = 4" (10cm) in stockinette
Check your gauge. Norah insists, and so do we.

Techniques
4/4RC K/K: Slip 4 stitches to cable needle and hold in back of work, p1, k2, p1, then p1, k2, p1 from cable needle.
4/4RC K/P: Slip 4 stitches to cable needle and hold in back of work, p1, k2, p1, then p4 from cable needle.

SLIPPING STITCHES TO CREATE A SELF-CORDED EDGE: On right-side rows, slip stitches with the yarn in front: on wrong-side rows, slip stitches with the yarn in back.

Abbreviations
4/4RC K/K 4 over 4 right-cross cable, knit stitches over knit stitches
4/4RC K/P 4 over 4 right-cross cable, knit stitches over purl stitches • **cont** continu(e)(ing)
cn cable needle • **k** knit • **p** purl • **rep** repeat
RS right side(s) • **sl** slip • **st(s)** stitch(es)
WS wrong side(s) • **wyb** with yarn in back: hold yarn in back of work
wyf with yarn in front: hold yarn in front of work

Tip
• To bring out the soft hand of the yarn when blocking, hand-wash your scarf and lay flat to dry.

Pattern Stitch
Cast on 57 sts.
ROW 1 (WS): Sl 3 wyb, k3, p3, *k4, p2, k6, p2, k4, p3; rep from * once more, k3, p3.
ROW 2 (RS): Sl 3 wyf, p3, *k3, p4, k2, p6, k2, p4; rep from * once more, k3, p3, k3.

ROWS 3 AND 5: Rep Row 1.

ROW 4: Rep Row 2.

ROW 6: Sl 3 wyf, p3, *k3, p4, k2, p1, 4/4RC K/K, p3; rep from * once more, k3, p3, k3.

ROW 7: Sl 3 wyb, k3 p3, *k4, (p2, k2) twice, p2, k4, p3; rep from * once more, k3, p3.

ROW 8: Sl 3 wyf, p3, *k3, p3, 4/4RC K/P, p1, k2, p4; rep from * once more, k3, p3, k3.

ROW 9: Rep Row 1.

Row 10: Rep Row 2.

ROWS 11 – 20: Rep Rows 1 – 10.

ROWS 21 – 34: Rep Rows 1 and 2 seven times.

Rep Rows 1 – 34 until piece measures about 56" (142 cm), ending with Row 23. Bind off in pattern.

Finishing

Weave in ends.

Block to finished measurements.

Cable Pattern

end row 23 —

end RS rows;
beg WS rows

21-st repeat
work twice

beg RS rows;
end WS rows

☐   k on RS; p on WS

▣   p on RS; k on WS

▨   4/4RC K/P

▨   4/4RC K/K

PRINCESS GARDEN SKIRT ...
Designed by Justine Turner

This adorable skirt, definitely designed for a princess, includes a beautifully embellished border. The gorgeous roses and leaves can be sprinkled across the skirt, as you will. Of course, if your princess prefers her skirts flower-free, simply leave off the roses. This skirt is utterly fun to knit and totally girl-worthy.

 Skill Level: ROCKING CHAIR

Things You'll Need to Know
- Cable cast-on
- Knitting in the round
- Simple lace knitting
- Picking up stitches

Sizes
1 year (2T, 4T, 6, 8, 10)
Shown in size 4T
Instructions are given for the smallest size, with larger sizes shown in parentheses. When only one number is given and no size is mentioned, that number applies to all sizes.

Finished Measurements
Waist circumference: 20¼ (22½, 24, 26¼, 28¼, 29¾)" [51.5 (57, 61, 66.5, 72, 75.5)cm]
Length: 11½ (13, 14, 16, 19, 20)" [29 (33, 35.5, 40.5, 48.5, 51)cm]

Yarn
Rowan Yarn *Pure Wool DK* (100% wool); 137 yds [125m]/1¾ oz [50g]; DK/light weight [3]; **COLOR A:** 2 (3, 3, 3, 4, 4) balls; **COLOR B:** 1 (1, 1, 1, 1, 1) ball, shown in colors Raspberry #028 (A) and Avocado #019 (B)
Yarn used for the roses and leaves on this skirt were remnants of the Rowan colors used to make the skirt, plus Debbie Bliss *Baby Cashmerino* in color baby pink #601; Dale of Norway *Dale Baby Ull* in color pastel pink #4711; and Shepherd *Baby Wool 4 Ply* in color #0333.

Needles
Size US 6 (4mm) needles, 16" (40cm) circular needle, or size needed to obtain gauge
Size US 4 (3.5mm) needles, 16" (40cm) circular needle
Size US 1 or 2 (2.25 or 2.75mm) needles for smaller roses;
Size US 4 or 5 (3.5 or 3.75mm) needles for larger roses

Notions
Stitch marker
Small and medium-size safety pins
Blunt tapestry/yarn needle
18 (19, 20, 21, 23, 25)" [45.5 (48.5, 51, 53.5, 58.5, 63.5)cm] of ½" (1.3cm) wide elastic

Gauge
22 sts and 31 rnds = 4" (10cm) in stockinette using larger needles
Your little girl will be most unhappy if you make this the wrong size because you didn't check your gauge.

Techniques
CABLE CAST-ON: An easy cast-on, once you're clear how it works. Keep it loose, or you'll get into trouble. Start with a slip knot. Knit into the slip knot, leaving the stitch on the left needle. *Knit into the gap between the two stitches on the left needle. Place knitted stitch that's now on the right needle onto left needle. And so on.
Thanks to www.KnittingHelp.com for the info. (Seeing the video of this cast-on makes all the difference.)

Abbreviations

beg begin(ning) • **BO** bind off • **cont** continu(e)(ing) • **dec** decrease • **dpn** double-pointed needle **k** knit • **k2tog** knit 2 stitches together (1 stitch decreased) • **k3tog tbl** knit 3 stitches together through back of loops (2 stitches decreased)

m1 make 1: With tip of left needle, lift the strand of yarn between the last stitch worked and the next stitch by inserting the needle from front to back, then knit through the back of the loop to twist it (1 stitch increased). • **ndl(s)** needle(s)

p3tog tbl purl 3 stitches together through back of loops (2 stitches decreased) • **pm** place marker **rep** repeat • **rem** remain • **rnd(s)** round(s) **RS** right side(s) • **skp** slip, knit pass: Slip 1 stitch purlwise, knit 1 stitch, pass the slipped stitch over (1 stitch decreased). • **sk2p** slip, knit 2 together, pass: Slip 1 stitch purlwise, knit 2 stitches together, pass the slipped stitch over (2 stitches decreased). **sl** ship • **st(s)** stitch(es) • **St st** stockinette stitch **tog** together • **WS** wrong side(s) • **yo** yarn over

Tips

• It may be easier to keep track of the skirt shaping by placing a stitch marker before each decrease on the first regular decrease round above the hem.

• To customize this skirt, experiment with different yarns and needle sizes for the roses and leaves.

Pattern Stitch

LEAF LACE PATTERN (multiple of 10 sts + 3)

RND 1: K1, k2tog, k3, yo, k1, yo, k3, *sk2p, k3, yo, k1, yo, k3; rep from * to last 3 sts, skp, k1.

RND 2 AND ALL EVEN-NUMBER RNDS: K.

RND 3: K1, k2tog, k2, yo, k3, yo, k2, *sk2p, k2, yo, k3, yo, k2; rep from * to last 3 sts, skp, k1.

RND 5: K1, k2tog, k1, yo, k5, yo, k1, *sk2p, k1, yo, k5, yo, k1; rep from * to last 3 sts, skp, k1.

RND 7: K1, k2tog, yo, k7, yo, *sk2p, yo, k7, yo; rep from * to last 3 sts, skp, k1.

RND 9: K2, yo, k3, sk2p, k3, yo, *k1, yo, k3, sk2p, k3, yo; rep from * to last 2 sts, k2.

RND 11: K3, yo, k2, sk2p, k2, yo, k1, *k2, yo, k2, sk2p, k2, yo, k1; rep from * to last 2 sts, k2.

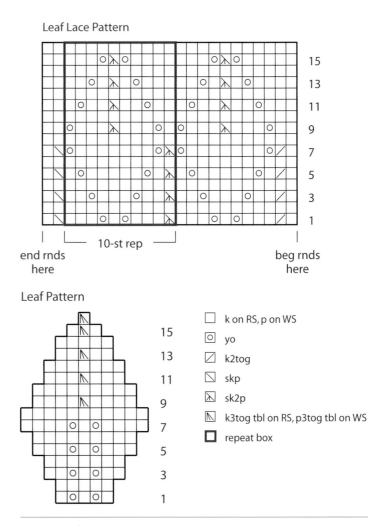

Leaf Lace Pattern

10-st rep

end rnds here

beg rnds here

Leaf Pattern

☐ k on RS, p on WS
◉ yo
⟋ k2tog
⟍ skp
⋏ sk2p
⋈ k3tog tbl on RS, p3tog tbl on WS
☐ repeat box

RND 13: K4, yo, k1, sk2p, k1, yo, k2, *k3, yo, k1, sk2p, k1, yo, k2; rep from * to last 2 sts, k2.

RND 15: K5, yo, sk2p, yo, k3, *k4, yo, sk2p, yo, k3; rep from * to last 2 sts, k2.

RND 16: K.

BOTTOM EDGE

Using larger ndl and B, cast on 133 (153, 163, 183, 203, 203) sts using cable cast-on. Pm for beg of rnd. Join to work in the rnd, making sure not to twist sts; rnds beg at center back.

Work 16 rnds of Leaf Lace Pattern.

Change to smaller ndl and A. Work 4 rnds of St st, marking first st of first rnd with a small safety pin.

NEXT (PICOT) RND: K1, *yo, k2tog; rep from * to end. K 1 rnd. Change to larger ndls. Work 3 rnds of St st.

JOINING HEM: With left ndl, pick up top of loop of st marked with safety pin, knit it and first st of rnd tog, *pick up top of loop of next st with left ndl, knit it and next st tog; rep from * to end.

SHAPING

Sizes 1 year (4T, 6, 8): K13 (27, 13, 14), k2tog, *k24 (52, 24, 27), k2tog; rep from * 4 (2, 6, 6) more times, k14 (26, 12, 13)—128 (160, 176, 196) sts.

SIZE 2T: K4, k2tog, k to end—152 sts.

SIZE 10: K4, m1, k to end—204 sts.

K 15 (9, 11, 11, 11, 12) rnds even.

NEXT (DEC) RND: *K30 (36, 38, 42, 47, 49) sts, k2tog; rep from * to end—124 (148, 156, 172, 192, 200) sts.

K 15 (9, 11, 11, 11, 12) rnds even.

NEXT (DEC) RND: *K29 (35, 37, 41, 46, 48) sts, k2tog; rep from * to end—120 (144, 152, 168, 188, 196) sts.

Cont dec every 16th (10th, 12th, 12th, 12th, 13th) rnd, 2 (5, 5, 6, 8, 8) more times, with 1 fewer st between dec each time—112 (124, 132, 144, 156, 164) sts.

Work even until piece measures about 10½ (12, 13½, 15, 18, 19)" [26.5 (30.5, 34.5, 38, 45.5, 48.5) cm] from bottom edge.

WAISTBAND

Change to smaller ndl. P 1 rnd. K 4 rnds and place small safety pin in 6th st of first rnd.

NEXT RND (EYELET HOLES FOR CORD): K52 (58, 62, 68, 74, 78), yo, k2tog, k4, k2tog, yo, k to end.

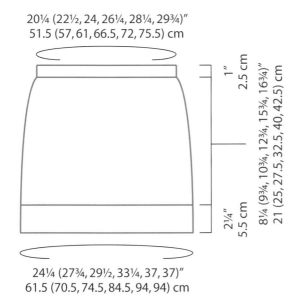

20¼ (22½, 24, 26¼, 28¼, 29¾)"
51.5 (57, 61, 66.5, 72, 75.5) cm

1"
2.5 cm

8¼ (9¾, 10¾, 12¾, 15¾, 16¾)"
21 (25, 27.5, 32.5, 40, 42.5) cm

2¼"
5.5 cm

24¼ (27¾, 29½, 33¼, 37, 37)"
61.5 (70.5, 74.5, 84.5, 94, 94) cm

K 2 rnds.

Change to larger ndl and B. K 2 rnds.

Change to smaller ndl. K 8 rnds.

NEXT RND: K5, pick up top of loop of st marked with safety pin using left ndl, k tog with first st of rnd, *pick up top of loop of next st with left ndl, k tog with next st, rep from * to last 5 sts of rnd.

BO rem 10 sts.

Cut yarn, leaving a tail about 12" (30.5cm) to sew rem opening.

Finishing

Weave in ends. Block to measurements, pinning lace to form points as shown.

Cut elastic to comfortable waist measurement, plus 1" (2.5cm). Using larger safety pin, thread elastic through waistband. Lap ends of elastic and adjust to fit. Sew ends of elastic tog. Slip under waistband, then sew rem opening closed.

Twist a cord from 2 lengths of color B, each about 48" (122cm), as follows: Tie pieces of yarn tog at each end, sl one end over a door handle or hook and place a dpn in the other end. Hold yarns with no slack in the middle, twist the end you're holding until the yarn is highly twisted and wants to twist up on itself. Carefully remove the end from the door or hook in one hand while holding onto the other end. Fold the strand so the 2 ends are tog and the other hand holding the middle and allow the yarn to twist on itself, forming a cord.

Tie a knot in each end for desired length. Trim ends and thread the cord through the picot holes.

ROSES AND LEAVES:

ROSE

Using needle size appropriate for yarn, cast on 6 sts, leaving a long tail.

Work back and forth, and work 2 rows of St st.

ROW 3 (RS): *K1, yo; rep from * to last st, end k1—11 sts.

ROW 4 (WS): P.

Rep the last 2 rows twice more—41 sts. BO loosely and cut yarn, leaving a long tail.

Starting with the end with the tail from the bind-off, spiral the piece from the center out to form a rose shape.

Thread the tail from the bind-off into a blunt tapestry/yarn ndl and use this end to sew a couple of sts in the center of the rose, through all layers at the base of the flower.

Draw the ndl down through the center of the flower to the underside, next to the tail from the cast-on, and tie both ends tightly tog. Use both ends to attach the rose to the skirt.

Make the desired number of roses with rem yarn remnants. 10 light-pink roses, 7 medium-pink roses, 6 dark-pink roses, and 1 large rose were made for this skirt.

LEAVES

Using size US 3 (3.25mm) ndl and B, cast on 3 sts. Work back and forth.

ROW 1 (RS): (K1, yo) twice, k1—5 sts.

ROWS 2, 4, 6, 8, 10, 12, AND 14 (WS): P.

ROW 3: K2, yo, k1, yo, k2—7 sts.

ROW 5: K3, yo, k1, yo, k3—9 sts.

ROW 7: K4, yo, k1, yo, k4—11 sts.

ROW 9: K4, k3tog tbl, k4—9 sts.

ROW 11: K3, k3tog tbl, k4—7 sts.

ROW 13: K2, k3tog tbl, k2—5 sts.

ROW 15: K1, k3tog tbl, k1—3 sts.

ROW 16: P3tog tbl. Fasten off rem st.

Cut yarn leaving a long tail and use to sew leaf to skirt.

SPIRAL GALAXY PILLOW ...

Designed by Daniel Yuhas

As a designer, Daniel is totally obsessed with spirals. He loves the way the simple lines radiate from the center of this handsome pillow—and so do we. Knitting in the round from the center out is quick and fun, and can give you quite gorgeous results from a very simple pattern. Beware—knitting spirals is addictive!

Skill Level: WING CHAIR

Things You'll Need to Know
- Disappearing loop cast-on
- Three-needle bind-off

- Working in the round on double-pointed and circular needles
- Increasing stitches by knitting into the front and back of the loop

Finished Measurements
16" (40.5cm) diameter

Yarn
Debbie Bliss *Donegal Luxury Tweed* (85% wool/15% angora); 93 yds [85m]/1¾ oz [50g] balls; worsted weight/medium [4]; 4 balls, shown in color Natural #07

Needles

Size US 7 (4.5mm) needles, one 16" (40cm) circular needle (optional), two 24" (60cm) and 32" (80cm) circular needles, and one set of 4 or 5 double-pointed needles or size needed to obtain gauge

Notions

16 stitch markers
Blunt tapestry/yarn needle
14" (35.5cm) round pillow form

Gauge

About 22½ sts and 24 rnds = 4" (10cm) in spiral pattern
How many gauges does it take to change a lightbulb? We have no idea, but please check the gauge yourself.

Techniques

DISAPPEARING-LOOP CAST-ON: The disappearing-loop method allows a large number of stitches to be cast on for center-out knitting without leaving a hole. An illustrated tutorial can be found at www.MoltingYeti.com/help/disappearingloop.html.

MORE ON THE DISAPPEARING-LOOP CAST-ON

ALONG WITH DANIEL'S SUPERB TUTORIAL FOR THE DISAPPEARING-LOOP CAST-ON (WWW.MOLTINGYETI.COM/HELP/DISAPPEARINGLOOP.HTML), HE ALSO OFFERS URLS FOR ADDITIONAL METHODS THAT LIVE ON THE WEB:

★ Emily Ocker's circular cast-on from Bagatell (a crochet cast-on)

★ Fleegle's Blog—simple ring beginning for circular shawls (a really elegant ring made with one knitting needle)

★ The line-art wizardry of TechKnitting™: Casting on From the Middle—Disappearing-loop method

★ You might find some of Daniel's other tutorials helpful: www.moltingyeti.com/help/techniques.html

STEP 1: Make a slip knot and place it on a double-pointed needle, leaving a tail 7" (18cm) long.

STEP 2: Hold a second double-pointed needle below and parallel to the first. Form a figure eight by *bringing the yarn down behind and under the bottom needle to the front, then up over the top of the bottom needle and to the back between both needles. Wrap yarn around back of top needle and bring over to the front, then down under the top needle and to the back between both needles.

STEP 3: Repeat from *, making figure eights until the top needle has the desired number of stitches, plus one extra.

STEP 4: Thread the tail through a blunt tapestry/yarn needle. Holding the working yarn in place, carefully remove the bottom needle.

STEP 5: Drop the slip knot off the left end of the remaining needle. Thread the tail through the empty bottom loops, from right to left. Gently tug the slip knot to undo it.

STEP 6: Distribute the stitches evenly over three double-pointed needles and begin working in the round. After you've worked five or six rounds, pull the tail snug and reinforce it by threading it through the loops a couple of times, always inserting needle into the stitches from the same direction.

THREE-NEEDLE BIND-OFF: Divide stitches evenly on two needles. Hold both needles in left hand with right sides together and needles parallel. Using a third needle in your right hand, knit together the first stitch from both needles. *Knit together the next stitch from both needles. Lift first stitch on right needle over top of second stitch, then off the needle—1 stitch remains on right needle; repeat from * until all stitches have been bound off. Fasten off remaining stitch on right needle.

Abbreviations

beg begin(ning) • **BO** bind off
cont continu(e)(ing)
dpn(s) double-pointed needle(s) • **k** knit
kfb knit into the front loop, then through the back loop of the same stitch (1 stitch increased)
ndl(s) needle(s) • **p** purl • **pm** place marker
rem remain(ing) • **rep** repeat

rnd(s) round(s) • **sl** slip

ssk slip, slip, knit: Slip one stitch from left needle to right needle, knitwise (as if to knit), slip second stitch same way, insert left needle through front of loops on right needle, then wrap yarn around right needle. With left needle, bring loops over the yarn wrapped around the right, which will knit them together through the back of the loops (1 stitch decreased).

st(s) stitch(es) • **WS** wrong side(s)

Tips

• This is a good pattern for learning to "read" your knitting. In each repeat of the pattern, your increases will be made into the bump created by the increase in the round below.

• This pillow is worked from the center out. To determine how long to knit your pillow, measure the pillow form by placing a tape measure across the top of the pillow from one edge to the edge on the opposite side. Divide this measurement in half; multiply the result by the row gauge to determine how many rounds you'll need to knit.

• Scaling this pattern is simple. This pattern will work for a circular pillow form of any diameter; just keep knitting until the cover is the same size as the pillow. The amount of yarn used in this pattern is for a pillow with a 16" (40.5cm) diameter; for larger pillows, make sure to purchase additional yarn.

• Because the raised stitches spiral to the left, the beginning point of the round will move to the left as well.

• Use a beginning-of-round marker that is a different color than the other markers, or use a removable marker to mark the line that will spiral at the beginning/end of every round.

• Markers denote the beginning of rounds and each increase; slip markers as you come to them.

Pattern Stitch

Using the disappearing loop cast-on, cast on 15 sts. Divide sts evenly over 3 dpns—5 sts on each ndl.
Rnds 1–2: K.
RND 3: Kfb in each st—30 sts.
RNDS 4–5: *K1, p1; rep from * to end.

RND 6: S 1, pm to mark new beg of rnd, *kfb, pm, k1; rep from * to end, remove end of rnd marker—45 sts.

RNDS 7–8: Sl 1, pm to mark new beg of rnd, * kfb, ssk; rep from * to end, remove end of rnd marker.

RND 9: *K to 1 st before marker, kfb, k1, rep from * to end; remove end of rnd marker—60 sts.

RND 10: Sl 1, pm to mark new beg of rnd, *k to 1 st before marker, kfb, ssk; rep from * to end, remove end of rnd marker.

RND 11: Sl 1, pm to mark new beg of rnd, *k to 1 st before marker, kfb, ssk; rep from * to end, remove end-of-rnd marker.

Rep rnds 9–11 until piece measures 8" (20.5cm), or desired length from center of pillow, changing to cir ndl when there are too many sts to fit on dpns. Cut yarn, leaving a tail about 6" (15cm) long to weave in, leave sts on ndl and set aside.

Make second side to match first side; do not cut yarn. Weave in ends before joining.

Joining

Hold both sides of pillow with WS tog and working yarn on top. Use three-needle bind-off to bind off about half of the stitches.

Insert the pillow form. Continue binding off until all sts have been worked and pillow form is completely covered.

Fasten off rem st and weave in tail.

Our 8th Secret

Learn to Soar Patternless

and Feel the Freedom

We all love patterns, directions, tales told so that we can pick up the sticks and follow the path to a sweater . . . a scarf . . . a pair of mittens.

Yet even with the most marvelous patterns in the world, some of us feel compelled to deviate. We embellish with a ruffle. We resize, we add embroidery, we remove a cable. Some of us go so far as to create.

And some of us leap off the patterned path and soar.

How can soaring patternless be laidback? In fact, freeing yourself, giving yourself permission to knit patternless, is quintessential laidbackness.

How to step off the patterned path is our eighth Secret.

It's bold; it's brave; it's fun.

All you need is one thing: resources. By "resources" we mean:

- Books you can learn from and ones that become invaluable references.
- Web sites that dig you out of a hole. www.KnittingHelp.com
- DVDs and YouTube-style sites that *show* you how to accomplish your goal.

FIRST, YOU NEED A LIBRARY

Some favorite books, videos, and web sites that have allowed us to step off the patterned path:

Vogue Knitting: The Ultimate Knitting Book, by the editors of *Vogue Knitting*

Knitting Without Tears, by Elizabeth Zimmermann, Schoolhouse Press

Barbara Walker's *Knitting Treasuries*. Originally published by Scribner, now by Schoolhouse Press

VICKI WOULDN'T BE WITHOUT:

Knitter's Almanac, *Knitting Around*, *Knitting Workshop*, *The Opinionated Knitter*, all by Elizabeth Zimmermann, Schoolhouse Press

Knitting for Anarchists, by Anna Zilboorg, Unicorn Books

The Knitter's Book of Wool and *The Knitter's Book of Yarn*, both by Clara Parkes, PotterCraft

America Knits, Melanie Falick, Artisan

Knitting America, by Susan M. Strawn, Voyageur Press

Knitting Art, by Karen Searle, Voyageur Press

Mary Thomas's Knitting Book, by Mary Thomas, Dover

Knit Fix, by Lisa Kartus, Interweave

Knitting in Plain English, by Maggie Righetti, St. Martin's Press

100 Flowers to Knit & Crochet, by Lesley Stanfield, St. Martin's Press

At Knit's End, by Stephanie Pearl-McPhee, Storey Publishing

200 Knitting Tips, Techniques & Trade Secrets, by Betty Barnden, St. Martin's Press

LISA'S MUST-HAVES:

Confessions of a Knitting Heretic, by Annie Modesitt, Modesitt Press

Knitting in the Old Way, by Priscilla A. Gibson-Roberts, Nomad Press

Color Works: The Crafter's Guide to Color, Interweave

Designing Knitwear, by Deborah Newton, Taunton Press

150 Crochet Trims, by Susan Smith, St. Martin's Griffin

Knitting on the Edge and *Knitting Over the Edge*, both by Nicky Epstein, Sixth Spring Books

The Intentional Spinner, by Judith McKenzie McCuin, Interweave Press

Homespun Handknit, by Linda Ligon, Interweave

Color in Spinning, by Deb Menz, Interweave

Natural Dyes and Home Dyeing, by Rita J. Adrosko, Dover

Dyer's Garden, by Rita Buchanan, Interweave

Dover Books has oodles of charted design books. Lisa recommends any of them.

Imagine singing this song urging women to knit for the troops during WWII. Oh my.

Knitting comic books. How cool are these?

OUT OF PRINT BUT QUITE FABULOUS:

The Principles of Knitting, by June Hemmons Hiatt, Simon and Schuster

Knitting in the Nordic Tradition, Vibeke Lind, Lark Books

Creative Knitting, Mary Walker Phillips, Dos Tejedoras

DVDs

"Knitting Workshop" by Elizabeth Zimmermann, and any other Zimmermann DVDs

Spinning DVDs by Patsy Zawitoski, Yarn Barn of Kansas

Any Lucy Neatby knitting DVD

NEXT, TRAVEL THE WEB

Explore such great sites as:

www.KnittingHelp.com

www.KnittersReview.com

www.PhilosophersWool.com

www.Ravelry.com

And, of course, YouTube!

THIRD, TIME TO EXPERIMENT

Our first attempts at going patternless:

My *first* experience of stepping away from a pattern was when I ran out of yarn to complete a sleeve for a lavender sweater. I was in shock, but when I realized that I could pick a ball of PINK and make a Design Element (in the words of EZ), I was set free.

SOME KNITTERS DEFINITELY SOAR IN DIFFERENT DIRECTIONS:

THE MUSEUM OF SCIENTIFICALLY ACCURATE FABRIC BRAIN ART (As featured in SCIENCE and the NATIONAL REVIEW) The world's largest collection on the web of anatomically correct fabric brain art has been inspired by research from neuroscience, dissection, and neuro-economics. The current exhibition features a rug based on MRI imaging, a knitted brain from dissection, and three quilts with functional images from PET. The artists are Marjorie Taylor and Karen Norberg; Bill Harbaugh, curator (www.Harbaugh. uoregon.edu/Brain). The museum only "Lives" on the Web.

AND IF KNITTED BRAINS WEREN'T ENOUGH . . .

England Darwin's Leftovers: Once he finished *On the Origin of Species*, what did Darwin do with his vast collection of stuffed reptiles, mammals, fish, and birds? Honestly, we're not sure. But some British knitters found the concept amusing and created Darwin's Leftovers. This collection of astonishing knit flora and fauna "leftovers" was created by more than 60 knitters. The knit beasts and plants were displayed at the Oxford University Museum of Natural History.

The *second Aha!* moment was when I realized that garments were mostly just shapes, simple or complicated, and with a little math and a tape measure I could figure out how to duplicate the shape of my favorite store-bought sweater. I kept all of my schematics and pencil drawings in a black artist's book that bulges with bits of yarn to commemorate each garment. I still go patternless, to this day. ~ LISA

I was knitting a scarf, a pattern I'd knit several times before. But this time I was bored. So I added a ruffle on the edge. It looked great! By the time I finished that scarf, it was a different animal from when I began it. I liked that.

I started patternless on my next scarf, casting on lots of stitches lengthwise. Then I knit a flare using short rows, and then added ribs and holes and lace! When I cast off, I realized I'd created one Frankenstein-ugly scarf. Yet old Frankie had taught me more about which stitches and motifs worked with what than I'd ever learned before. Sadly, Frankenstein has gone missing. But what I learned has stayed with me. And I continue the fun adventure of going patternless. ~ VICKI

WHAT NOW? HOW TO START ...

- Add a vertical stripe to a sweater.
- Add a lace edge on a shawl.
- Scrumble together a bunch of stitches and rows.
- Knit a favorite sweater pattern without the sleeves, or shorten it.
- For a pillow, knit free-form intarsia shapes into a basic square.
- Sketch a hat on paper, then knit it.
- Imagine knitted shapes and knit some.
- Create a knitted toy.
- Explore yarns and stitch styles and knit a wall hanging.
- Have fun with it.

Is there anything you've ever wanted to knit? Any confection? Creation? Go for it. The beauty of knitting is that you can always rip it out. Who knows, you might even create art.

Now . . . where did my Frankenstein scarf go?

THE PATH OF ARTIST RANIA HASSAN

Katharine Cobey, Debbie New, Reina Mia Brill, Adrienne Sloane, Lisa Anne Auerbach, Mark Newport—all are artists who have taken the craft of knitting and expanded it to reach beyond the expected. They've all stepped off the patterned path into the world of imagination. So has up-and-coming fiber artist *Rania Hassan.*

Born in New York City in 1975, Rania has also called Dubai, London, Houston, and Beirut home. Perhaps that global POV is what allowed her to step off the patterned path and craft something new and fresh and invigorating.

Rania's art is about connectivity—to today's knitters and to generations past. Her themes address how knitting "anchors you. How it ties you to home." Her mixture of painting and hard materials and knitting instantly captures the imagination. Her work exudes energy and life.

In 2009, Rania was awarded an Artist Fellowship Grant from the DC Commission on the Arts and Humanities. She's also received the Craft Award of Distinction from the James Renwick Alliance, a national organization associated with the Smithsonian American Art Museum, for her "Knit Together" series.

Rania didn't learn to knit from her mom or her grandma; rather, friends showed her the ropes as recently as 2005. She was a fast learner. What happened might be called spontaneous combustion, for she felt an instant kinship with and passion for the craft. As she says, "I always have my knitting with me. Always."

A journey that began with scarves and garments soon evolved to one of telling tales with fiber. An artist by education, Rania felt an almost instant need to illuminate how knitting ties you to home and to family and to history. Bloggers and online magazines like Knitty inspired her to grow her art, which she continues to craft. She works patternless—"randomly," as she calls it. "Things take shape as I'm working on them," she says. She most often knits her sculptures with Habu silk or wool and steel. Even things she knits for herself, she now knits patternless. As she says, "It's my way."

Her newest pieces incorporate drawers, which she describes as "pensive. How, when you knit, you weave your thoughts into the work. The drawer symbolizes recalling thoughts and memories and putting them away.

"I'm still astonished that with one strand of thread," she says, "you can make anything you want. Anything." Rania Hassan does just that.

KNITTER, ARTIST, DESIGNER, TEACHER, HISTORIAN:
Deborah Valoma, Artist Statement from her Web site:

I learned to stitch lace from my grandmother, descendant of Armenian survivors of the Turkish massacres; I learned to knit in Jerusalem from a Polish refugee of the Holocaust; and I learned to twine basketry from one of the few living masters of Native American basket weaving in California. These dedicated women tenaciously pull the threads of survival forward. When memory fails, hands remember. With each stitch, with each thread, they trace the breathless pause between loss and beauty.

We could not have said it better ~ LISA AND VICKI

Yarn Bombing . . . What?

Sheds and buses, trees and street lamps, parking meters and bridges—yarn bombers have covered them all with knitting. Picture hats on bronze busts, mittens on marble sculptures, and scarves on Celtic stones. All knit. All surprises.

What is yarn bombing? Also known as knit graffiti, yarn bombing was launched in Houston, Texas, by a bunch of gals who called themselves *Knitta Please*.

According to founder *Magda Sayeg*, "On city street corners, around telephone posts, through barbed wire fences, and over abandoned cars, a quiet revolution is brewing. 'Knit graffiti' is an international guerrilla movement that started underground and is now embraced by crochet and knitting artists of all ages, nationalities, and genders. Its practitioners create stunning works of art out of yarn, then 'donate' them to public spaces as part of a covert plan for world yarn domination!"

—from *Yarn Bombing: The Art of Crochet and Knit Graffiti,* by Mandy Moore and Leanne Prain (Arsenal Pulp Press, 2009).

SOME LEARN-TO-KNIT RHYMES FOR ENGLISH "THROW" KNITTING

IN THROUGH THE FRONT DOOR,
ONCE AROUND THE BACK,
PEEK THROUGH THE WINDOW,
AND OFF JUMPS JACK!

AND TO PURL:
UNDER THE FENCE,
CATCH THE SHEEP,
BACK WE COME,
OFF WE LEAP!

ANOTHER KNIT:
IN THE WOODS GOES THE HUNTER,
ROUND THE TREE GOES THE DOG,
OUT POPS THE RABBIT,
AND OFF THEY RUN.

ANOTHER PURL:
IN THROUGH THE BACK,
ROUND THE FRONT,
OUT THE BACK DOOR,
JACK MUST BE DRUNK.

WE LOVE OUR KNITTING MAGAZINES, BOTH PRINT AND ONLINE

Print:

Cast On • *Creative Knitting* • *Interweave Crochet* • *Interweave Knits* • *Knitscene* • *Spin-Off* • *Fiberarts* • *PieceWork* • *Knit Simple* • *Knitter's Magazine* • *Vogue Knitting* • *Rowan Knitting and Crochet Magazine* • *Debbie Bliss Knitting Magazine* • *Verena Knitting* (European, in English) • *Sandra* (German, in English) • *Let's Knit!* (British) • *Knit Today* (British) • *Knitting* (British) • *Simply Knitting* (British) • *Yarn Forward* (British) • *Rebecca* (Eu) • *Selvedge* (British)

Online:

Knit Circus (www.KnitCircus.com) • Twist Collective (www.TwistCollective.com) • Crochet Uncut (www.CrochetUncut.com) • Knitty (www.Knitty.com) • Knitter's Review (www.KnittersReview.com) • Loom Knitters Circle (www.LoomKnittersCircle.com) • Knitch (www.KnitchMagazine.com) • Knit on the Net (www.KnitOnTheNet.com). • PetitePurls (www.PetitePurls.com) • Tension Magazine (www.TensionMagazine.com)

Can't remember when they're coming out? Sign up for your favorite magazine's e-mailed newsletter. Easy-peasy, and you needn't worry about missing an issue.

JELLYCAT PIG STEPS OUT...

Designed by Shirley Craig

Why, oh, why, would we place Shirley Craig's marvelous JellyCat Pig outfits for Hermione (in the full outfit) and Calliope (in the shirt) in our Soar Patternless chapter? Easy. Shirley knit them long before she designed them.

When I admired (lusted) after her JellyCat Pig pattern, Shirley said, "I just made it up. You know, I knit it for Calliope." At our request, Shirley wrote up the pattern. And, so, yes, a pattern now exists, but Jellycat Pig Steps Out is an homage to all those who take that leap of faith and soar patternless. As Shirley says, "Your pig will be warm and happy, and if your pig is happy, you'll be happy, too!" ~ VICKI

 Skill Level: **RECLINER**

Things You'll Need to Know
• Mirrored decreases—i.e., decreases that are paired, one on each end or side of the item.
• Working two sets of stitches at the same time (for pant legs).
• Making a twisted cord.

Size
To fit 15" (38cm) tall "Jellycat" Pig

Finished Measurements
PULLOVER
Chest: 13½" (34.5cm)
Length: 6¾"–7" (17–18cm)
Sleeve length: 4¼" (11cm)
PANTS
Hips: 17" (43cm)
Length: 9¼" (23.5cm)
Leg length: 4" (10cm)

Yarn
Red Heart *Super Saver* (100% acrylic); 244 yds [223m]/5 oz [141g] skein; worsted weight/medium {4}; 1 skein, shown in colors Painted Desert Print #303 and Aspen Print #305

Needles
Size US 8 (5mm) needles, or size needed to obtain gauge

Notions
Blunt tapestry/yarn needle
Removable markers or safety pins

Gauge
17 sts and 23 rows = 4" (10cm) in stockinette
Hermione and Calliope will be thrilled if you check your gauge.

Abbreviations
beg begin(ning) • **BO** bind off • **dec** decrease
k knit • **k2tog** knit 2 stitches together (1 stitch decreased) • **p** purl • **rep** repeat • **RS** right side(s)
ssk slip, slip, knit: Slip one stitch from left needle to right needle, knitwise (as if to knit), slip second stitch same way, insert left needle through front of loops on right needle, then wrap yarn around right needle. With left needle, bring loops over the yarn wrapped around the right, which will knit them together through the back of the loops (1 stitch decreased).

St st stockinette stitch • **st(s)** stitch(es)
tog together • **WS** wrong side(s)

Tips

• When casting on, leave a long tail about 12" (30.5cm) for sewing the pieces together.
• To work both legs of the pants at the same time, the pattern tells you to join a second ball of yarn. Simply take the other end from the skein you're working from and join that to your work, or wind off about 5–6 yards (4.5–5.5m) from the other end to make a separate ball.

PULLOVER

FRONT: Cast on 36 sts. Working back and forth, work 5 rows of k2, p2 rib.

BEG WITH A RS ROW and work 8 rows of St st.

NEXT ROW (RS), k2tog, k to last 2 sts, end ssk—34 sts. Work 5 rows even.

Rep these 6 rows 3 more times, then rep dec row once more—26 sts.

Work even for 1–3 more rows; piece should measure about 6¾"–7" (17–18cm) from beg.

K 4 rows even for neckband. BO knitwise.

BACK: Work back same as front.

SLEEVES (make 2): Cast on 20 sts.
Working back and forth, work 20 rows of St st.
Work 6 rows of k2, p2 rib. BO in pattern.

Finishing

Sew front and back tog at sides of neckband, leaving the 6" (15cm) open at top edge for neck opening. Use removable markers and mark the center of both sleeves. Sew sleeves to sides of body with markers at shoulder seams, sewing through cast-on loop of sleeve and making sure sides of sleeves are evenly spaced from shoulder on front and back. Sew tog at sides of body and along underarm edges of sleeves.

PANTS: **FRONT:** Cast on 36 sts.

Working back and forth, work 3 rows of k2, p2 rib.

BEG WITH A WS ROW and work 30 rows of St st; piece should measure about 5¾" (14.5cm) from beg.

LEGS: NEXT ROW (WS): P18, attach a 2nd ball of yarn and p18.
Working each leg separately, work 15 rows even.
Work 5 rows of k2, p2 rib.
BO in pattern.

BACK: Work back same as front.

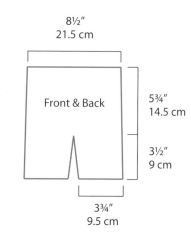

Sleeves
4¼"
11 cm

4¾"
12 cm

6"
15 cm

Front & Back

2¼"
5.5 cm

4½ - 4¾"
11.5 - 12 cm

8½"
21.5 cm

8½"
21.5 cm

Front & Back

5¾"
14.5 cm

3½"
9 cm

3¾"
9.5 cm

Finishing

Sew pants tog along sides, and legs tog along inseams.
If desired, make a twisted cord with 2 strands of yarn held tog. Beg and end at center of front, thread cord through rib at waist.

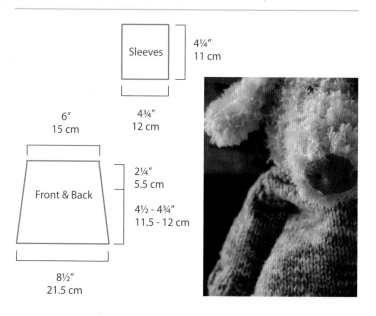

AMBER WAVES ...

Designed by Vicki Stiefel

I created Amber Waves for Charlene Schultz's magnificent Angora Blizzard ("Blizz" for short") yarn, a combo of yarn from her adorable angora rabbits and merino. Blizz's loft, warmth, and ethereal qualities are exceptional.

Again, why a pattern in a patternless chapter? Simply because I created the scarf first, then wrote up the pattern. When I decided to concoct a scarf out of Blizz, I adapted a blanket's pattern repeat to make the scarf and so Amber Waves was born.

BTW, as a friend of mine did, you can use the pattern as a jumping-off point. Widen it, embellish it, narrow it.

Skill Level: RECLINER

Things You'll Need to Know
Simple lace knitting

Finished Measurements
Width: 7" (18cm)
Length: 68" (172.5cm)

Yarn
HoneyBunns *Angora Blizzard* (85% angora rabbit hair, 15% merino hand-dyed); 100 yds [109m]/1¾ oz [50g]; sport/fine weight [2]; 4 skeins; 1 skein each color, shown in colors Orange Sun (A), Amber Light (B), Waves of Grain (C), and Bronze Gold (D)

Needles
Size US 9 (5.5mm) needles, or size needed to obtain gauge

Notions
Blunt tapestry/yarn needle

Gauge
19½ sts and 30 rows = 4" (10cm) over pattern
It's not the end of the world if you don't check your gauge on this one. Just don't blame us if you run out of yarn!

Abbreviations
k knit • **k2tog** knit 2 stitches together (1 stitch decreased) • **rep** repeat • **st(s)** stitch(es)
yo yarn over

Wave Pattern

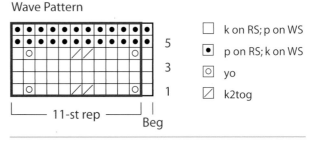

	k on RS; p on WS
●	p on RS; k on WS
○	yo
╱	k2tog

11-st rep — Beg

ROW 3: K.

Rep rows 1–3 for pattern.

Using A, cast on 34 sts.

ROWS 1–21: Work Wave Pattern 7 times.

ROWS 22–39: Change to B. Work Wave Pattern 6 times.

ROWS 40–60: Change to C. Work Wave Pattern 7 times.

ROWS 61–81: Change to D. Work Wave Pattern 7 times.

ROWS 82–111: Change to A. Work Wave Pattern 10 times.

ROWS 112–147: Change to B. Work Wave Pattern 12 times.

ROWS 148–183: Change to C. Work Wave Pattern 12 times.

ROWS 184–252: Change to D. Work Wave Pattern 23 times.

ROWS 253–291: Change to C. Work Wave Pattern 13 times.

ROWS 292–321: Change to B. Work Wave Pattern 10 times.

ROWS 322–351: Change to A. Work Wave Pattern 10 times.

ROWS 352–375: Change to D. Work Wave Pattern 8 times.

ROWS 376–399: Change to C. Work Wave Pattern 8 times.

ROWS 400–420: Change to B. Work Wave Pattern 7 times.

ROWS 421–441: Change to A. Work Wave Pattern 7 times.

Bind off loosely purlwise. Weave in ends.

Tips

• For balanced stripes, when working your own color combination, make sure to use no more than half of the yarn by the time you reach half of the desired length for the scarf.

• The light, lofty appearance of the scarf is achieved by knitting with a needle size larger than that recommended for the yarn. Using a very lofty (i.e., fuzzy) yarn adds to the loftiness of the scarf.

• Any weight yarn can be used for this scarf; make sure to adjust your needle size accordingly to achieve the desired effect.

• For a narrower scarf, cast on 23 stitches and work two repeats of the pattern across each row.

• This scarf is reversible, as the stitch pattern uses a three-row repeat. To have a "right side" and a "wrong side," change colors on the same side every time, and repeat the three rows twice to complete a six-row repeat.

Pattern Stitch

WAVE PATTERN (multiple of 11 sts + 1)

ROW 1: K1, *yo, k3, (k2tog) twice, k3, yo, k1; rep from * to end.

ROW 2: P.

> "Sabrina fair, / Listen where thou art sitting / Under the glassy, cool, translucent wave, / In twisted braids of lilies knitting / The loose train of thy amber-dropping hair." —JOHN MILTON

Do It with Hooks

Just Like One Hand Clapping

Crochet in a knitting book? Absolutely! You may not yet have the skill in your toolbox, or maybe you even came to knitting via crochet. But either way, knowing how to crochet is like being bilingual—it only makes you a better knitter. Whether you simply keep a crochet hook in your knitting bag to retrieve a dropped stitch or you're able to crochet up a tornado, crochet is a skill that can enhance your knitting.

Crochet might make a simple and sturdy edging for your knitted piece, a chained loop to secure a button, a luxurious and cozy cashmere beanie, or a wild, free-form fabric. Crochet is a perfect partner to knitting and can be a relaxing and laidback addition to your time spent with yarn running through your fingers.

CROCHET EDGINGS

While you may fall in love with crochet but may not be sure you're ready for one of our patterns, how about giving a crocheted edging a shot. I love that adding a crocheted edging to a knit piece seems to add a whole other dimension to the article, whether it's a scarf, a pillow, or a skirt. Crocheted edgings fit right into my hunger for embellishments on dishcloths, scarves, and hats.

131

A neat way to experiment is to edge one of your swatches. Now you can see how the yarn and stitches work together. A favorite embellishment of mine is to edge a pillow with a special yarn, say pure tussah silk. I love the play of light on the edge compared to the matte look of wool. Lisa notes how important crocheted edges are in a knitter's repertoire. She has used a variety of edges in her finished garments for kids. Her favorite go-to crocheted edge is a nice, firm chain edging, which allows her to go around and around, incorporating button loops. It makes for a nice edging for V-neck sweaters, as well. Even better? Invent your very own use for crocheted edging. ~ VICKI

Here are some Web sites with dozens and dozens of crocheted edging links:

> http://Home.InReach.com/marthac/edging.html
> http://BarbsCraftBooks.tripod.com/barbscrochet/id44.html
> www.CrochetPatternCentral.com/directory/edgings.php

Seven of our favorite crochet edges:

> Single crochet
>
> Scallop edge
>
> Lattice edge
>
> Picot edge
>
> Rope edge
>
> Curlicue fringe
>
> Little clovers (not so easy, but so pretty)

Here are some marvelous crochet books that will help you learn the skill:

Teach Yourself Visually Crocheting, by Kim P. Werker and Cecily Keim, Visuall

Crochet in Color, by Kathy Merrick, Interweave

Freeform: Serendipitous Design Techniques for Knitting & Crochet, by Prudence Mapstone, Prudence Mapstone Publishing

150 Crochet Trims, by Susan Smith, St. Martin's Griffin

100 Flowers to Knit and Crochet, by Lesley Stanfield, St. Martin's Griffin

200 Crochet Tips, Techniques and Trade Secrets, by Jan Eaton, St. Martin's Press

Crocheting in Plain English, by Maggie Righetti and Theresa Shaw, St. Martin's Press

The Crochet Stitch Bible, by Betty Barnden, Krause Publications

Interweave Crochet magazine will inspire you.

Online you'll find some terrific free learn-to-crochet videos. Just Google "Crochet videos for beginners."

"How can she **knit** with so many?" the puzzled child thought to herself. "She gets more like **a porcupine every minute!**"

Through the Looking Glass,
BY LEWIS CARROLL

TOM CLARK,
THAT BEANIE-CAP GUY

After the meals were served and the dishes done, Grandma Amy would sit quietly by the big living-room window that looked out over a rolling green pasture and work on her crocheting.

She always seemed so happy and peaceful working with her yarns. I must have been about five or six when Grandma Amy taught me how to crochet. I remember her telling me that she'd taught my dad and uncle to crochet when they were little, to keep them still when they were home sick from school. She never explained why she taught me to crochet, but I've loved it ever since.

Not long after Grandma taught me to crochet, my family moved to Italy, where we lived for many years in the countryside north of Rome. It was in Italy where my fascination with natural fibers began. I relish the buttery softness of cashmere and the ethereal lightness of qiviut. I love collecting natural fibers as much as I love working with them.

I've enjoyed many interests and activities over the years, yet nothing has ever displaced my crocheting. The rhythm of the hook through the yarn stills my busy mind and allows me to relax.

Though sometimes a wanderer, I made my home in Southern California. There, at Laguna Beach, I began to notice surfers pulling on beanie caps when they'd emerge from the cold Pacific waters. The look wasn't new, but what was novel was that even in summer the surfers would leave their beanie caps on long after they'd changed back into their street clothes and warmed up.

I saw something I liked in those beanies and the way they looked on the surfers. So one Sunday morning, I stopped at a surf shop to find myself one. They had lots of them in lots of colors, but they were all acrylic. Not exactly what I'd been hoping for. That was the moment, standing there at Surf & Sport in Laguna Beach, when I came up with the idea to crochet a beanie out of some natural and beautiful fiber.

I bought myself a couple of hundred dollars worth of Italian cashmere and other fine yarns. A few hits and misses later I came up with a beanie style I liked. Friends saw mine and wanted them, too, and I was in the beanie-making business.

Six years later I'm still crocheting beanie caps from some of the world's most luxurious natural animal fibers. I now also crochet Nekkers, which are similar to beanies, only they're open on both ends so that they can be slid down over the head and worn around the neck like a scarf or an old-fashioned dickey. While Nekkers are the newest addition to the Pussy Cap collection, at the end of the day it's still the beanies that will always take center stage. (www.PussyCap.com) ~ TOM CLARK

U.K.-Speak

In case you pick up a U.K. crochet book or find some drool-worthy pattern from across the pond, here's a list of basic U.S. and U.K. terms and abbreviations:

U.S. on the left, U.K. the on right. Only one term? They're the same.

Chain (ch)

Single crochet (sc)—Double crochet (dc)

Half double crochet (h.dc)— Half treble (h.tr)

Double crochet (dc)—Treble (tr)

Treble (tr)—Double treble (d.tr)

Double treble (d.tr)—Triple treble (tr.tr)

Triple treble (tr.tr)—Quadruple treble (q[uad] tr)

Quadruple treble (q[uad] tr)— Quintuple treble (q[uin] tr)

Slip stitch (sl st)

Fasten off—Cast off

Skip—Miss

Gauge—Tension

Work even—Work straight

Yarn over (yo)—Yarn over hook (yoh)

Knitted brain coral

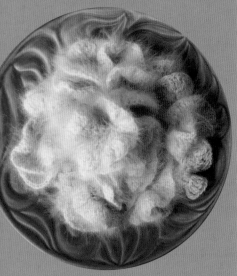

Crocheted hyperbola

Let's Hear It for the Boys!

Well, OK, the guys . . . the men . . . the fellas who work and play in fibers. They're out there and they kick butt. Our own wonderful *Daniel Yuhas* and *Tom Clark* rock the house. Knitty.com gives us this wonderful list:

James Norbury (1904–1972): wrote numerous knitting books.

Kaffe Fassett (1937–): Incomparable. Need we say more?

Eugene Bourgeois (contemporary): See www.PhilosophersWool.com.

Izo Matukawa (dates unknown): Fabulous Japanese knitter and author.

Barry Klein (contemporary): Author.

Franklin Delano Roosevelt (1882–1945): President and knitter.

Brian Sawyer, (contemporary): Crafter, photographer, knitter.

And our list:

Franklin Habit: marvelous cartoonist and knitter.

David Cole: fabulous knitting-machine artist.

Brandon Mably: designer for *Vogue Knitting* and Rowan Yarns; works with Kaffe Fassett.

Nathan Vincent: crochet artist.

Alan Dart: designer of amazing knitted creatures.

Drew Emborsky: The Crochet Dude author of how-to crochet books, designer.

Michael del Vecchio: knitting book writer and tech editor.

Joe: of Queer Joe's Knitting Blog. http://queerjoesblogspot.com

Stephen West: designer, author

Jared Flood: Brooklyn Tweed, designer, photographer, author

Bruce Weinstein: designer, author

Brian Crimmons: BrianKnits.com, Hogger

We're sure there are more. Check out: www.menwhoknit.com

Not sure it counts, but Charles Dickens gave us the most famous knitter of all time: *Madame Thérèse Defarge* appears in his classic novel, *A Tale of Two Cities*. We'd like to think Charles knit, too.

BTW, to our knowledge, Russell Crowe does not knit. The famous Crowe knitting photo was doctored in Photoshop.

Odd, how sometimes the fellas feel shut out of the knitting realm. They shouldn't. In days gone by, when guilds held sway in pre-industrialized times, only men were allowed to join the knitter's guild. Thus, women might knit, but they sure couldn't sell their knitted goods. Only men could do that.

With the dawn of the age of industrialization and of mechanized knitting machines, men could no longer make a living knitting. So they ceded their place in knitting to women, who have held fast to it ever since.

PARK CITY POSH BEANIE ...
Designed by Tom Clark

Tom Clark's beautiful beanie is luxuriously soft and decadent, a cap that you or the one you love will reach for over and over again when the air gets a little crisp. The cashmere used is top of the line for softness, but you can choose myriad fibers, remembering that around your face, the softer the better.

 Skill Level: **RECLINER**

Things You'll Need to Know
• Basic crochet
• Carrying strands of yarn up back of work
• Decreasing stitches in crochet

Finished Measurements
Circumference: 19"/48.5cm
Length: 12½"/32cm

Yarn
Lisa Souza *Hand Spun Hand Dyed Cashmere* (100% cashmere); 80 yds of blue, 80 yds of sand; DK/Worsted; **MC**: 2¼ oz/64g; **CC**: 1¼ oz/33g, shown in colors Warm Gold (MC) and Tudor Blue (CC)

Hook
Size K crochet hook, or size to obtain gauge

Gauge
11 sts and 15 rnds = 4" (10cm) in single crochet
Aw, c'mon, take time to check that gauge.

Abbreviations
beg begin(ning) • **CC** contrast color
ch chain • **MC** main color • **rep** repeat
rnd(s) round(s) • **sc** single crochet
sl slip • **st(s)** stitch(es) • **WS** wrong side(s)

Tips
• The fit is easy to adjust by adding to or subtracting from the number of chains at the beginning.

If you change the number of chains, remember to adjust the top shaping accordingly.
• Stitches often tighten as the work progresses; be sure to measure your head accurately and allow some room for the tightening of the stitches.
• This cap is worked without joining the last stitch of every round to the first stitch at the completion of every round; work progresses as a spiral and there will be a distinct jog in the stripes along the side of the cap.

Pattern Stitch
Using MC, ch 51. Join with sl st in first ch to form ring, making sure ch is not twisted. Hold with smooth side of ch to inside throughout.
RND 1: Ch 1, work 1 sc in each ch to end.
RND 2: Without joining, work sc across rnd. Do not cut yarn.
RND 3: Join CC. Ch 1, work sc across rnd. Do not cut yarn.

RND 4: Bring MC up along WS and ch 1. Work sc across rnd.

RND 5: Twist both yarns to carry CC up 1 rnd. Rep rnd 2.

RND 6: Bring CC up along WS and ch 1. Work sc across rnd.

Rep rnds 4–6 until cap measures about 9¾" (25cm) from beg, end with CC rnd.

Shaping

NEXT RND: Using MC, *work 16 sc, skip next st; rep from * to end—48 sts.

NEXT RND: *Work 8 sc, skip next st; rep from * to last 3 sts, end 3 sc—43 sts.

NEXT RND: Using CC, *work 9 sc, skip next st; rep from * to last 3 sts, end 3 sc—39 sts.

NEXT RND: Using MC, *work 6 sc, skip next st; rep from * to last 4 sts, end 4 sc—34 sts.

NEXT RND: *Work 5 sc, skip next st; rep from * to last 4 sts, end 4 sc—29 sts.

NEXT RND: Using CC, *work 6 sc, skip next st; rep from * to last st, end 1 sc—25 sts.

NEXT RND: Using MC, *work 4 sc, skip next st; rep from * to end of rnd—20 sts.

NEXT RND: *Work 3 sc, skip next st; rep from * to end of rnd—15 sts.

NEXT RND: Using CC, *work 2 sc, skip next st; rep from * to end of rnd—10 sts.

NEXT RND: Using MC, *work 1 sc, skip next st; rep from * to end of rnd—5 sts. Fasten off both colors, leaving ends about 7"/18cm. Pull ends through to inside and knot tog. Weave in ends at beg of cap.

HEIRLOOM MOTIF CROCHET SCARF ...
Designed by Therese Chynoweth

Welcome especially love this scarf for combining an heirloom feel with a modern point of view. The scarf represents the best of both worlds in crochet—the more traditional coupled with a fresh outlook. We see it as yumalicious.

 Skill Level: **WING CHAIR**

Things You'll Need to Know
- Working crochet in the round
- Joining motifs as you work
- Puff stitch
- Picots

Size
5" x 41" (13 x 104cm)

Yarn (use either)
Bijou Basin Ranch *Bijou Spun Yak/Bamboo* (75% yak / 25% bamboo); 180 yds [165m] per 2 oz [56g]; sport/fine [2]; 1 skein, shown in color Creamy Natural

Spud & Chloë. *Fine* (80% superwash wool/20% silk); 248 yds [227m] per 2¼ oz [65g]; fingering/superfine [1]; 1 skein, shown in color Anemone #7805

Hook
Size D/3 (3.25mm) crochet hook, or size needed to obtain gauge

Gauge
Each square measures approx 3" x 3" (7.5 x 7.5cm), blocked
You know you want to take time to check your gauge, right? Please.

Techniques
BEGINNING PUFF STITCH: (Insert hook in base of chain, yarn over and draw through a loop, making

sure loop is same length as chain at beg of rnd, yarn over) twice, insert hook in base of chain yarn over and draw through a loop (6 loops on hook), yarn over and draw through all loops on hook (1 loop remains).

PUFF STITCH: *Insert hook in base stitch, then yarn over and draw through a loop, making sure to lengthen the loop (2 loops on hook). Yarn over (3 loops on hook); repeat from * twice more, then insert hook in base st and draw through another loop (8 loops on hook). Yarn over and draw through all loops on hook (1 loop remains).

3-CHAIN PICOT: Chain 3, join with a slip stitch in first chain made to form a loop.

5-CHAIN PICOT: Chain 5, join with a slip stitch in first chain made to form a loop.

JOINING MOTIFS AS YOU WORK: Hold motif section of work to the left of the edge to which it will be joined and with crochet hook at lower right, and yarn under the pieces. Work a slip stitch in the center of the chain the piece is being joined to by inserting hook from the top down. Work to next joining point and join the same way. Work to final joining point, then join motif in third spot as before. Complete the round, then fasten off.

Abbreviations

beg begin(ning) • **ch** chain • **dc** double crochet
hdc half double crochet • **rep** repeat
rnd(s) round(s) • **sc** single crochet
sl st slip st • **st(s)** stitch(es) • **tr** treble crochet

Tips

• The puff stitch is worked by inserting the crochet hook into the same stitch each time you need to draw through another loop.

• When pinning the scarf to finished measurements, it's helpful to pin each motif to 3" [7.5cm] square along the length of the piece, then place pins in the long chain loops along each side to give the edges a lacy look, as shown. Place pins in the corners of each motif as well as at the center along the outside edges of each motif.

1ST MOTIF

FOUNDATION

Ch 5. Join with sl st in first ch to form a ring.

RND 1: Ch 1, work 15 sc around ring. Join with sl st in ch at beg of rnd.

RND 2: Ch 2, work 1 beg puff st in base of ch, *ch 5, skip next st, work puff st in next st; rep from * 6 more times, ch 2, work dc in top of ch at beg of rnd.

RND 3: * Ch 5, 1 sc in ch-5 loop of previous rnd; rep from * 6 more times, ch 2, 1 dc in top of dc from previous rnd.

RND 4: Ch 4, (2 dc, 1 hdc) over dc that joined last rnd, *ch 3, (1 sc, ch 3, 1 sc) in next ch-5 loop, (1 hdc, 2 dc, 1 tr, 3-ch picot, 5-ch picot, 3-ch picot, 1 tr, 2 dc, 1 hdc) in next ch-5 loop; rep from * twice more, ch 3 (1 sc, ch 3, 1 sc) in next ch-5 loop, (1 hdc, 2 dc, 1 tr, 3-ch picot, 5-ch picot, 3-ch picot) in ch-2 loop at end of rnd, then join with a sl st in top of ch at beg of rnd. Fasten off.

2ND MOTIF

Beg each additional motif and work through rnd 3 same as first motif.

RND 4: Ch 4, 2 dc, 1 hdc over dc that joined last rnd, *ch 3, (1 sc, ch 3, 1 sc) in next ch-5 loop, ch 3 (1 hdc, 2 dc, 1 tr, 3-ch picot, 5-ch picot, 3-ch picot, 1 tr, 2 dc, 1 hdc) in next ch-5 loop; rep from * once more. (1 hdc, 2 dc, 1 tr, 3-ch picot, ch 2, join with sl st to center of 5-ch picot at lower right corner of previous motif, ch 2, join with sl st to first ch (forms the 5-ch picot at corner), 3-ch picot, (1 tr, 2 dc, 1 hdc) in same ch-5 loop, ch 3, 1 sc in next ch-5 loop, ch 1, join with sl st to center of ch-3 loop from previous motif, ch 1, 1 sc in same ch-5 loop, ch 3, (1 hdc, 2 dc, 1 tr) in ch-2 loop at end of last rnd, 3-ch picot, rep join at corner as previous corner, 3-ch picot. Join with a sl st in top of ch at beg of rnd. Fasten off. Make 11 more motifs in same manner as 2nd Motif, joining each to scarf as you go.

EDGING

RND 1: Beg at one corner. Work 1 sc in ch-5 picot, [ch 1, 1 sc in next picot, *ch 6, skip next ch-3 loop, 1 sc in next ch-3 loop at center of next ch-3 loop, ch

6, skip next ch-3 loop, 1 sc in next ch-3 picot, ch 5, 1 sc in ch-3 picot of next motif; rep from * to last 3-ch picot of side, ch 1, work 3 sc in ch-5 picot at corner] 4 times, ending last rep 2 sc in ch-5 picot at end of rnd. Join with sl st to first sc at beg of rnd.

RND 2: Ch 1, *work 1 sc in each sc and ch from previous rnd to end of first side, ending with 1 sc in last st (the 2nd sc in corner of previous rnd), ch 1, 1 sc in same st; rep from * to end of rnd, ending with 1 sc, ch 1 in last st. Join with sl st to ch at beg of rnd.

RND 3: Ch 2, [skip 1 st, *1 sc in next st, ch 2, skip 2 sts; rep from * to 1 st before the ch at corner, ch 1, skip 1 st, (1 sc, ch 1, 1 sc) in corner ch, ch 1] to end of rnd. Join with a sl st in 2nd ch at beg of rnd.

RND 4: Ch 3, *(1 dc, ch 2, 1 dc) in next ch-2 space; rep from * to end of rnd, working ch 3 at each corner, and ending with a complete rep. Join with a sl st in top of ch at beg of rnd.

RND 5: Ch 3, *[1 sc in next ch-2 space, ch 5, 1 sc in next ch-2 space, ch 2] to end of first side, ending with a ch 5, (1 sc, ch 2, 1 sc) in next ch-2 space; rep from * to end of rnd, ending with a sl st in base of ch at beg of rnd. Fasten off.

Finishing

Pin piece out to finished measurements and steam to block.

Check Out Jo Hamilton to see some amazing crochet art: JoHamiltonArt.com/index.htm

Connect the Dots

It Really Is a Small World ... from Local to National to the International Community of Knitters

Guild meetings • Spinning clubs • Library knitalongs • the Internet • Chat boards • E-mail • Knitter's Review • Knitty.com • Twist Collective • Facebook • Twitter • Ravelry • the NBT (Next Big Thing)

This is our last secret, Lisa's and Vicki's. But, of course, the secret also encompasses all the local and national and international neighborhoods of knitters. Join us.

The community of knitters, crocheters, spinners, and fiber fanatics is vast, and we are a sea of people connected by a passion. We are doctors and plumbers and sailors. We are writers and artists and candlestick makers. We are children and grannies, hipsters and preppies, straights and gays.

We are Argentina and Israel and the U.S. We are South Africa and Mongolia and New Zealand. We are rural; we are the burbs; we are the cities. We are synapses that fire with the terms "yarn over," "worsted," "double points."

We are a universal language that's spread across the globe in a viral heat wave that's unstoppable.

We are male and female, all ages, all lifestyles.

E.M. Forster wrote, "Only connect." We do.

Connected, we are stronger than the sum of our parts. Connected, we hold our

141

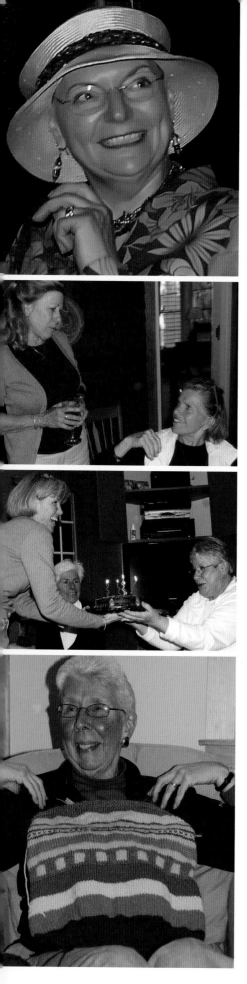

hands out to others who need help. Connected, we raise our hands to add to the chain of strength.

We are mighty. We are powerful. We are legion.

CINDY'S KNITTERS

When I met Cindy, she was wearing a red-and-yellow flowered dress, a matching head scarf, and a broad grin. Cindy grinned a lot, even though she'd had a death sentence for eleven years. It took another year for us to become close friends. We bonded over—what else?—fiber.

Of all my pals, Cindy was the one who understood and shared my fiber addiction.

Cindy wore her smile dimples like a badge, even after an oxygen tank became her constant companion and her hair had grown in to pixie length. No more chemo for Cindy. At the time, I didn't understand what that meant. Cannulas in her nose, oxygen "puppy" beside her, Cindy read and knit and crafted jewelry; she attended concerts and cooked organic meals and shepherded her two daughters toward adulthood. I admired her intensely.

Because of the risk of infection, she couldn't go to fiber festivals, so I'd bring back skeins of merino and alpaca and cashmere-silk. I'd carry home books and buttons and needles. And I'd take a million photos. And we'd hunker in her comfy living room and laugh at the photos and pet the yarn and yap about how we'd spin together someday.

The summer of 2006, we were complaining about finishing the sweaters we'd knit, about weaving in the ends and sewing the seams. Cindy suggested we have a finishing party. Soon, my living room was stuffed with our buddies. We knit; we wove; we sewed. We yapped; we drank; we ate. And we laughed and laughed and laughed.

That was the real beginning of Cindy's Knitters.

Cindy died two months later.

When the snow was piled high outside my French doors, over sauvignon blanc and brie—favorites of Cindy's—my dear friend Kim and I reminisced and reflected on Cindy. We'd also brought our knitting and our tears. We remembered the finishing party and how much fun we'd all had.

And so we asked a few friends to join us the following Thursday for wine and cheese and knitting. And they did. And we called ourselves Cindy's Knitters, to honor our friend. And to this day we meet on Thursdays, every other week.

We are a living memory of Cindy and her knitting and her lust for life. Through the years, we've learned that the stitches we knit bind us in both real and virtual ways. Our hands form a chain, a circle that when one of us aches, the others soothe; when one of us stumbles, the others pick us up; when one of us loses—a husband, a friend, a mother, a brother—the others hold us close.

We are Cindy's Knitters.

What's a Knitalong or KAL?

Simple: an organized event where people get together to knit in person or on the Internet for a common goal.

But there's more:

Knitalongs often come together around a common project or theme.

The Knitting Olympics could be called a knitalong. So could a scarf-along. A one-skein knitalong. A mystery KAL, where the finished piece is a mystery, since each chapter or portion of the pattern is revealed separately in sequence.

You can participate in your own Real World knitalongs at your guild, your LYS, or simply with your buddies.

Web-based knitalongs are always popping up, and while they generally take place over a finite amount of time, new ones are launched with great frequency, often based around a new pattern on Ravelry or a new book pattern. Some even offer prizes and giveaways. Just Google "knitalong" or visit Ravelry's knitalong directory: www.Ravelry.com/groups/browse/alongs/knitting.

A huge plus of participating in a KAL is that you have knitters to commiserate with if you get stuck on a pattern or have a question. Go ahead and choose that challenging pattern—you'll be in good company!

A super book on KALs: *Knitalong: Celebrating the Tradition of Knitting Together* by Larissa Brown and Martin John Brown.

WHAT THE HECK IS THE KNITTING OLYMPICS?

Back in 2006, *Stephanie Pearl-McPhee* issued a challenge on her blog (YarnHarlot.ca) to join her in the first Knitting Olympics for the Torino, Italy, Games. The rules were simple.

From Stephanie's blog for the 2010 Winter Games:

ELIGIBILITY: Any knitter who, embracing the "Citius, Atius, Fortius" ideal, would like to challenge themselves while embracing the Olympic spirit, and is just whacked enough to play along with me.

CONCEPT: You must cast on a project during the Opening Ceremonies of the Winter Olympics and finish before the Olympic flame goes out Sunday. That's seventeen days.

BRIT-SPEAK

★ A "GANSEY" IS AN ARAN OR FISHERMAN'S SWEATER, JUST IN CASE YOU WERE CURIOUS

★ A "WAISTCOAT" IS A VEST.

★ A "JUMPER" IS A SWEATER, AND THE BRITS HAVE EVEN KNIT THEM FOR DEFEATHERED CHICKENS AND BABY LAMBS. (WE COULDN'T MAKE THIS STUFF UP.)

Are You a Lefty?

A lefty knitter? Check out this great article from www.Knitty.com: www.knitty.com/ISSUEwinter03/FEATmirror.html. BTW, most lefties knit the same way righties knit.

Flying the Friendly Skies?

Of course, you want to take your knitting onboard. Can you?

The Transportation Security Administration (TSA) decides what we can carry on a plane. As of this writing, knitting needles are permitted. That may change by the time you read this. And then change again.

The best thing to do is go to www.Tsa.gov and search using the term "knitting." That will give you the most up-to-date info on whether you can carry your knitting needles, scissors, etc., onboard a plane that departs from the U.S. Flying international? Each country is different and, as with the U.S., each country changes its rules often. Check with individual airlines, consulates, countries for that information. No single database exists.

(KNITTING OLYMPICS CONT.) RULES:

1. The project must be a challenge for you to complete in seventeen days.

2. There are no rules about what a challenge would be. Like the real Olympics, there are many areas to compete in. If you are a new knitter, then a garter-stitch baby sweater might do . . . If you are experienced, use your own conscience.

3. While this is intended to be somewhat difficult (like the Olympics) it is not intended to ruin your life. Don't set yourself up for failure. This is intended to (like the Olympics) require some measure of sacrifice and be difficult, but it should be possible to attain.

4. No casting on before the flame is lit. (If you can't watch, pick a time in there.)

5. Finish before the flame goes out.

6. You may swatch before the games. (I consider this "training.")

Medals? The Knitting Olympics has only a gold medal. (There is only do—or do not.) Finishers get a gold-medal button for their blog, their name entered into a draw for a chance at a prize from me, and the joy of knowing that they are an Olympic level knitter, no matter how experienced they are. You are only competing against yourself. (Well. And the Olympic schedule.)

More than 4,000 knitters signed up for the Winter 2010 Olympic games at Stephanie's site. In addition, Ravelry held its own Ravelympics, and other sites did the same. So sharpen your sticks and get prepared for the 2012 Summer Olympics. Let the games begin!

"It's a small world, after all . . . "
(Now you can't get it out of your head, can you?)

Thanks to *Debbie Stoller* and her groundbreaking *Stitch 'N Bitch, The Knitter's Handbook, Stitch and Bitch groups* have been founded throughout the U.S. and the world. A personal favorite of mine is *Stitch London*. It's one of the richest and most innovative knitting groups I've seen.

At Stitch London, everyone's welcome. The group's London Knit Crawl is famous, as is its wrapping of the 550-foot "Lion Scarf" around the chilly Trafalgar Square lions. Members have knit blankets for breast cancer and worn hand-knit goatees for the first-ever Goatee Knitting Race.

The group's unquenchable joy of knitting and unbeatable verve for life inspires me as a knitter and planet dweller. (www.StitchLDN.co.uk) ~VICKI

The earliest knitted garments ever unearthed were a pair of socks discovered in Egypt from the first millennium.

JIVE SWEATER ...
Designed by Ashwini Jambhekar

A lover of ruffled, or bell, sleeves on sweaters, Ashwini nonetheless finds this feature impractical for her job as a research scientist. (Yup, you read that right.) She designed this sweater to have the femininity of lace or ruffles without the worry of excess fabric getting in the way.

Ashwini personifies the idea of a worldwide community of knitters. While she learned to knit here, in the U.S., her knitting baseline is international. She learned to knit from her mother, who learned in India. Yet Ashwini uses the same language as all knitters: knit and purl and yarn over and on and on and on.

 Skill Level: **WING CHAIR**

Things You'll Need to Know
- Easy lace knitting
- Picking up stitches
- Reading knitting charts

Sizes
S (M, L, XL)

Instructions are given for size S, with larger sizes in parentheses. When only one number is given and no size is mentioned, that number applies to all sizes.

Finished Measurements
Bust: 32½ (35½, 41½, 44½)" [82.5 (90, 105.5, 113) cm]
Length: 22¼ (22¾, 23¼, 24)" [56.6 (58, 59, 61)cm]

Yarn
Classic Elite Yarns *Wool Bam Boo* (50% wool, 50% bamboo); 118 yds [108m]/1¾ oz [50g] ball; DK weight/light [3]; 8 (9, 10, 11) balls, shown in color Key Lime #1635

Needles

Size US 6 (4mm) needles, straight and 24" (60cm) circular needles, or size needed to obtain gauge
Size US 4 (3.5mm) straight knitting needles
Size US D/3 (3.25mm) or E/4 (3.5mm) crochet hook

Notions

2 stitch holders
Blunt tapestry/yarn needle

Gauge

22 sts and 30 rows = 4" (10cm) in stockinette on larger needles
22 sts and 34 rows = 4" (10cm) in Rhombus Lace on larger needles
Let's get it together and swatch, swatch, swatch!

Techniques

PICK UP STITCHES WITH A CROCHET HOOK: Use a crochet hook with a straight shank, not one with a separate handle. Hold the crochet hook as you would a knitting needle. *Insert hook through stitch at edge and hold yarn under hook. Draw a loop through to the right side; repeat from *, sliding stitches up along handle of crochet hook as you work, then off onto a knitting needle.

Abbreviations

approx approximately • **beg** begin-(ning) • **BO** bind off • **cont** continue **dec** decrease • **inc** increase • **k** knit
k2tog knit 2 stitches together (1 stitch decreased) • **ndl(s)** needle(s) • **p** purl **rem** remain • **rep** repeat
rnd(s) round(s) • **RS** right side(s)
sl slip • **st(s)** stitch(es)
St st stockinette stitch • **tog** together **WS** wrong side(s) • **yo** yarn over

Pattern Stitch

RHOMBUS LACE (multiple of 8 sts + 2)
ROW 1 (RS): K1, (k2tog, yo) twice, *k4, (k2tog, yo) twice; rep from * to last 5 sts, end k5.
ROW 2 AND EVERY WS ROW: P.
ROW 3: (K2tog, yo) twice, k1, *k3, (k2tog, yo) twice,

Rhombus Lace Pattern

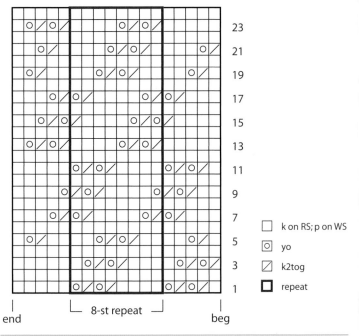

k on RS; p on WS
yo
k2tog
repeat

end   ⌐ 8-st repeat ⌐   beg

k1; rep from * to last 5 sts, end k5.
ROW 5: K1, k2tog, yo, k2, *k2, (k2tog, yo) twice, k2; rep from * to last 5 sts, end k2, k2tog, yo, k1.
ROW 7: K3, k2tog, yo, *k2tog, yo, k4, k2tog, yo; rep from * to last 5 sts, end k2tog, yo, k3.
ROW 9: K2, k2tog, yo, k2tog, *yo, k4, k2tog, yo, k2tog; rep from * to last 5 sts, end yo, k4.
ROW 11: Rep row 1.
ROW 13: K5, *(k2tog, yo) twice, k4; rep from * to last 5 sts, end (k2tog, yo) twice, k1.
ROW 15: K4, k2tog, *yo, k2tog, yo, k4, k2tog; rep from * to last 5 sts, end yo, k2tog, yo, k2.
ROW 17: Rep row 7.
ROW 19: Rep row 5.
ROW 21: K2tog, yo, k3, *k1, (k2tog, yo) twice, k3; rep from * to last 5 sts, end k1, k2tog, yo, k2.
ROW 23: Rep row 13.
ROW 24: P.
Rep rows 1–24 for pattern.

K2, P2 RIB (multiple of 4 sts)
ROW 1: *K2, p2; rep from * to end.
ROW 2: K the k sts and p the p sts.
Rep these 2 rows for pattern.

BACK

Using larger ndls, cast on 90 (98, 114, 122) sts. Work back and forth in garter st for 4 rows (k every row).

Beg Rhombus Lace Pattern and work until piece measures 9 (9, 9, 9¼)" [23 (23, 23, 23.5)cm] from beg, ending with either 6th, 12th, 18th, or 24th row of pattern.

Change to smaller ndls. Work k2, p2 rib for 2" (5cm).

Change to larger ndls. Beg St st. Work until piece measures 14¼ (14¼, 14¾, 15)" [36 (36, 37.5, 38) cm] from beg, ending with a WS row.

SHAPE ARMHOLES: BO 5 (5, 6, 7) sts at the beg of next 2 rows—80 (88, 102, 108) sts.

Dec 1 st at each end of every RS row 5 (6, 11, 11) times—70 (76, 80, 86) sts rem.

Work even until armhole measures 7 (7½, 7½, 8)" [18 (19, 19, 20.5)cm].

SHAPE NECK AND SHOULDERS: Next row, work 20 (22, 23, 25) sts, sl next 30 (32, 34, 36) sts to holder, join second ball of yarn, then work remaining 20 (22, 23, 25) sts.

Work each side of back separately and dec 1 st at each neck edge every row 2 (2, 3, 3) times.

AT SAME TIME, when armhole measures approx 7½ (8, 8, 8½)" [19 (20.5, 20.5, 21.5) cm] and 0 (0, 1, 1) neck dec have been worked, BO from armhole edge 9 (10, 10, 11) sts twice—0 sts rem.

FRONT

Work front same as back to armholes.

SHAPE ARMHOLES: BO 5 (5, 6, 7) sts at the beg of next 2 rows—80 (88, 102, 108) sts.

Dec 1 st at each end of every RS row 5 (6, 11, 11) times. AT SAME TIME, when armhole measures 2¼ (2½, 2½, 3)" [5.5 (6.5, 6.5, 7.5)cm], shape neck.

SHAPE NECK & SHOULDERS: Mark center 28 (30, 34, 36) sts. Cont armhole shaping and work to center marked sts, sl center 28 (30, 34, 36) sts to holder, attach a second ball of yarn and work to end.

Working each side of front separately, dec 1 st at each neck edge every row 3 times.

Work even until armhole measures 7 (7½, 7½, 8)" [18 (19, 18, 20.5) cm].

When armhole shaping is complete, 18 (20, 20, 22) sts rem.

BO from armhole edge 9 (10, 10, 11) sts twice— 0 sts rem.

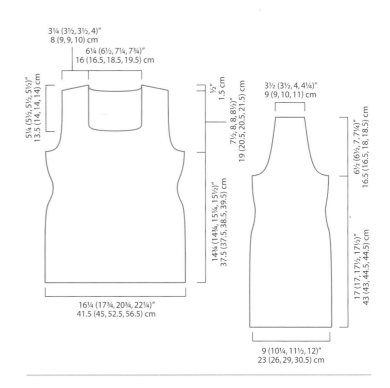

3¼ (3½, 3½, 4)"
8 (9, 9, 10) cm

6¼ (6½, 7¼, 7¾)"
16 (16.5, 18.5, 19.5) cm

5¼ (5½, 5½, 5½)"
13.5 (14, 14, 14) cm

½"
1.5 cm

7½ (8, 8, 8½)"
19 (20.5, 20.5, 21.5) cm

3½ (3½, 4, 4¼)"
9 (9, 10, 11) cm

6½ (6½, 7, 7¼)"
16.5 (16.5, 18, 18.5) cm

14¾ (14¾, 15¼, 15½)"
37.5 (37.5, 38.5, 39.5) cm

16¼ (17¾, 20¾, 22¼)"
41.5 (45, 52.5, 56.5) cm

17 (17, 17½, 17½)"
43 (43, 44.5, 44.5) cm

9 (10¼, 11½, 12)"
23 (26, 29, 30.5) cm

SLEEVES (make 2)

Using larger ndls, cast on 50 (58, 66, 66) sts. Work back and forth in garter st for 4 rows (k every row). Beg Rhombus Lace Pattern and work until piece measures 11 (11, 11½, 11½)" [28 (28, 29, 29)cm], or desired length from wrist to above elbow. Change to smaller ndls. Work in k2, p2 rib for 2" (5cm).

Change to larger ndls. Beg St st. AT SAME TIME, inc 1 (0, 0, 1) st at each end of 15th row—52 (58, 66, 68) sts. Work even until sleeve measures 17 (17, 17½, 17½)" [43 (43, 44.5, 44.5)cm].

SHAPE CAP: BO 5 (5, 6, 7) sts at beg of next 2 rows—42 (48, 54, 54) sts. Cont to shape cap for each size as follows:

SMALL: Dec 1 st at each end of every 4th row 11 times—20 sts rem.

MEDIUM: Dec 1 st at each end of every 3rd row 6 times, every 4th row twice, then every 3rd row 6 times—20 sts rem.

LARGE: Dec 1 st at each end of every 3rd row 16 times—22 sts.

X-LARGE: Dec 1 st at each end of every 3rd row 5 times, every 4th row 5 times, then every 3rd row 5 times—24 sts.

ALL SIZES: BO rem sts loosely.

Finishing
Sew front and back tog at shoulders.

NECKBAND
Using larger circular ndl and with RS facing, beg at left shoulder and pick up and p 32 (33, 36, 37) sts along left neck edge (approx 3 sts per every 4 rows and 2 sts over the 3 dec rows on side of neck edge), p sts from front holder, pick up and p 32 (33, 36, 37) sts along right neck edge to shoulder, 3 (3, 4, 4) sts along left back neck edge, p sts from back holder, then 3 (3, 4, 4) sts along right back neck edge to shoulder—128 (134, 148, 154) sts.

Join to work in the rnd, and mark beg of rnd. P 2 rnds. Bind off purlwise. Sew sleeves into armholes. Sew front and back tog at sides and sleeves tog along underarms.

PROSPERO HOODIE ...
Designed by Justine Turner

Just like our young man in the photos, this is a sweater for the intrepid adventurer—rough, tough, and ready to go. All a kid needs in a hoodie is for it to be warm, hard-wearing, and very cool.

We love hoodies, for adults and for kids. The idea for a kid's hoodie in our book came from the Midwest; the yarn, from California; the designer, from New Zealand. Somehow, to us, this represents the mash-up of the global knitting community. And how beautifully the parts so often fit.

 Skill Level: WING CHAIR

Things You'll Need to Know
- Knitting in the round
- Simple cables
- Provisional cast-on
- Cable cast-on
- Kitchener stitch
- Three-needle bind-off
- Suspended bind-off

Sizes
4 (6, 8, 10, 12) years
Shown in size 4
Instructions are given for size 4, with larger sizes in parentheses. When only one number is given, it applies to all sizes.

Finished Measurements
Chest: 25½ (27½, 29½, 31½, 33½)" [65 (70, 75, 80, 85)cm]
Length: 12¾ (14, 15¼, 16¾, 17¾)" [32.5 (35.5, 38.5, 42.5, 45)cm]

Yarn
Lisa Souza *Hand Dyed Superwash Merino* (100% superfine merino wool); 560 yds [512m]/8 oz [227g]; worsted/medium weight [4]; 2 (2, 2, 2, 2) skeins, shown in color Cam-oh!

Needles

Size US 6 (4mm) needles, two 16" (40cm) circular needles, and one set of double-pointed needles
Size US 7 (4.5mm) needles, 16" (40cm) circular needle and one set of double-pointed needles, or size needed to obtain gauge

Notions

Cable needle
8 stitch markers in one color for marking cables and sleeves
2 stitch markers in another color for marking the center front and back
6 safety pins or small stitch holders
Blunt tapestry/yarn needle
1 yard (91.5cm) of cord for hood (optional)

Gauge

21 sts and 32 rnds = 4" (10cm) in Cornrow Rib using larger needles
How many gauge swatches does it take to check? Just one! Do it!

Techniques

CABLE CAST-ON: An easy cast-on, once you're clear how it works. Keep it loose, or you'll get into trouble. Start with a slip knot. Knit into the slip knot, leaving the stitch on the left needle. *Knit into the gap between the two stitches on the left needle. Place knitted stitch that's now on the right needle onto the left needle. And so on. Thanks to www. KnittingHelp.com for the info. (Seeing the video of this cast-on makes all the difference.)

KITCHENER STITCH (OR GRAFTING OR WEAVING): In other words, you're joining two sets of live stitches without leaving a seam. Great tutorials are online at www.KnittingHelp.com (video) and www.Knitty. com. You'll need a tapestry needle for this.

PROVISIONAL CAST-ON: Choose a smooth yarn of similar weight to the item. Cast on the number of stitches as normal, knit one row in the waste yarn, then start knitting your item with the actual yarn. When you remove the waste yarn, unravel it one stitch at a time and pop that stitch onto the needle.

SUSPENDED BIND-OFF: Knit 2 stitches, *lift the first stitch over the second stitch and off the needle as for a normal bind-off, but place this stitch on the left needle. Knit the second stitch on the left needle and slip both this stitch and the bound-off stitch from the left needle, dropping the bound-off stitch—2 stitches on the right needle; repeat from * until all stitches have been worked.

THREE-NEEDLE BIND-OFF: Divide stitches evenly on two needles. Hold both needles in left hand with right sides together and needles parallel. Using a third needle in your right hand, knit together the first stitch from both needles. *Knit together the next stitch from both needles. Lift the first stitch on right needle over top of second stitch, then off the needle—1 stitch remains on right needle; repeat from * until all stitches have been bound off. Fasten off remaining stitch on right needle.

Abbreviations

2/2LC 2 over 2 cable, left cross: Slip 2 stitches to cable needle and hold in front of work, knit 2 stitches, knit stitches from cable needle.

2/2RC 2 over 2 cable, right cross: Slip 2 stitches to cable needle and hold in back of work, knit 2 stitches, knit stitches from cable needle.

beg begin(ning) • **BO** bind off

cont continu(e)(ing) • **dec** decreas(e)(ing)

dpn(s) double-pointed needle(s)

inc increas(e)(ing) • **k** knit

k2tog knit 2 stitches together (1 stitch decreased)

LT Left twist: Slip 1 stitch to cable needle and hold in front of work, knit 1 stitch, knit stitch from cable needle.

ndl(s) needle(s) • **p** purl

p2tog purl 2 stitches together (1 stitch decreased)

pm place marker • **rem** remain(ing)

rep repeat • **rnd(s)** round(s) • **RS** right side(s)

RT right twist: Slip 1 stitch to cable needle and hold in back of work, knit 1 stitch, knit 1 stitch from cable needle. • **sl** slip

ssk slip, slip, knit: Slip one stitch from left needle to right needle knitwise (as if to knit), slip second stitch same way; insert left needle through front of loops on right needle, then wrap yarn around right needle. With left needle, bring loops over the yarn wrapped around the right, which will knit them together through the back of the loops (1 stitch decreased).

st(s) stitch(es) • **St st** stockinette stitch

tbl through the back of loops

tog together • **WS** wrong side(s)

Tips

- Please examine the stitch pattern in your gauge swatch. See how there are columns of "fat" purl stitches? These are created when you purl a stitch that had been knit on the previous round. Understanding how your stitches behave will help you when working decreases later in the pattern.
- The suspended bind-off creates a stretchy bound-off edge.
- The body is worked in the round to the underarms, then the sleeves are joined and the yoke is worked in the round.
- Stitch markers are used to separate pattern areas and mark the beginning/end of rounds; slip all markers as you come to them.
- The hoodie pictured has a "pixie"-style hood; directions are also given for an optional rounded hood.
- When working raglan shaping, work decreases as k2tog before each marker and ssk after each marker.

Pattern Stitches

CORNROW RIB (multiple of 2 sts)

ROW/RND 1: P when working in the round; k when working back and forth.

ROW/RND 2: *K1, p1; rep from * to end.
Rep rows/rnds 1–2 for pattern.

SIDE SEAM CABLE PATTERN (worked over 20 sts)

RND 1: P2, k4, p2, RT, LT, p2, k4, p2.

RNDS 2 AND 4: (P2, k4) 3 times, p2.

RND 3: P2, 2/2LC, p2, LT, RT, p2, 2/2RC, p2.
Rep rnds 1–4 for pattern.

BODY

Using smaller circular ndls, cast on 140 (150, 162, 174, 186) sts using cable cast-on and place markers

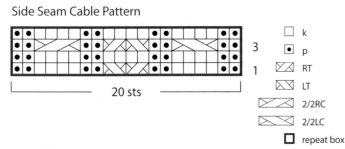

Side Seam Cable Pattern

	k
•	p
RT	
LT	
2/2RC	
2/2LC	
	repeat box

20 sts

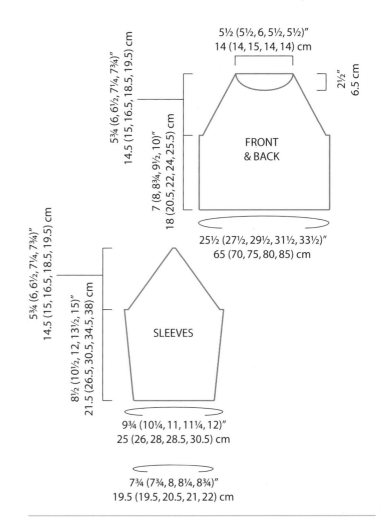

5½ (5½, 6, 5½, 5½)"
14 (14, 15, 14, 14) cm

2½"
6.5 cm

5¾ (6, 6½, 7¼, 7¾)"
14.5 (15, 16.5, 18.5, 19.5) cm

FRONT & BACK

7 (8, 8¾, 9½, 10)"
18 (20.5, 22, 24, 25.5) cm

25½ (27½, 29½, 31½, 33½)"
65 (70, 75, 80, 85) cm

5¾ (6, 6½, 7¼, 7¾)"
14.5 (15, 16.5, 18.5, 19.5) cm

SLEEVES

8½ (10½, 12, 13½, 15)"
21.5 (26.5, 30.5, 34.5, 38) cm

9¾ (10¼, 11, 11¼, 12)"
25 (26, 28, 28.5, 30.5) cm

7¾ (7¾, 8, 8¼, 8¾)"
19.5 (19.5, 20.5, 21, 22) cm

as follows: cast on 50 (55, 61, 67, 73), pm, cast on 20 sts, pm, cast on 50 (55, 61, 67, 73), pm, cast on 20 sts, pm in a different color for beg of rnd. Join to work in the rnd, being careful not to twist sts.

RND 1 (SET-UP): *[K1, p1] to next marker, (p2, k4) 3 times, p2; rep from * once more.

NEXT RND: *Work rnd 1 of Cornrow Rib to first marker, rnd 1 of Side Seam Cable Pattern over next 20 sts; rep from * once more.

Cont patterns as established until 10 rnds have been worked. Change to larger circular ndl. Work in patterns until piece measures about 7 (8, 8¾, 9½, 10)" [18 (20.5, 22, 24, 25.5)cm] from beg, end with rnd 1 of Cornrow Rib.

Cut yarn, leaving a tail to weave in.

Sl last 7 sts back to left ndl, sl next 6 sts from right ndl to safety pin. Set body aside.

SLEEVE (make 2)

Using smaller dpns, cast on 42 (42, 44, 46, 48) sts using cable cast-on. Pm for end of rnd. Join to work in the rnd, being careful not to twist sts.

Beg Cornrow Rib AT SAME TIME, inc 1 st each end of rnd every 10th (11th, 11th, 12th, 13th) rnd 6 (7, 8, 8, 9) times—54 (56, 60, 62, 66) sts.

Work even until piece measures about 8½ (10½, 12, 13½, 15)" [21.5 (26.5, 30.5, 34.5, 38)cm] from beg; end with a rnd 1 of pattern rep.

Cut yarn, leaving a tail to weave in.

Sl last 3 sts back to left ndl, then sl 6 sts from left ndl to safety pin.

YOKE

Join pieces for yoke as follows: K1, work next rnd over 46 (48, 52, 54, 58) sts of left sleeve, k1, pm. Work front sts: k1, (k1, p1) 3 times, work pattern as established to next marker, cont Cornrow Rib over next 6 sts, k1, pm, sl next 6 sts to safety pin. Work right sleeve sts same as left. Work back sts same as front, pm for end of rnd—224 (238, 258, 274, 294) sts. Join to work in the rnd.

NEXT RND: K1, *work in pattern to 1 st before next marker, k2; rep from * 3 more times, ending last rep k1.

Rep last rnd.

NEXT RND (DEC): *Ssk, work in pattern to 2 sts before next marker, k2tog; rep from * 3 more times—216 (230, 250, 266, 286) sts.

Cont shaping yoke for each size as follows:

SIZE 4: Dec on body every following 3rd rnd 10 times, then every 2nd rnd 6 times. AT SAME TIME, on sleeves, dec every following 2nd rnd 22 times.

SIZE 6: Dec on body every following 3rd rnd 9 times, then every 2nd rnd 9 times. AT SAME TIME, on sleeves, dec every following 2nd rnd 23 times.

SIZE 8: Dec on body every following 3rd rnd 11 times, then every 2nd rnd 8 times. AT SAME TIME, on sleeves, dec every following 2nd rnd 25 times.

SIZE 10: Dec on body every following 3rd rnd 8 times, then every 2nd rnd 15 times. AT SAME TIME, on sleeves, dec every following 3rd rnd 2 times, then every 2nd rnd 24 times.

SIZE 12: Dec on body every following 3rd rnd 6 times, then every 2nd rnd 20 times. AT SAME TIME, on sleeves, dec every following 3rd rnd 2

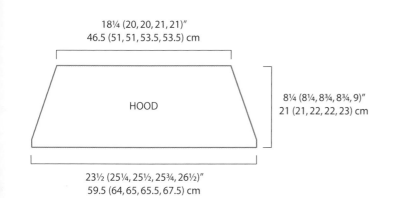

18¼ (20, 20, 21, 21)"
46.5 (51, 51, 53.5, 53.5) cm

HOOD

8¼ (8¼, 8¾, 8¾, 9)"
21 (21, 22, 22, 23) cm

23½ (25¼, 25½, 25¾, 26½)"
59.5 (64, 65, 65.5, 67.5) cm

times, then every 2nd rnd 26 times.

AT SAME TIME, after 29 (32, 35, 41, 44) rnds have been worked for the yoke, mark the center 14 (17, 17, 15, 15) sts of front.

Cut yarn, leaving a tail to weave in. Sl the sts for the left sleeve and left side of front to the neck edge to the right ndl.

SHAPE FRONT NECK: Reattach yarn. Bind off marked center front sts using suspended bind-off, then work to end of rnd, then cont to left neck edge.

Working back and forth, work rem raglan shaping and dec 1 st at each side of neck every RS row 6 (5, 6, 6, 6) times—38 (39, 45, 43, 43) sts rem.

NEXT ROW: BO rem sts using suspended bind-off.

PIXIE-STYLE HOOD

Using smaller circular ndl, cast on 123 (132, 134, 135, 139) sts using provisional cast-on.

*Work back and forth in St st for 7 rows, end with a RS row.

Remove provisional cast-on and sl resulting loops to 2nd smaller circular ndl; there will be 1 fewer st on second ndl.

NEXT ROW: With WS facing, hold both needles with WS tog. P tog the first st on both ndls, *p tog the next st on both ndls; rep from * until all sts have been worked—123 (132, 134, 135, 139) sts.

Change to larger circular ndl. Work 5 rows in Corn-row Rib.

NEXT ROW: Work next row of pattern and dec 1 st at each end—121 (130, 132, 133, 137) sts.

Work 3 rows even.

Rep last 4 rows 11 (11, 12, 11, 12) more times, then rep dec row once more—97 (106, 106, 109, 111) sts.**

Work even until piece measures about 8¼ (8¼, 8¾, 8¾, 9)" [21 (21, 22, 22, 23)cm] from fold edge.

Divide sts with 48 (53, 53, 54, 55) sts on one ndl, and rem 49 (53, 53, 55, 56) sts on second ndl. Hold ndls with RS tog, bind off using three-needle bind-off.

ROUNDED HOOD

Using smaller circular ndl, cast on 122 (132, 134, 136, 138) sts using provisional cast-on. Pm after 61 (66, 67, 68, 69) sts for center of row.

Work same as Pixie-Style Hood from * to **—96 (106, 106, 110, 110) sts rem.

NEXT ROW: Work to 2 sts before marker, ssk, k2tog, work to end—94 (104, 104, 108, 108) sts.

Rep last row 5 (5, 5, 6, 6) more times, working dec on WS rows as p2tog tbl, p2tog—84 (94, 94, 96, 96) sts.

Divide sts evenly onto 2 ndls, with 42 (47, 47, 48, 48) sts on each ndl. Hold ndls with RS tog, BO using three-needle bind-off.

Finishing

Pin hood into neck opening, placing seam at center of back, and edges meeting at center of front, having open ends of hem above neck edge.

Sew hood into neck.

Sew underarm edges using Kitchener st. Weave in ends.

Wash according to manufacturer's instructions.

Lay out to finished measurements and allow to dry.

Thread cord through hem at front of hood.

Theresa Rebeck's play Loose Knit is a contemporary comedy about a weekly knitting circle. Of course, it represents a microcosm of life.

MELVIN THE MUSICAL MONSTER ...
Designed by Rebecca Danger

Melvin is a rock-and-roll kind of monster. His favorite thing to do is to get together with his monster friends and play covers of his favorite band, Melvin and the Monsterettes. Secretly though, he dreams of dancing the role of the Prince in *The Nutcracker*. We say, "Go for it, Melvin!" Dreams do come true. Ours have.

What's most beautiful about Melvin is that he can be loved by Democrat or Republican, Greek or Aussie, black or red or yellow or white, Jew or Buddhist, Christian or Muslim.

Melvin, like so much in knitting, transcends race and religion and politics and locale. Don't you just love it?

 Skill Level: **RECLINER**

Things You'll Need to Know
- Knitting in the round on circular and double-pointed needles
- Three-needle bind-off
- Backward loop cast-on
- Increasing stitches by knitting into the front and back of the loop

Size
About 14" (35.5cm) tall and 10" (25.5cm) wide before stuffing

Yarn
Plymouth Yarn *Baby Alpaca Grande* (100% baby alpaca); 110 yds [100m]/3½ oz [100g]; chunky weight/bulky [5]; **MC:** 1 skein; **CC:** 1 skein
MELVIN #1: MC, Purple #2213; CC, Lime #1310
MELVIN #2: MC, Tomato #69; CC, Gold #1709

Needles
Size US 10 (6mm) needles, one set of double-pointed needles and one 16" (40cm) circular needle, or size needed to obtain gauge

Notions
Stitch markers
Row counter
Scissors
Straight pins
Blunt tapestry/yarn needle
1 set approx ¾" (18mm) safety eyes
White or off-white felt for teeth
Fiberfill stuffing
Fabric glue (such as Unique Stitch)
Small amount of yarn in a dark or contrasting color for belly button

Gauge
13 sts and 17 rnds = 4" (10cm) in stockinette; 13 sts and 18 rnds = 4" (10cm) in body pattern
Melvin will not die if you don't check your gauge, but his sister, Bernice, will be pretty ticked off.

Techniques
BACKWARD LOOP CAST-ON: *Hold the needle in your right hand, with yarn coming from the needle

between your left index finger and thumb, around
the back of your thumb and back into your palm;
hold the yarn with the other three fingers of your
left hand. Insert the tip of the needle up from under-
neath the strand next to your thumb, just above
where your other fingers are holding the strand.
Slip the loop off your thumb and gently pull on the
strand to tighten. Repeat from * until you have as
many stitches as you need.

THREE-NEEDLE BIND-OFF: Divide stitches evenly on
two needles. Hold both needles in left hand with
right sides together and needles parallel. Using a
third needle in your right hand, knit together the
first stitch from both needles. *Knit together the
next stitch from both needles. Lift the first stitch on
the right needle over the top of the second stitch,
then off the needle—1 stitch remains on right needle; repeat from * until all stitches have been bound
off. Fasten off remaining stitch on right needle.

Abbreviations

beg begin(ning) • **BO** bind off • **CC** contrast color
dpn(s) double-pointed needle(s) • **k** knit
k2tog knit 2 stitches together (1 stitch decreased)
kfb knit into the front loop, then through the back
loop of the same stitch (1 stitch increased)
MC main color • **ndl(s)** needle(s)
rep repeat • **rnd(s)** round(s) • **RS** right side(s)
st(s) stitch(es) • **WS** wrong side(s)

Tips

• Any mistakes made while knitting your Melvin
will just give him more character!
• When gluing Melvin's teeth to his head, stack
some heavy books on Melvin's face to hold the teeth
in place until the glue dries. Cruel, I know, but trust
me, Melvin will thank you for it when his teeth stay
securely attached to his face.
• It is easy to use any yarn and needle combination
you choose for this project. Just use needles about
two sizes smaller than those recommended on the
yarn label to create a tight-knit fabric that the stuffing won't show through.

LEG (make 2)

Using dpns, cast on 6 sts in MC. Join to work in the rnd, making sure not to twist sts.

RND 1: Kfb in all sts–12 sts.

RND 2: *Kfb, k1; rep from * to end–18 sts.

RNDS 3–16: K. At end of last rnd, cast on 9 new sts using backward loop cast-on–27 sts.

Cut yarn, leaving a tail about 12" (30.5cm) long and slip these sts to circular ndl.

When the second leg is complete, cut yarn leaving a tail about 12" (30.5cm) long.

Slip the 9 new sts and next 9 sts of the second leg to the left ndl of the same circular ndl as the first leg, and the rem 9 sts to the right ndl—54 sts.

The new sts should be on opposite sides of the ndl, with both legs between them. Place marker for beg of rnd at one side of body, and place marker for other side of body with 27 sts between markers.

BODY

Join to work in the rnd and place marker for beg of rnd—54 sts.

RNDS 1–6: With MC, k.

RND 7: With CC, k.

RNDS 8–10: P.

RND 11: K.

RNDS 12–31: Rep rnds 8–11 five more times.

RNDS 32–34: P

RNDS 35–38: With MC, k.

RND 39: *K2tog, k25; rep from * once more—52 sts.

RND 40: K.

RND 41: *K24, k2tog; rep from * once more—50 sts.

RND 42: K.

RND 43: *K2tog, k23; rep from * once more—48 sts.

RND 44: K.

RND 45: *K22, k2tog; rep from * once more—46 sts.

RND 46: K.

RND 47: *K2tog, k21; rep from * once more—44 sts.

RND 48: K.

RND 49: *K20, k2tog; rep from * once more—42 sts.

RND 50: K.

RND 51: *K2tog, k17, k2tog; rep from * once more—38 sts.

RND 52: *K2tog, k15, k2tog; rep from * once more—34 sts.

RND 53: *K2tog, k13, k2tog; rep from * once more—30 sts.

Turn piece with WS facing and divide sts evenly on 2 ndls. Use 3-needle bind-off to BO all sts.

ARMS (make 2)

Using dpns, cast on 15 sts in MC. Join to work in the rnd, making sure not to twist sts.

RNDS 1–19: K.

RND 20: K2tog 8 times, k3tog—7sts.

Cut yarn, leaving a tail about 6" (15cm) long. Using a blunt tapestry or yarn needle, draw tail through rem sts and tighten.

EYE PATCH

Using dpns, cast on 6 sts in CC. Join to work in the rnd, making sure not to twist sts.

RND 1: Kfb in each st—12 sts.

RND 2: Kfb in each st—24 sts.

RND 3: K.

RND 4: BO all sts purlwise.

Finishing

Weave ends. Use blunt tapestry or yarn needle and contrast yarn to embroider a cross st on front at lower edge of CC.

Stuff only the "hands" at the ends of the arms.

Attach the arms to the body, using straight pins to hold arms in place while adjusting placement, making sure both arms are evenly placed.

Sew both arms to the body.

Pin the eye patch to the face, adjusting placement to your satisfaction.

Sew around the edge of the eye patch to tack down the sides.

Attach one safety eye by placing the post through the center of the eye patch, to the inside, and secure according to package instructions.

Attach second safety eye, adjusting so it's even with the first eye.

Stuff the body and legs, and sew bottom closed. A little extra stuffing around the hips will give Melvin a cute shape.

Cut a small rectangle from the felt, using Melvin's face as a gauge for width. Cut up and down in a zig-zag line along one long edge to create little teeth.

Pin the teeth to the face, positioning them to your liking. Use fabric glue to glue teeth to the head.

RESOURCES

Sources for the Yummy Yarns Used in the Book

Berroco www.berroco.com

Bijou Basin Ranch www.bijoubasinranch.com

Brown Sheep Co. www.brownsheep.com

Buffalo Gold www.buffalogold.com

Cascade Yarns www.cascadeyarns.com

Classic Elite www.classiceliteyarns.com

Debbie Bliss www.debbieblissonline.com

Decadent Fibers www.decadentfibers.com

Foxfire Fiber and Designs www.foxfirefiber.com

Freshisle Fibers: freshislefibers.com

Great Northern Yarns www.greatnorthernyarns.com

Habu Textiles www.habutextiles.com

HoneyBunns 540 Forest Rd, Lyndenborough, NH 03082

Lion Brand Yarn www.lionbrand.com

Lisa Souza Knitwear and Dyeworks www.lisaknit.com

Louet North America www.louet.com

Mission Falls www.missionfalls.com

Noro Yarns www.knittingfever.com

Plymouth Yarn www.plymouthyarn.com

Qiviuk Yarn www.qiviuk.com

Red Heart www.redheart.com

Rowan www.knitrowan.com

Spud & Chloë www.spudandchloe.com

Fiber CSAs

Here's our listing, but as with anything in our fast-moving world, some may have vanished. We'll try to keep these updated in our Web site, but the best way to find them is to Google "fiber" or "yarn CSA."

• Call of the Wool in Oregon (www.callofthewool.com)

• Foxfire Fiber & Designs in Massachutsetts (www.foxfirefiber.com)

• Grand View Farm in Vermont (www.grandviewfarmvt.net)

• Juniper Moon Farm in Virginia (www.fiberfarm.com)

• Serenity Sheep Farm in Montana (www.homesteadblogger.com/serenitysheepfarm)

• Trailhead CSA, is a collective of fiber farms in Pennsylvania (www.trailheadcsa.com)

• Wool and Feather Farm in Wisconsin (www.etsy.com/shop/woolnfeatherfarm)

How to Find the LaidBack Knitters and the Authors:

The LaidBack Knitters Web site: www.laidbackknitters.com

Vicki's Web site: www.vickistiefel.com
Lisa's Web site: www.lisaknit.com

Check us out on Twitter:
@knittingnews http://twitter.com/knittingnews
@lisaknit http://twitter.com/lisaknit

Visit our Ravelry Groups:
LaidBack Knitters (& Crocheters)
Lisa Souza Love
Vicki is the LaidBackKnitter and Lisa is LisaSouza

DESIGNER BIOS

Therese Chynoweth (page 137). A woman of many talents, Therese came to us as a tech editor extraordinaire. Little did we realize that she is also an amazing knitting and crochet designer. Her recent book, *Norwegian Sweater Techniques for Today's Knitter*, (Wiley, 2010) as well as her acres of work for Dale of Norway and Interweave stand her in good stead. While her Heirloom Motif Crochet Scarf harks back to the past, it's incontrovertibly modern in style and feel.

Tom Clark (page 135) is one of a kind. So are the caps he designs. See his profile in Chapter 9.

Audrey F. Clarke (page 63) began creating scarves for her daughter, because they were one of the few articles of clothing that both mother and daughter agreed upon. Soon after, Audrey began making fingerless gloves to match her scarves, so her daughter could type her college papers into the wee hours without freezing her hands off. Scarves and mitts became a fashion statement for her daughter (who still receives envious looks while wearing her matching sets at work). Yet they barely scratch the surface of Audrey's creative wearable works of art. If you ask her husband, he'll say the sweater she made him one Christmas pretty much resulted in their tying the knot.

Audrey's creative work extended far beyond that of knitting. Her ability to create beauty was endless.

~ GABRIELLE CLARKE

Linda Cortright (page 78). Before she began her career as a wild and wonderful globe-trotting publisher, Wild Linda designed. Boy, did she ever. Read her profile in Chapter 5.

Shirley Craig (page 125) was born and grew up on Martha's Vineyard. Although she's traveled the world and brings an international sensibility to any project she tackles, she's a Vineyarder at heart. Wife to famed mystery author Philip R. Craig, the words angler, writer (*Delish*, a fabulous 2006 cookbook published by Vineyard Stories), teacher, and, now, knitting-pattern designer all fit Shirley Craig, a unique talent and human being.

Rebecca Danger (page 155) got into knitting at age 12, when she visited her grandma in California. "I insisted she show me how to knit. I haven't put down the needles since, and I knit my way through high school and college. After running a different business to the point of exhaustion, I started Danger Crafts as a sort of healing project. Except when I sat down to knit clothes and hats, monsters and teddy bears seemed to come off my needles more easily. I don't necessarily know where the monsters come from, although every time I look at my two pugs I see that monster underbite that I like to include on all of my monster faces. I think the pugs' behavior might have something to do with all the monsters as well."

You can visit Rebecca and meet more of Rebecca's monsters at www.RebeccaDanger.typepad.com.

Kathleen Day (page 13). There have been few days in the last 50 years that Kathleen Day hasn't had knitting in her hands. Beginning at age 12, she knit her way through public school, boarding school, and college, twice!

She knit during lunch breaks when working as a nurse, while waiting for the kids at dance lessons, and for her college sweetheart/husband, two children, five grandchildren, for friends and charities. In the course of knitting 1,300 premie hats for Children's Hospital in Omaha, NE, she designed many fancy ones to make knitting them fun for her and to bring smiles to the faces of the parents and the hospital staff.

Kathleen's designs and patterns include hats for all ages and sizes, scarves and stoles, women's and children's vests and tops. Besides hand-knitting, she cranks socks on antique circular sock-knitting machines.

More of Kathleen's designs can be found at Lisa's Web site, www .LisaKnit.com.

Norah Gaughan (page 108), a legend in knitwear design, is also one of the knitting world's most generous and gracious people. Currently Berroco's design director, Norah creates knitting designs that are indelible and have appeared in magazines, on the web, and in numerous books. Her design themes most often come from the natural world, and if you spy a Gaughan design, it's instantly recognizable as a "Norah."

Sivia Harding (page 27) needs no introduction. Her creations of lace and beads remind us of fairy wings and spiderwebs—gossamer creations that illuminate the art of knitting. Yet Sivia crafts heartier fare, too, which reflects her unconfined soul.

Her gentle heart is coupled with a fine sense of humor. "Knitted lace is my first and enduring love, and when I learned how wonderfully lace combines with beads, I began incorporating beads into most of my designs. Socks and fingerless gloves have become the latest additions to my design repertoire."

Published extensively, from *Interweave Knits* to Twist Collective, Sivia defines the term "knitting designer." See her Web site www.siviaharding .com.

Holly Haynes (page 60), a knitter since childhood, combines her love of yarn, texture, and handbags by designing felted bags and writing the knitting patterns to go along with them. Never one to stick to a written knitting pattern she was off and knitting in 2005, when a friend asked her to create a felted bag pattern. Since then Holly has developed a line of felted-bag knitting patterns that she sells on the Internet at www.Felted-Bags.com. Her designs focus on bags with unusual shapes and closures. When she isn't knitting, she enjoys weaving, spinning, and collecting old recipes for her cooking Web site, www.Heritage Recipes.com.

Anne Hennessey (page 7). She's our Wise Woman and the creator of Anne's Wings. See Secret 1.

Marion Hester (page 37) lives on glorious Manitoulin Island in Canada, populated by Suffolk sheep, as well as people.

Her story of the watermelon sock yarn: "I had been hand-dyeing and selling our wool for about a year when I discovered a book with watermelon socks by Kathleen Taylor. I loved those watermelon socks but

wanted to make them work for our Suffolk yarn. After many tries at dyeing and much swatching, I succeeded in creating my watermelon yarn. But I keep secret the method for the dots/seeds. They're difficult and time-consuming! I contacted Kathleen Taylor, who gave her blessing to my selling my watermelon yarn, which was quite different from hers. And so I began. My family has many, many pairs of 'reject' socks! Visit her on the Web at www.Fresh isleFibers.com.

Rosemary (Romi) Hill (pages 82 and 85). Fiery and passionate, Rosemary Hill does everything with gusto. From her knit jewelry to her shawl pins to her lace extravaganzas, Rosemary (or Romi) infuses each piece with craftsmanship and life. Her patterns have been extensively published. Yet Romi would most likely say that her greatest accomplishment is her two marvelous boys. Visit her at www.DesignsbyRomi .com.

Ashwini Jambhekar (page 145). *10 Secrets* contains Ashwini's first published knitting pattern. A huge knitting enthusiast, Ashwini is a scientist in her "other" life. "My doctorate is in biochemistry—which qualifies me to juggle tubes containing colorless drops of liquid! I work at Mass General Hospital in Boston, in the molecular biology department." On weekends, when she's not knitting, Ashwini practices ballet—or, as she puts it, "I pretend to be a ballerina."

While Ashwini was born in America, her parents are natives of India. Ashwini learned to knit from her mom, who was taught to knit in school. Why school? Gandhi deemed that schools should teach craft as well as academics. He believed craft would stand Indians in good stead if they wished to begin or contribute to cottage industry. Gandhi would surely be proud of Ashwini and her budding design career.

Janice Kang (page 40) designs, knits, and spins in Northern California, where there is a lively fiber-arts community. In design, she charts and swatches, then launches into knitting the first sample, writing the pattern along the way. She gravitates toward intricate lace, traveling stitches, and novel construction in her personal projects as well as in her designs. Read her blog: KnitFlix .blogspot.com.

Kimberly K. McAlindin (page 21) has been cooking up knitting patterns for years. She's done some extravagant work for Decadent Fibers. You can find more of Kimberly's designs at Decadent Fibers.

Brenda Patipa (page 53). According to Brenda Patipa, she learned two important things from her grandmother: how to knit and how to make excellent chicken soup. Both have stood her in good stead. In elementary school, she knit bookmarks to sell. That was probably the first of many of her entrepreneurial endeavors.

After she graduated with a BFA in Graphic Design from California College of the Arts, she began designing and making custom knits for women. Eventually, she focused on publishing her designs for others to knit. When she met Lisa Souza, her design career took off. She's been published in a variety of venues, including www.Knitty.com.

The Queenie Sisters (page 105). Read all about the Queenies in our Chapter 7 profile.

Judy Sumner (pages 45 and 67) designed her first sock in 1997 and hasn't looked back. In addition to designing for Lisa's Lisa Souza Knitwear and Dyeworks, Judy has designed for Lorna's Laces, Lion Brand Yarns, Knitter's, *Interweave Knits*, and many others. She's won acclaim for *Knitted Socks East and West: 30 Designs Inspired by Japanese Stitch Pat-*

terns. She often compares knitting a sock to writing a haiku. Visit her at www.KnoxSocks.com.

Justine Turner (pages 110 and 149). A native of New Zealand, Justine, aka Just Jussi (rhymes with "fussy"), is a *Brady Bunch* mom with a blended family of five girls. While most of her kids have flown the coop, Justine still has plenty to keep her busy. In addition to her vibrant knit-design career for babies and children, she's also been known to enter her cat in New Zealand's Next Top Cat Model. While her kitty didn't win on her first outing, we suspect, with Justine at the helm, she'll ultimately triumph. Visit her at www.justjussi.com.

Daniel Yuhas (page 115), aka Molting Yeti, taught himself garter stitch during what he calls "a lonely fall break at college, fumbling over the illustrations in a teach-yourself book. After a friend saw what I was up to and taught me to purl, I was off. I soon found myself spending long, dreamy afternoons poring over the stitch dictionary in the back of *Vogue Knitting*. The more I learned, the more I wanted to know."

"It never ceases to amaze me how string, two sticks, and two simple stitches can be combined in such an astonishing number of ways." His designs have appeared in *Interweave, Knits Yarn Forward, Creative Knitting,* and more. His Web site is www.MoltingYeti.com.

INDEX